No Ordinary Moments

Books by Dan Millman

The Peaceful Warrior Series
Way of the Peaceful Warrior
Sacred Journey of the Peaceful Warrior

Guidebooks
No Ordinary Moments
The Life You Were Born to Live
The Laws of Spirit
The Inner Athlete

Especially for Children
Secret of the Peaceful Warrior
Quest for the Crystal Castle

For information about Dan Millman's tapes and trainings,
please see the back pages of this book.

No Ordinary Moments

A Peaceful Warrior's Guide to Daily Life

Dan Millman

H J Kramer Inc
Tiburon, California

Published by H J Kramer Inc
P.O. Box 1082
Tiburon, CA 94920

Editor: Nancy Grimley Carleton
Cover Art: T. Taylor Bruce
Cover Design: Spectra Media
Composition: Classic Typography
Book Production: Schuettge & Carleton
Manufactured in the United States of America
10 9 8 7 6 5 4

Library of Congress Cataloging-in-Publication Data

Millman, Dan.
    No ordinary moments : a peaceful warrior's guide to daily life
/ Dan Millman.
        p. cm.
    ISBN 0-915811-40-5 : $12.95
    1. Spiritual life. 2. Millman, Dan. I. Title.
BL624.M49 1992
291.4'48—dc20
                                                    92-9545
                                                    CIP

To Our Readers
The books we publish
are our contribution to
an emerging world based on
cooperation rather than on competition,
on affirmation of the human spirit rather
than on self-doubt, and on the certainty
that all humanity is connected.
Our goal is to touch as many
lives as possible with a
message of hope for
a better world.
Hal and Linda Kramer, Publishers

About the Editor

Nancy Grimley Carleton, a senior editor for H J Kramer Inc, edits all of Dan Millman's adult books. Also a licensed psychotherapist and certified hypnotherapist, she has a broad background in psychospiritual disciplines, which has enabled her to help Dan shape both the writing and spirit of his work. She lives and practices in Berkeley, California.

About the Illustrator

T. Taylor Bruce, commercial artist, has illustrated numerous book projects, including Dan Millman's children's books and his recent book covers. She and her husband, both professional artists, live in Petaluma, California.

Contents

List of Action Items

Acknowledgments

My appreciation to Hal and Linda Kramer for their consistent support, encouragement, feedback, and faith. They, along with my gifted editor (and sometimes counselor), Nancy Grimley Carleton, have taught me that "no one is smarter than all of us."

Thanks to Michael Greenberg, M.D., Ed Kellogg, Sid Kemp, Sharon Marcillac, Joy Millman, Charles Root, and Jan Shelley for reviewing an unpolished draft of the manuscript.

Carl Weisbrod, Ph.D., kindly granted permission to adapt excerpts from a talk on psychological defense mechanisms, edited by Bill Harris, M.D., and originally printed in the December 1991 newsletter of the Vegetarian Society of Honolulu.

With their blessing, I've adapted a few paragraphs from HOPE Publication's superb "Start Taking Charge" booklet "Adapting to Stress."

I extend grateful acknowledgment to Oscar Ichazo of Arica Institute, from whose "Nine Doors of Compensation" training I drew the concept for the primary avenues of stress release outlined in Chapter 5.

Michael Bookbinder, an inspiring teacher and colleague in spirit, showed me practical ways to integrate the Way into daily life, including methods for opening the heart in Chapter 13. He also inspired the final words in Chapter 15.

Appreciation to Cherie Carter-Scott, who wrote the original "Rules for Being Human" on which I've based the "Rules" on page 43 of this book.

Deepest thanks to all my past teachers, students, and other sources of inspiration, too numerous to name, who are now a part of me. And to my family, for their patience, love, and support.

Preface

If a person sweeps streets for a living,
he should sweep them as Michelangelo painted,
as Beethoven composed, as Shakespeare wrote.
Martin Luther King, Jr.

In the years following publication of my first book, *Way of the Peaceful Warrior,* I received questions from thousands of people all over the world who wanted to know more about a peaceful warrior's approach to life.

I wrote *No Ordinary Moments* as a comprehensive guide to the way of life I teach, and live, to the best of my ability. This volume contains universal principles and practices designed to benefit readers whether or not they have read my previous books.

For those new to my writings—and as a review for those familiar with my work—I want to summarize a key incident described in *Way of the Peaceful Warrior,* because it gave birth to the title and tone of this book.

Late one night, months after meeting Socrates, an unusual old gas station attendant who became my mentor in the peaceful warrior's way, I asked him yet another in an endless string of questions: "Soc, do you think I could ever learn to read other people's minds?"

"First," he said, "you'd better learn to read your own; it's time you looked inside to find your answers."

"I don't *know* the answers; that's why I'm asking you."

"You know far more than you realize, but you don't yet trust your inner knower." Socrates turned and gazed out the window and took a deep breath. He always did this when he was deciding something. "Go out back, Dan—behind the station. You'll find a large flat stone. Remain on that stone until you have something of value to tell me."

"What?"

"I think you heard me."

"This is some kind of test, right?"

He said nothing.

"Right?"

No one could clam up like Soc.

With a sigh, I went outside, found the stone, and sat down. "This is silly," I muttered to myself. To pass the time, I started thinking of all the concepts I'd learned. "Something of value . . . something of value . . . "

Hours passed; it was getting cold. The sun would rise in a few hours.

By dawn, I came up with something—not too inspired, but the best I could do. I rose on stiff, sore legs and hobbled into the warm office. Socrates sat at his desk, relaxed and comfortable, preparing to end his shift. "Ah, so soon?" he said, smiling. "Well, what is it?"

What I told him isn't worth repeating and wasn't good enough—so back to the rock.

Socrates soon left and the day shift came on. As the sun passed slowly overhead, my classes came and went. I missed gymnastics practice. How long would I have to stay here? Desperate, I racked my brain for something of value to tell him.

Socrates returned before dusk, gave me a quick nod, and entered the office. After dark I came up with something else. I limped inside, rubbing my back, and told him. He shook his head and pointed toward the rock. "Too mental; bring me something from your heart and from your guts—something more *moving.*"

As I continued to sit, I muttered to myself, "Something more moving . . . more moving." *What did he want from me, anyway?* Hungry, sore, and irritable—and so stiff I could hardly think anymore—I stood up on the rock and began to practice a few flowing movements of t'ai chi, just to get some energy moving.

I bent my knees and gracefully moved back and forth, my hips turning, my arms floating in the air, and my mind emptied. Suddenly an image came to me: A few days before, I had been out running and came to Provo Square, a little park in the middle of the city. To loosen up and relax, I started practicing a slow-motion t'ai chi routine Socrates had shown me. My mind and body relaxed into a peaceful state of balance and concentration. I became the movements, swaying like seaweed, floating to and fro on gentle ocean currents.

A few students from the local high school stopped to watch me. Focused on each movement, I hardly noticed them—until I finished the routine, picked up my sweatpants, and started pulling them over my running shorts. As my ordinary awareness asserted itself, my attention began to drift.

The students who had been watching me caught my attention—especially a pretty teenage girl, who pointed at me, smiled, and said something to her friend. I guess they were impressed, I thought, as I put both legs into one pant leg, lost my balance, and fell on my butt.

The kids laughed. After a moment of embarrassment, I lay back and laughed with them.

Sitting on that rock outside the gas station, I smiled as I remembered the incident. In the next instant, a wave of energy overwhelmed me as I was struck by a realization so profound it was to change the course of my life: I realized that I had given my full attention to the movements of t'ai chi, but not to the "ordinary" movements of putting on my pants. *I had treated one moment as special and the other as ordinary.*

Now I knew I had something of value to tell Socrates. I strode into the office and announced, *"There are no ordinary moments."*

He looked up and smiled. "Welcome back," he said. I collapsed on the couch; he made us tea. As we sipped the steaming brew, Socrates told me: "Athletes practice their athletics; musicians practice their music; artists practice their art. The peaceful warrior *practices everything.* That is a secret of the Way, and it makes all the difference."

I finally understood why, several years before, Socrates had insisted, "Walking, sitting, breathing, or taking out the trash deserve as much attention as a triple somersault."

"That may be true," I had argued, "but when I do a triple somersault, my *life* is on the line."

"Yes," he replied, "but in *every* moment, the *quality* of your life is on the line. Life is a series of moments. In each, you are either awake or you are asleep—fully alive, or relatively dead." I vowed never again to treat any moment as ordinary.

As the months passed, I would ask myself, at random: In this moment, am I fully alive, or relatively dead? I resolved to practice every action with full attention.

I've learned that the quality of each moment depends not on what we get *from* it, but on what we bring *to* it. I treat no moment as ordinary, no matter how mundane or routine it appears. I practice writing, sitting, eating, and breathing with my full attention. In doing so, I've begun to enjoy daily life as I once enjoyed gymnastics. Life hasn't changed; *I* have. By treating every action with respect and every moment as sacred, I've found a new relationship with life, filled with passion and purpose.

All I've described comes naturally, almost effortlessly, once we clear the internal obstructions in our lives. This book outlines how we can accomplish this.

If *No Ordinary Moments* serves, in a small way, to make your daily life more peaceful, happy, and healthy, then my efforts will have been rewarded and my joy multiplied in the mirror of your lives.

Dan Millman
San Rafael, California
Spring 1992

Part I
The Peaceful Warrior's Way

Introduction

Beneath the surface of daily life lies a deeper quest – a journey up a mountain path toward our hopes and dreams. *No Ordinary Moments* serves as a map up that mountain to a new way of life – through the same process of insight, disillusion, discovery, and inspiration I encountered and described in *Way of the Peaceful Warrior.*

The term *peaceful warrior* seems to contradict itself. How can we be both peaceful and a warrior? Famous warriors from every culture, in spite of their violent image, have demonstrated qualities of courage, commitment, and inner strength; yet few of these warriors had a peaceful heart. The peacemakers of history have shown qualities of loving-kindness and compassion; yet only a few of these peacemakers possessed a warrior's spirit. The peaceful warrior combines courage and love – a warrior's spirit with a peaceful heart.

Now we begin our journey: The first part of this book provides a revealing look at the issues and challenges of the peaceful warrior's way through the dark forest – a necessary preparation for our climb above the clouds and into the light.

In order to enhance the journey through this book, I have included a number of *action items* – exercises designed to convey the experience behind the words. Most of these items take only a little time to complete. If you do them, you will measurably increase your ability to translate the principles into real outcomes in daily life.

1

Heart of the Warrior's Way

Peace comes not from the absence of conflict,
but from the ability to cope with it.
Anonymous

Somewhere in the American West, a softly moaning wind blows dust and tumbleweeds across the vast desert wilderness, a barren land stretching across open country with no human life except for a few small, isolated frontier towns.

The cry of a coyote sounds above the howling wind, when out of the dust emerges a lone figure, striding softly across the desert floor, barely leaving any footprints. Walking gracefully, at an unhurried pace, he nods respectfully to a jackrabbit. As he passes, we see he wears an old hat and carries a small bag and bedroll tied around his chest. His face, unlined and serene, reveals a man without past or future—a man who lives completely in the present moment.

We sense in him great courage, power, and strength, and at the same time, a quality of compassion and kindness. Warrior and priest, he lives to protect life and to serve those in need; soft-spoken, gentle, and refined in manner, a Shaolin priest well trained in the martial arts, he lives as a healer and counselor whose wisdom derives from the natural world. An archetype of the peaceful warrior, his name is Kwai Chang Cain—a character created by Ed Spielman and played by David Carradine for the old "Kung Fu" television series.

Real-life examples of peaceful warriors include Mahatma Gandhi, Harriet Tubman, Martin Luther King, Jr., Joan of Arc, Albert Schweitzer, and many others who have applied

3

a warrior's spirit to the cause of peace. They reflect the potential within each of us.

The Way of the Peaceful Warrior

Happiness, or Spirit, surrounds us and permeates every cell of our being. We only feel this inspiration in rare moments, however, because of internal obstructions in our body, mind, and emotions. The way of the peaceful warrior directly confronts and clears these internal obstructions so we can feel the happiness that is our natural birthright.

As peaceful warriors, we strive to travel the paths of life with courageous spirits, but we recognize that true healing ultimately comes from the heart. We realize that we help to shape our lives, and that by changing ourselves we can change our world. The way begins where we are. It works at every level. The method is simple action. The time is now.

Peaceful warriors have the patience to wait
until the mud settles and the waters clear.
They remain unmoving until the right time,
so the right action arises by itself.
They do not seek fulfillment, but wait with open arms
to welcome all things.
Ready to use all situations, wasting nothing,
they embody the Light.

Peaceful warriors have three great treasures:
simplicity, patience, and compassion.
Simple in actions and in thoughts,
they return to the source of Being.
Patient with both friends and enemies,
they live in harmony with the way things are.
Compassionate toward themselves,
they make peace with the world.

Some may call this teaching nonsense;
others may call it lofty and impractical.
But to those who have looked inside themselves,
this nonsense makes perfect sense.
And for those who put it into practice,
this loftiness has deep roots.

Adapted from a poem by Lao-tzu

Warriors in Training in the School of Daily Life

Imagine, in the midst of daily life, a moment when your mind clears and becomes serene, your emotions open as blissful energy, and your body feels strong, supple, relaxed, and alive. As extraordinary as that may sound, it describes your normal state—when you were two months old.

We all once embodied this warrior's state, and we can do so again. We don't need to learn anything new; we only need to clear the obstructions that block our natural experience. By cutting free our programs, fears, and beliefs with the sword of awareness, we can experience with our whole body what it feels like to reawaken the bright innocence of our childhood while retaining the hard-earned wisdom of experience.

Sometimes Earth seems to function as a spiritual boot camp—a place where we learn about the material realm, the realm of changes. Here, even our loved ones eventually pass out of our lives. The demands of life develop the best within us; we are all peaceful warriors in training. Earth provides our schooling; daily life becomes our training ground.

Within each of us beats the heart of a peaceful warrior. When we gaze at our reflection and look deeply into our own eyes, we can begin to see a glimmer of who we are becoming.

♦

The Face of a Peaceful Warrior

1. Find a mirror and look at your face for one minute.
   - See yourself as if looking at someone you've never seen before.
   - Look with compassion and stay open to whatever feelings arise.
2. Gaze into your eyes with the feeling that you are looking into the eyes of a peaceful warrior.

♦

The Three Selves

Body, mind, and emotions form one kind of trinity that comprises the human being. Another powerful trinity called the *three selves* offers a useful model for appreciating the scope of the peaceful warrior's way. I refer to the Basic Self (or subconscious), the Conscious Self (or ego), and the Higher Self (or spiritual self). Insight into these three distinct forms of consciousness provides powerful leverage for attaining greater awareness, motivation, enjoyment, and inspiration in our lives.

The Basic Self

The *Basic Self* has sometimes been called our "inner child" because the qualities, motives, and characteristics of this consciousness closely resemble those of a four- to seven-year-old child. Like young children, Basic Selves share common qualities, yet some Basic Selves show more strength, confidence, and understanding than others. Although I sometimes use the terms *subconscious* or *inner child*, I generally prefer the broader term, *Basic Self*, because I refer to a consciousness whose functions go beyond those of the popular image of the "inner child."

Separate and distinct from the conscious mind, the Basic

Self closely identifies with the physical body and manifests as our body wisdom—our instinct, intuition, gut feelings, latent drives and abilities, and memory. In charge of our body, the Basic Self works through the autonomic (involuntary) nervous system to maintain our body's functions and generate our energy for life.

Like most children, the Basic Self remains highly open to suggestion (hypnosis), programming, visualization, or any form of healing that works with the subconscious. If secure and happy, the childlike Basic Self demonstrates playfulness, energy, inspiration, loyalty, determination, and spontaneity. But if our conscious mind ignores, devalues, or suppresses the Basic Self (as often happens), then it tends to withdraw, block energy, lower immune response, and sabotage our endeavors. By becoming more conscious of how our subconscious works, we can access energy and courage and improve our health and sense of well-being. The Basic Self serves as a foundation from which we can leap to higher states of awareness.

The Conscious Self

The *Conscious Self* serves as the center of logic, reason, and discrimination—all necessary tools for life. Its major function involves conscious learning so that we can better adapt to and thrive in our environment. I use the terms *Conscious Self, conscious mind,* and *ego* interchangeably.

When working in harmony, our Conscious Self *guides, educates, and reassures* our Basic Self as a parent would a child, helping it understand life while allowing the Basic Self to express its own unique capacities. When out of balance, the Conscious Self tends to use logic and reason to devalue the feelings and intuitions of the Basic Self the way some adults tend to devalue the feelings of children. This results in an estrangement between mind and body; we lose touch with our feelings and our deepest intuitions. To heal this imbalance, our Conscious Self can learn to reestablish rapport with our Basic Self, which leads to a renewed sense of vitality, pleasure, and health.

The peaceful warrior values reason, logic, and the other functions of the Conscious Self but also recognizes their limitations. As we begin to see our Conscious Self in perspective, we recognize that life works better when our Basic Self and Conscious Self cooperate under the loving dominion of the Higher Self.

The Higher Self

The *Higher Self*, a radiant aspect of our consciousness sometimes referred to as our "guardian angel," completes the trinity of the three selves. The Higher Self manifests qualities of selfless courage, love, compassion, wisdom, altruism, and joy. It serves as a "cheerleader to the soul," reminding the Conscious Self of the spiritual possibilities beyond the material world and the limits of the conscious mind.

The Higher Self has deep empathy for the Conscious Self and Basic Self but exists in a state of loving detachment; it gently guides without interfering, allowing the Conscious Self to make its own choices and learn whatever lessons it needs.

By mastering the powers of the Basic and Conscious Selves, we can enjoy great success in the world, but staying in touch with our Higher Self adds the dimensions of joy, love, and an experience of the higher possibilities of life.

Experiencing the Three Selves

1. Experience your Basic Self by tuning into your body; recall the last time you had a feeling, hunch, or intuition about something. Notice how your body responds to your thoughts and feelings, giving you signals to help guide you.
2. Experience your Conscious Self by noticing your thoughts and judgments right now. Watch how you gather information, apply logic, or learn something.

3. Experience your Higher Self by tuning into your heart and your higher feeling dimension. Recall those special moments when you felt inspired or uplifted – when your mind stopped, your body relaxed, and your heart opened to feel the embrace of your Higher Self.

◆

Aspects of the Way

The cumulative wisdom and highest practices of humanity embodied in the peaceful warrior's way have existed for centuries. Today, we are translating this ancient, universal wisdom into forms appropriate to modern men and women. Thousands of paths, approaches, methods, systems, schools, sects, and seminars exist, each with a slightly different approach. Some work primarily with the Basic Self; others emphasize the Conscious Self or Higher Self. Some place special attention on body, mind, or emotions. The way of the peaceful warrior works to integrate all these aspects of ourselves.

Body, Mind, and Emotions

When facing a razor-sharp sword in mortal combat, the ancient samurai knew the importance of physical skill, but they also knew that skill alone was not enough if their minds were distracted or their emotions in turmoil. These warriors didn't play to win or lose; they played to live or die. If they had a weakness, they could not ignore it or pretend it didn't exist. The ancient warriors knew that, like a chain, our lives break at the weakest link. Their lives depended on complete and equal training of body, mind, *and* emotions. If our lives are to count for something, we, too, need to strengthen our weakest link.

◆

The Weakest Link

1. Any difficulty we have encountered in life involves a weakness in body, mind, or emotions. Recall one or more difficulties you have faced in your life.
2. For each one, consider whether that difficulty relates more to body, mind, or emotions. Do you notice a pattern?

◆

Simple awareness of our weakest link serves as the first step toward strengthening it.

A Balanced Life

To achieve a state of harmony and inspiration, we need to integrate our body, mind, and emotions as well as our three selves—connecting heaven and earth with our head in the clouds and our feet on the ground.

> *Heaven is under our feet*
> *as well as over our heads.*
> Henry David Thoreau

As Ram Dass once said, "We can be lost in cosmic bliss, but still be responsible for remembering our zip code."

Courage and Love

Courage and love form two key precepts of the warrior's way; it takes courage to stay open and vulnerable. Courage entails feeling the fear and taking whatever action is necessary or remaining still. Love involves accepting all things as they are even while working toward positive change. Some of us have made great strides in the domain of courage; others have opened our hearts wide in the domain of love. The peaceful warrior's way embraces both.

A Way of Action

Many of us live in our heads, connected to everyday reality through a filter of our concepts. We *think* we understand ideas like living in the now, self-trust, and commitment, but real understanding only comes by *doing*; only action has the power to turn knowledge into wisdom. The way of the peaceful warrior rests on spontaneous, heartfelt action.

> *On the day of judgment,*
> *we shall not be asked what we have read,*
> *but what we have done.*
> Thomas à Kempis

Sometimes the highest action is none at all. Nature's rhythms reveal "a time for every purpose under heaven." The warrior values times of contemplation and stillness, when the highest wisdom accepts the natural course of life.

Light and Shadow

In the ancient traditions, in all cultures, warriors have had to confront and work with both the lighter *and* darker elements of the world, and of the psyche—meeting and embracing the disowned parts of the self. Unable to afford the luxury of comforting illusions, warriors have always dealt with the realities of life and death, acknowledging the dark forces of fear, insecurity, and self-doubt as sparring partners here to strengthen us. Shadows are only cast in the presence of a greater Light; the Light always reigns supreme. Secure in this knowledge, we stay open to all possibilities, while respecting the natural laws that govern the material level of reality.

The Battleground

Martial arts can serve as a metaphor of life; yet the peaceful warrior's way has little to do with fighting external opponents. Our greatest battles lie deep within our own psyches as we face fear, insecurity, and self-doubt. These internal adversaries pose a far greater threat to our lives and our well-being than the external difficulties of daily life.

> *Be kind, for everyone you meet*
> *is fighting a hard battle.*
> Plato

How many times have we heard the saying "We are our own worst enemy" without realizing how this principle applies to us? How many times, for example, have we become angry with someone else instead of using the energy of our anger to confront our inner opponents of fear, insecurity, and self-doubt? All significant battles are waged within the self.

> *We have seen the enemy and it is [within] us.*
> Pogo

The Moment of Truth

Some years ago, on a quiet evening just after dusk, Michael started to back his car into a parking space on a city street when the driver of the car parked behind him honked his horn. Michael stopped and checked behind him to see what was the matter but could find nothing amiss; it was a legal space, and he had a right to park there. Assuming that the man could not be honking at him, he continued pulling into the space.

The fellow honked again and flashed his lights. "What's going on?" Michael asked himself. A little irritated and puzzled, he put on the brake, got out of the car, and walked over to the driver's side window. "Excuse me," he asked, "is there a problem here?"

Michael froze as the man raised a twelve-gauge shotgun barrel to his face. For one instant, he didn't know whether the man was going to shoot him—whether this was his last breath, his last moment on Earth. Needless to say, it was no longer a quiet evening.

After another long instant, the man just said, "Get your car out of here."

Michael felt a moment of profound relief and elation. He was probably going to live another day. "Yes, sir," he said, getting back into his car and quickly pulling away. As he drove off, he noticed another man backing out of a nearby liquor store with a shotgun in one hand and a sack in the other; apparently Michael had been blocking the getaway car.

This incident affected Michael deeply, not just because it was frightening. As the hours and days passed, he relived the moment many times—staring down that gun barrel, wondering if in the next instant that man would relieve him of everything above his shoulders.

And he asked himself, "If I died, suddenly, right now—do I feel complete? Have I accomplished all I set out to do? What have I postponed until tomorrow? Is there anyone I still need to forgive, or to ask for their forgiveness? What old business have I left unfinished?"

When Michael told me about this incident and how his life had changed as a result, I understood even more deeply that there are no ordinary moments. It took a man with a gun to drive the point home—that each moment is precious; that each moment *counts* for something and we dare not waste it; that *this* is the moment of truth.

2

In the Arena of Daily Life

A pupil from whom nothing is ever demanded
which he cannot do,
never does all he can.
John Stuart Mill

Ups and Downs

At the end of *Way of the Peaceful Warrior*, I shared a deep realization in the only words I could find:

There is no need to search . . . achievement leads no-where . . . makes no difference at all. Just be happy now. Release your struggle, let go of your mind, throw away your concerns, and relax into the world. No need to resist life. Open your eyes and see that you are far more than you think. You are already free.

Lofty words, coming from an ecstatic moment of illumination. A few years later, however, they seemed like the words of a stranger; I could remember them, but I couldn't *feel* them. Lofty words don't satisfy us if our body is in pain, if our relationship is troubled, or if we're wondering how we're going to pay our bills this month.

During this down cycle in my life, doors slammed in my face and opportunities dried up. Despite my past realizations, I felt lost and frustrated. Doing what I could to support my family, I worked two jobs, starting at 4:30 A.M. and finishing at 6:00 P.M. I was working as a typist—the only skill I could market at the time. Deep in debt, I handled what was in front

14

of me, stayed open to opportunities, and faced life one day at a time.

Something Socrates had said helped sustain me through this dry spell. He reminded me that life has cycles—that whatever goes up, comes down, and what falls can rise again. Progress can be slow: We remember, then we forget, then we remember; we take two steps forward, then one step back. No matter how enlightened we become, we still face the realities of daily life.

A young man had spent five arduous years searching for truth. One day, as he walked up into the foothills of a great mountain range, he saw an old man approach from above, walking down the path, carrying a heavy sack on his back. He sensed that this old man had been to the mountaintop; he had finally found one of the wise—one who could answer his heart's deepest questions.

"Please, Sir," he asked. "Tell me the meaning of enlightenment."

The old man smiled, and stopped. Then, fixing his gaze on the youth, he slowly swung the heavy burden off his back, laid the sack down, and stood up straight.

"Ah, I understand," the young man replied. "But, Sir, what comes after enlightenment?"

The old man took a deep breath, then swung the heavy sack over his shoulders and continued on his way.

Socrates once told me, "A flash of enlightenment offers a preview of coming attractions, but when it fades, you will see more clearly what separates you from that state—your compulsive habits, outmoded beliefs, false associations, and other mental structures." Just when our lives are starting to get better, we may feel like things are getting worse—because for the first time we see clearly what needs to be done.

"After illumination," Socrates continued, "difficulties continue to arise; what changes is your relationship to them. You see more and resist less. You gain the capacity to turn your problems into lessons and your lessons into wisdom."

The Simple Life

Mahatma Gandhi, nonviolent leader and political activist, advised all of us to "live simply, so that others may simply live." Gandhi did indeed live according to these high ideals; wearing a loincloth or other simple garb and spinning his own cotton, he took only what he needed, and he gave whatever he could. But Gandhi had help from others. Said one Indian industrialist who donated millions of dollars to Gandhi's cause, "It cost me a fortune to keep Gandhi simple."

What constitutes simplicity may differ for each of us, depending upon our age, circumstances, and life purpose. Few of us are destined to embody Gandhi's high ideals or extremes of simplicity, or to live in isolated caves or forests like the wandering ascetics. We are more likely to deal with the everyday realities of modern society such as getting an education, earning a living, having relationships, and perhaps raising families, and facing the challenges that go with all of these. Still, we can all practice inner simplicity—a quiet mind in the midst of a busy lifestyle.

In the Fires of Daily Life

A man once said to me, "I'd like to live like a peaceful warrior and do more spiritual practices, but with a family to support, and a full-time job, I just don't have the time."

He didn't yet realize that his family and his job—his relationship with his wife, the responsibilities of children, and the pressures of his profession—*were* his spiritual practice. Such a practice often demands and develops more than sitting in a cave and meditating. I speak from experience, because I've done both.

There is a place for inner work—for stopping the world and getting away for a while—but for the peaceful warrior *daily life is the arena of training;* we use the demands of life as the means to reveal our weak areas, transform them into strengths, and develop body, mind, and emotions.

Near the end of our time together, Socrates reminded me, "I've shown you the way *of* the peaceful warrior, not the way *to* the peaceful warrior. The journey itself creates the warrior; daily life is your journey and is the means of your training. When you recognize this, every moment takes on a larger purpose."

Daily life offers so much potential for growth precisely because it makes so many demands. We all recognize the issues that test and train us: work or career, finances, relationships, education, housing, health, diet and exercise—and finding our purpose, meaning, and direction.

Relationships

If life is a dance, we need a dancing partner. A primary, committed relationship is a stabilizing influence; it frees time and attention for other issues. Because sexuality plays an integral role in most of our lives, and because we have a sexual drive, if we do not have a stable relationship we often either resign ourselves to masturbation in lieu of an intimate relationship, or spend our lives searching for a partner.

No matter what other qualities of attraction exist, most couples are also drawn together by mutual sexual need. In nearly every relationship, one person has a greater need for sexual release, so every relationship involves a dynamic tension.

The bubbling pot of relationship also contains issues of intimacy and affection, companionship and privacy, support and loyalty, honest feedback and open communication.

The demands of relationship—for intimacy, openness, sharing, sacrifice, adaptability, emotion, passion, honesty, and vulnerability—can compromise or threaten the pure self-interest of the Conscious Self, which tends to hold its own individual needs as paramount. Relationships, in other words, represent an affront to the ego; after the honeymoon period, couples, by nature, don't get along easily. Committed relationships such as marriages offer one of the most challenging spiritual disciplines on the planet, because they confront our tendency to withdraw from love and intimacy and spur us to mature beyond this tendency.

Some couples form unconscious contracts in order to tolerate each other. While each person's needs are met, they stay together, but if the liabilities start to outweigh the benefits, they legally or emotionally separate. Other more aware couples bring added psychological resources into the relationship. They form understandings, respect boundaries, make conscious agreements, and create a life together of mutual benefit and support.

In this regard, I feel proud of my parents, and other couples like them, who, despite their issues and blind spots, have remained together in a loving relationship for fifty-nine years. They have even retained their sense of humor, which probably accounts for the longevity of their relationship. This kind of commitment represents a rare spiritual achievement, through which they have matured in ways that surpass some of my sophisticated young friends who know all about "levels of consciousness."

The responsibility of parenthood, for all its joys, makes emotional and financial demands and calls for sacrifices that offer one of the most maturing forms of spiritual training life provides us. I once read a poster that said, "Mature adults don't make children; children make mature adults."

Those of us who don't choose to have children can benefit from spending quality time with nephews, nieces, or other children, because it helps us reconnect with the simplicity, playfulness, and creativity of our Basic Self. Caring for a dog or another pet who enjoys attention and affection offers those of us who don't have children a chance to form a loving bond with a creature who embodies many qualities of the Basic Self.

In addition to our relationship with children or pets, many of us have issues to work out with our parents. We sometimes sweep these issues under the rug, because expressing them might mean "upsetting people" and "hurting feelings." For that very reason, our relationship with our parents offers a wonderful opportunity for courage, love, and growth.

I remind those who do not choose to get married or have children that these primary areas of growth are two of many; there is something for everyone.

On-the-Job Training

Most of us seek a meaningful career—a way to spend our time, a way to feel like a contributing member of the society in which we live. Office politics present a microcosm of life, and the relationships we develop at work offer numerous opportunities to "work things out" with peers, colleagues, and the office pain-in-the-butt (who may or may not be the boss).

Our work constantly asks us, Who are you? What are your values and priorities? What are you capable of? What do you deserve? How do you get along with others? Thus, in its demands, it has all the potential of marriage for aiding our internal development.

Living in this world costs money, and even if we are independently wealthy, right livelihood involves honoring our values and abilities while providing a service in the world. The amount of money we make is related both to our marketable abilities, chosen work, and self-esteem—what we feel we're worth. Money issues and work mirror our present state of functioning and are therefore ripe with potential for growth.

In the Mirror of the Body

Our body's health and physical shape reflect our current level of discipline, emotional clarity, and psychological functioning. We cannot easily fool ourselves when we look in a mirror. Beneath the cut of the clothing and the makeup, when we assess our level of energy and vitality, we have life's feedback about our present lifestyle, our degree of awareness and discipline, and even our level of self-esteem. Our issues with health, physical appearance, and fitness through diet, exercise, and a balanced life provide a constant demand for introspection and a means of taking stock—a valuable part of our training.

---◆---

Issues and Lessons of Daily Life

1. Which area(s) of life – work or career, finances, relationships, education, health (addictions, diet, exercise, etc.) have challenged you the most?
2. In one or two sentences, write or state aloud the main lesson you have learned or quality you have gained from that challenge.

---◆---

Forks in the Road

Daily life presents a series of choices. Do we get up or stay in bed? Do we get married or travel on our own? Do we get a job or go to school full-time? Do we opt for immediate goals or go the distance? Every choice we make has benefits and liabilities. Life issues push us to find our deeper values—to weigh them and make choices. Every choice has consequences that can teach us something. Therefore, every one of us who lives and works in the arena of daily life is engaged in full-time spiritual training along the path of the peaceful warrior.

3

When the Going Gets Tough

Life can be hard and dangerous;
those who seek happiness may find sorrow;
those who seek peace may find strife;
those who seek love may find disappointment.
Joy comes to those who do not fear solitude.
Life comes to those not afraid to die.
Adapted from Joyce Cary

Daily Life as a Difficult School

We learn a great deal here on Earth because daily life is a difficult school. From the first shock of birth, we inevitably meet pain as well as pleasure. In addition to the usual challenges and difficulties, the going can get so tough at times that we understand the Taoist sage who once said, "Those who celebrate at birth and mourn at death may have it backward."

Like ships at sea bound for different ports of call, sometimes we sail steadfastly, guided by the stars and a clear compass; other times, we feel lost—cut adrift. When the seas of our lives are calm, we settle into a comfortable routine—go on automatic pilot—but when a storm comes up, we have to draw upon our deepest inner resources.

Life is not always a matter of holding good cards,
but sometimes, of playing a poor hand well.
Robert Louis Stevenson

Although we can't always avoid the storms in our lives, we can control our response; we can trim the sails, batten down the hatches, and make the best of it. Depending on how we respond, life will either lift us up or grind us down. What doesn't kill us, if approached with the right attitude, will strengthen us.

Spiritual Weight Lifting

Anyone who has trained with weights knows that if we try to lift too much, we can tear down the muscles; on the other hand, if we don't lift enough, we don't develop our strength. The hardships of our lives serve as the weights we lift in order to strengthen our spirits. Adversity gives us the chance to discover our true capacity. We can only show courage in the face of fear.

> *Courage is like a muscle;*
> *we strengthen it with use.*
> Ruth Gordon

Some years ago, in a study of immune systems, scientists raised a group of chickens in an optimally comfortable, sterile environment: just the right temperature and the right food, no difficulties, traumas, threats, risks, or stress of any kind. After several generations, the scientists placed these chickens back in a normal environment; they all quickly died.

When we meet with adversity, rather than ask, "Why did this happen to me?," we can roll up our sleeves and remember that we are engaged in spiritual weight lifting. If life develops what it demands, the demands of hard times develop strong spirits.

> *In the midst of winter*
> *I discovered within me,*
> *an invincible summer.*
> Camus

The Blessings of Adversity

In 1966, the summer before my senior year at college, I felt in the best physical shape of my life. I had just bought a new Triumph motorcycle. Triumph—it seemed an appropriate name for this period of my life: I had just completed some stunt work for a Tony Curtis movie on the beach at Malibu; I would soon ride up to Berkeley, then catch a plane to Yugoslavia, where I had been invited, as a potential Olympian, to train with the world's best gymnasts before the World Championships.

Then, just two days before I was to leave for the World Championships, my motorcycle collided with a car making an illegal turn; my right thighbone smashed into about forty pieces. Those few moments changed the course of my life—not just externally, but internally. Something inside me changed.

Sometimes we turn to God
when our foundations are shaking
only to find out it is God
who is shaking them.

Anonymous

If I hadn't broken my leg, I might never have met the old man I called Socrates; I might never have considered life and death in the same way, or understood pain and suffering, or discovered the commitment, strength, and power I had inside me. In retrospect, that broken leg turned into one of the great blessings of my life. Adversity may turn out to be one of Spirit's greatest gifts. I do not recommend broken bones, however, as a method of awakening.

In *Way of the Peaceful Warrior*, Socrates told me the story of an old farmer and his son whose only horse ran away. The neighbors said it was bad luck, but then the horse came back with three wild horses following. This seemed like good luck—until the son, trying to ride one of the wild horses, fell off and broke his leg. Bad luck, it turned out—except that soon after the accident, the military generals swept through the valley, taking all able-bodied young men off to a terrible war. The son, of course, was spared. Within every gift lies adversity; within every adversity lies a gift.

One day, while reaching for some toilet paper, I noticed an ant crawling across the paper I was about to tear off the roll. With a puff of air, I blew the ant off the paper. From the ant's viewpoint this may have seemed like a big misfortune, unless it considered the alternative.

Learning From Adversity

1. Recall a circumstance in your life that felt painful or difficult.
2. Ask yourself these questions:
   • What felt most difficult about it?
   • What positive lesson(s) did it offer?
   • What do you see as the primary benefits of an otherwise painful situation?
   • How will this knowledge help you in the future?

The Bluebird's Lesson

One chilly autumn day, as thousands of birds took wing and flew south to escape the frozen winter, one little bluebird decided he wasn't leaving with the rest. "A waste of time," he reasoned. "After all, I'll just have to fly all the way back again next spring." Soon, however, a record cold spell descended upon the land, and the little bird realized he would have to leave. He winged his way up into the sky, but soon the icy air overcame him, his little wings froze, and he plummeted out of the sky. As fortune would have it, his nearly lifeless body landed in a large haystack, then fell onto the hard earth of a barnyard, near a group of cows.

Just as the little bluebird's heart, nearly frozen, was about to stop, a cow happened by and relieved itself directly over the little bird. The warm manure covered the bird, saving his life; his little heart started beating strongly, and his wings thawed out. Happy to be alive, the bluebird began to sing a beautiful song, which, as fate allowed, attracted the attention of the barnyard cat, who padded over, looked through the manure, found the little bird, and promptly ate him.

This story ends with two morals:

1. Not everyone who dumps on us is necessarily our enemy.
2. Not everyone who gets us out of the mess is necessarily our friend.

Difficult people and situations aren't the only doorways to transformation, but they may be one of the surest; they get our attention and reveal our weak areas. I remember a story told to me by a Catholic friend:

> *Saint Teresa of Avila was full of life, with a quick tongue, mischievous spirit, and ready wit. One stormy night she found herself in an old cart, holding the reins of two old oxen, as she bumped over a muddy road in Spain.*
>
> *Lightning flashed and thunder roared; in a panic, the startled oxen sped up, and the wheel of the wagon caught in a deep hole, throwing Teresa off the cart, where she landed face first in the mud.*
>
> *Teresa knew that she was supposed to thank God for everything, but this wasn't going to be easy. Just then she heard the voice of her beloved Jesus say, "Teresa, be not dismayed, but only strengthened—I offer this only to my most faithful friends."*
>
> *Teresa—her face and clothing covered with mud—*

*thought about this for a moment, then looked up and
answered, "Perhaps that's why you have so few."*

Pain as Awakener

All of us face physical, mental, and emotional pain in the
course of our daily lives. Physical pain confronts us in obvious forms. Mental pain manifests as worries, regrets, contradic-
tion, and confusion. Emotional pain comes as some variation
of fear, sorrow, or anger. Whatever the form, pain generates
the impulse to change, and serves to wake us sleepers from
our dreams.

> *Pain is the most heeded of doctors;*
> *to goodness and wisdom*
> *we only make promises;*
> *we obey pain.*
> Marcel Proust

Pain of any kind gives us feedback about something that
needs our attention—about our physical habits, about our beliefs, about our emotions.

Adversity can be a gift, because it offers us two clear
choices: Suffer the consequences of stagnation, or face the
challenges of change.

> *I admire those who can smile in times of trouble,*
> *who can gather strength from distress*
> *and who grow brave by reflection.*
> Thomas Paine

We can tolerate a little pain for a long time. Fearing the
unknown territory of transformation, we may choose familiar
suffering for years. We may continue to cope with dysfunctional relationships, numbing or dehumanizing work, or other
life-denying situations. Though Spirit has compassion and

patience, life is a stern teacher; pain, if untended or masked, continues to grow, until change or madness become our only choices.

At that crisis point, when there's no other option but futile resistance, if we choose the warrior's path, we go through the pain, like a dark bank of clouds, and emerge in a place of clarity; we come out from our hiding place and find the will to heal our lives. Most of all, we never give up.

The saints are the sinners who keep on trying.
Robert Louis Stevenson

Riding the Natural Cycles

Some of us interpret tough times as divine justice, a punishment from God. I'd like to suggest that God never punishes us, but only gives us opportunities to balance and to learn.

The wise learn from adversity;
the foolish merely repeat it.
Anonymous

All things move in cycles, like the seasons: Times of abundance, when fortune smiles, alternate with times of scarcity, when our best efforts bear little fruit. The wise use such hard times for their own purposes, sowing seeds, waiting out the storm or the dry spell, building foundations, preparing for opportunity when it comes.

It's better to prepare for an opportunity
that may never come
than to have an opportunity
but find ourselves unprepared.
Les Brown

Sparring in the Ring of Life

When we get up each day, we step into the ring with the challenges of daily life—not only the external challenges of other people and tasks, but the inner battles with fear, insecurity, jealousy, envy, and self-doubt.

Life comforts the disturbed and disturbs the comfortable. Sometimes, out of nowhere, Spirit lands a left hook that really shakes us up; we get slammed into the ropes, knocked to the canvas. Maybe the shock comes in the form of a financial crisis, a death in the family, a divorce, or an illness or injury.

Such stresses can shock and disorient us, but they also wake us from our comfortable slumber and catalyze our subconscious into generating the energy and focus we need to make life changes. They can expand our reference point so we ask ourselves, What is my life for? Who am I? Where have I been and where am I headed?

When we get broadsided by circumstance—if life lands a one-two punch and knocks us to the canvas—we can stay down or we can stand up. Standing up after a bad fall can require an act of great endurance and courage. When we finally get back on our feet, we can look our adversary in the eye, put our hands on our hips, and say, "Okay, you knocked me down, but I got up, and I'm going to keep getting up." Then you can sum up a warrior's attitude toward adversity with the words, "Was *that* your best shot? C'mon, give me your *best* shot."

> *Pray not for a lighter load,*
> *but for stronger shoulders.*
> St. Augustine

Hard times provide opportunities that don't come around when life is comfortable. Those of us who have spent time with children who have cancer or other life-threatening illnesses know that such tragedies also serve as an express elevator to Spirit. These children often transform into wise old sages in children's bodies.

When we open up, drop our guard, and stop our posturing, we become vulnerable to learning again; we lose face and become willing beginners again. The mind is like a parachute; it works best when it's open. Coming from the beginner's attitude, we remain open to new discovery.

> *I'm looking forward*
> *to looking back on all this.*
> Sandra Knell

The Teachings of Death and Separation

The stages of denial, anger, depression, and then acceptance apply to any major loss; we grieve the death of a relationship in much the same way we might mourn the death of a loved one. We need to take special care of our Basic Self in times of grief or loss. Our Conscious Self, relying on logic, may cling to rationalizations about why the relationship needed to end or believe it has a loved one's death "under emotional control." If we claim to be "just fine" after a major loss, we may benefit from a deeper look.

No matter how "strong" or reasonable we may act on a conscious level, our Basic Self will most likely feel fear—even terror—as well as confusion, insecurity, deep sorrow, and anger at the "unfairness" of our loss. Therefore, we need to give our Basic Self some tender, loving care and the space to grieve in spite of how resilient we *think* we are. Major changes of any kind, including birth and death, can shock and disorient our Basic Self. Whether or not our Conscious Self thinks it's necessary, self-compassion and appropriate ceremony can help heal and reassure our Basic Self.

Surviving the Death of a Loved One

From the transcendental perspective, birth and death mark apparent beginnings and endings within the cycles of changes; all things rise and fall and rise again, only in different forms. A person's death may be relatively dignified or very difficult, but no more difficult than birth, with its pain, blood, bodily fluids, and trauma. Transitions are both profound and challenging, both for those of us changing, and for the friends and loved ones who are left behind.

> *God gave us memories*
> *so that we might enjoy roses*
> *in December.*
>
> James Barrie

Specific visualizations can help our Basic Self to accept the loss of a loved one, especially if that loss is sudden, unexpected, or if the loved one died away from home.

———————————◆———————————

Saying Good-bye

1. Remember and picture the loved one who has died in a happy moment of laughter or kindness or calm.
2. Feel the joy of that moment, and recognize that no one can take away these internal memories, which you can enjoy at any time. Whenever you recall the one who has passed on, see that same happy image – something you still share in a very real sense. The physical part of that person has gone away, but the energy and memories will be with you as long as you wish.
3. Now, in your mind's eye and in your heart, picture and feel yourself saying a loving good-bye, in any way you wish, for as long as you need to. Imagine the kind of farewell you would

have liked to say if you had known that he or she would be dying.
4. Accept all the feelings that come up, including the courage to stand alone. Take within you the good and positive qualities of that person as a gift. And say good-bye.

---◆---

The End of a Relationship

Relationships do not necessarily last "till death do us part"—nor should they, despite best intentions and arbitrary instructions or expectations of others. People come together in relationships for a variety of purposes, and the relationships end when these purposes have been fulfilled. Some relationships are meant to last a long time; others, for shorter duration.

While a commitment to remain together helps create an atmosphere of spiritual growth through compromise, sacrifice, sharing, openness, trust, and cooperation, we are not necessarily meant to stick a relationship out no matter what.

Whether married or not, when a relationship ends we can wisely treat this ending with the same respect we would give any death or loss. One or both members of a couple may feel angry, resentful, or alienated—or they may remain good friends; in either case, *the relationship itself* deserves respect. We can appreciate the purpose a relationship has served, making the best possible use of it by way of a thorough "debriefing"—using it as an opportunity for learning and growth.

Death and divorce certainly have as much significance as birth and marriage, and are often much more educational. We create beautiful wedding ceremonies for the Basic Selves of all concerned; we may also benefit from a ceremony marking a separation.

Ideally, such a ceremony would take place with the two people before a group of close friends. If the estrangement feels too great, however, it can be read by one person, as a form of closure, substituting "I" for "we," and changing some of the language as appropriate.

◆

A Separation Ceremony

We are here to acknowledge the parting of two souls whose paths now go their separate ways.

Though we may seem to separate for negative reasons, with feelings of sorrow and anger, feelings both expressed and unexpressed, it is time to accept that whether or not we consciously desire this change, it will be for the highest good of all concerned no matter what reasons now appear for us to separate or to stay together. And it is up to all of us to make the best use of this separation, to learn about ourselves, and to grow and evolve, so that the time we've had together, and the time to part, will bear fruit in the future for each of us.

Take a few moments to remember a happy time together, without clinging to it, but knowing that these memories can last, in spite of the shadows and difficulties we now experience. [*Pause to remember.*]

Let us acknowledge what we have shared and created together; let us acknowledge each other for what we have been able to give of ourselves, whether we gave little or in abundance, recognizing that we did the best we were capable of at our present stage of evolution. [*Pause to give silent thanks.*]

We acknowledge ourselves for whatever painful feelings arise, and we accept that they will pass. We leave open the possibility that when the feelings heal, we may someday, sooner or later, share as friends, and offer the mutual support of those who understand each other.

We recognize that the end of one thing opens the space for another, and that grieving in time is washed away by the joys of new experience.

As two individual souls of value, we say good-bye. While

accepting our present feelings, we turn to the future with wisdom gained from experience.

◆

No matter what our Conscious Self finds rational, no reasons make up for the sense of loss. Our Basic Self grows attached to relationships and people. Here in the realm of changes, we cannot hold onto anything or anyone forever. By accepting the process of change, of gain and loss, we take one more step up the mountain path on the way of the peaceful warrior.

It Could Be Worse

Sometimes things go from bad to worse; sometimes, just when we see a light at the end of the tunnel, it turns out to be the headlight of an oncoming train.

> *Pete went to his doctor for a complete physical examination. The doctor called him a few days later and said, "The lab reports are in; I have bad news and worse news."*
>
> *Confused and troubled, Pete said, "Bad news and worse news? Well, what's the bad news?"*
>
> *"You have twenty-four hours to live," the doctor informed him. "The lab reports are conclusive."*
>
> *In shock, Pete could only say, "Twenty-four hours? But — what's the worse news?"*
>
> *"Oh, that," the doctor answered, casually, looking down at some papers. "I meant to call you yesterday."*

When we're hurting, it does very little good for someone to tell us "it could be worse." It *already* feels worse. On the other hand, what we call "troubles" are largely a matter of perspective. During a period when money felt scarce, our car broke down and the bill was much larger than I'd expected.

I didn't know how I was going to pay for it, and, feeling irritable, I got into an argument with my wife. I thought I had a problem; then I remembered a haunting picture I had seen showing the smiling faces of starving children living in absolute squalor and poverty in India.

A few weeks later, during a stressful period, I came down with a bad case of the flu; I was going to fall behind at work, and my next paycheck would hardly pay the rent. As I thought about my problems and flipped through the television channels, I saw images of the homeless in our cities and people struggling to stay alive in many countries of the world where starvation, disease, and painful death constitute business as usual.

I lay back in bed and started to laugh. I laughed at myself, and I laughed at the human condition. I laughed at a world in which the death of thousands comes as cataclysmic news to some, and a casual news item to others, sandwiched between local weather and sports. I laughed because otherwise I would have cried.

Since that time, my difficulties have never seemed so big. I like to remind myself that if I have clothing on my back and a place to live and food to eat, I don't have any real problems. This observation may not feel helpful to those of us whose partners just walked out the door and who are feeling deep emotional pain. But we can get so wrapped up in our own little world, our own personal concerns, that we lose sight of the bigger picture. We have lost perspective.

> *I cried because I had no shoes*
> *until I met a man who had no feet.*
> Persian saying

For anyone who has had a tough day recently, I offer the following accident report submitted by a bricklayer in the West Indies:

My supervisor asked me to bring down some excess bricks from the third floor, so I rigged a beam and pulley, hoisted up a barrel, and tied it in place. After filling the barrel with bricks, I returned to the ground and untied the rope, intending to lower the barrel to the ground.

Unfortunately, I misjudged the weight of the bricks. As the barrel started down, it jerked me off the ground so fast and so far I was unable to let go. Halfway up, I met the barrel coming down and received a severe blow on the shoulder.

I then continued to the top, banging my head against the beam and getting my fingers jammed in the pulley.

When the barrel hit the ground, it burst its bottom, allowing the bricks to spill out. I was now heavier than the barrel and so I started down again at high speed.

Halfway down I met the barrel coming up and received severe injuries to my shins. When I hit the ground I landed on the bricks, getting several painful cuts from the sharp edges.

At this point, I must have lost my presence of mind because I let go of the line. The barrel then came down, giving me another heavy blow on the head and putting me in the hospital.

The above story seems an apt metaphor not only of the tragicomedy of life but of how we humans create our own messes while trying to clean up after others; stumbling and bumbling, wearing the most pompous air, we walk with our noses in the air and trip over the curb. Perhaps the almost universal popularity of the Marx Brothers, Laurel and Hardy, and the Three Stooges stems from their uncanny resemblance to us all.

A Warrior's Faith

Pray as if everything depended on God,
and work as if everything depended upon man.
Francis Cardinal Spellman

Sometimes faith is our only way out. Times come when we can only find the courage to *assume* that whatever choice we've made and whatever circumstances we face are perfect for us, and we can then proceed with confidence.

Our choices will feel inherently "right" if we access the wisdom of our subconscious as well as our Conscious Self. If we try to figure out our lives with our mind alone, we may end up climbing to the top of the ladder only to find out it's leaning against the wrong wall. When we trust our deepest intuitions and gut feelings, we can also trust that whatever we choose will serve us well—that any decision we make is the right one.

Understanding Suffering

Spirit guides us in ways that our Conscious Self can't always understand or accept. For example, some people are challenged with physical ailments that send them on a long search to heal themselves. Only later do they realize that what seemed like pure adversity at the time really offered precisely the education they needed to become a resource for others, and to live out their life purpose as healers.

Sometimes our suffering enables us to understand the suffering of others. Along with the pain of illness or injuries comes the blessing of compassion. I've always found a gift hidden in every adversity. *That doesn't make adversity any easier; it only makes it more meaningful.*

Sometimes a health issue can be cured; other times, it will not improve much, for God's own reasons, and we can only practice acceptance, and make this challenge part of our training.

Pain, whether in body, mind, or emotions, is a fire storm that purifies all in its path, clearing old karmas and teaching new lessons. Don't seek pain, but when it comes, the path out of the fire reveals hard-earned wisdom. Giving birth involves labor pains, even when we are the one being reborn.

What is to give light must endure burning.
Viktor Frankl

Suffering happens, but it doesn't last forever, and every pain endured contains a lesson to be learned. A warrior's perspective can help us to understand and accept the natural cycles of good times and bad times, and to appreciate the uses of both. But when the going gets tough, we want to feel better, to stop hurting; we want life to get easier. When we're struggling in the quicksand, we don't want encouraging words — we want a tree branch or a rope! Sometimes, however, a word, or a phrase, or an uplifting idea are all we have to hang onto.

The Buck Stops Here

If we have nothing at all to do with creating our present situation (through past choices and actions), then we humans are merely passive victims of an arbitrary fate. In some ways, perhaps we are subject to the vagaries of fate, but certainly not in all ways, and we always have the power to choose our attitudes and our response to even the most capricious circumstances.

God can't make a Stradivarius violin
without Stradivarius.
Anonymous

If we take an active responsibility for helping to create our present situation, this empowers us with the recognition that we can change it. There comes a point in time when we come to understand the nature of our cooperative venture with Spirit, when we realize that we have free will and that God only wants volunteers. Then, and only then, can we throw off the heavy shackles of self-pity and accept the power to change our present situation. When life knocks us down, we can do our best to land on our back, because if we can *look* up, we can *get* up. That's what I so admire about human beings—lovers and fighters, we keep getting up and climbing back into the ring.

Part II
Up the Mountain Path

Introduction

Some years ago, while I was teaching gymnastics at Stanford University, a quiet young man in one of my classes handed me a wristband made of tiny beads of different colors. On the band he had woven Chinese characters. "It says, 'mountain path,'" he explained. In my mind's eye, the path appeared: I saw the depth of that young man's vision; the mountain peak awaits, above the clouds, where the sun shines brightly through the rarefied air, up in the high country of our psyches.

I found out, as do we all, that it takes time and effort to climb that winding mountain path, past pitfalls, risks, and distractions of every kind. On the way, we meet light and darkness, beauty and pain, fatigue and elation. We cover vast distances with small steps. In the process, we learn about ourselves and about the world around us. Whatever experiences await us on our own mountain path shall pass. As we climb, our horizons expand and our perspectives broaden. Each new challenge leaves us stronger and wiser. Looking back, we see with greater clarity, and what once appeared as difficulties now reveal themselves as blessings; from the heights, we see the breathtaking beauty of the world.

You cannot stay on the summit forever;
you have to come down again.
So why bother in the first place?
Because what is below does not know what is above,
but what is above knows what is below.
One climbs, one sees.
One descends, one sees no longer,
but one has seen.

There is an art of conducting oneself
in the lower regions
by the memory of what one saw higher up.
When one can no longer see,
one can at least still know.

Mt. Analogue

4

Getting Real

As the disoriented pedestrian learned,
it's what we don't see that can hurt us.
Anonymous

Life, Illusion, and Reality

If we walk down Main Street while we are feeling hungry, the "reality" we see is going to be filled with places to eat. If we're in a hurry, the road seems monopolized by Sunday drivers. We all live in different worlds—the worlds of our own minds. Our views of reality can be so different, I sometimes want to ask my friends, "What color is the sky in your world?"

If a pickpocket stands in a crowd of saints,
all he sees are their pockets.
Hari Dass Baba

Some philosophers believe that life itself is an illusion—in the words from Shakepeare's *Macbeth*, "a tale, told by an idiot, full of sound and fury, signifying nothing." But if we cross the street without looking and a truck runs over us, it has more impact than all our philosophies. If life gets our attention with a serious illness, we have no alternative but to deal with it.

However, if two people have an accident, or come down with the same illness, one person may perceive this misfortune as a tragedy or a punishment from God; the other person may see it as a challenge or opportunity. One may feel bitter; the other, grateful. Each person will respond differently based on his or her individual *perception* of the event.

42

Getting Real   43

Our values, attitudes, beliefs, and associations determine our perception of the physical reality "out there," and our sense of what is "real." As our beliefs change, we tune into different dimensions. Thus, two people may look at the same external world; one may perceive a paranoid "hell," and the other, a world of beauty and love.

Rules for Being Human

Whatever else it may be, this is also a physical world; it costs us money, energy, and time to function here. Food costs, shelter costs, clothing costs. Therefore, we need to work—to expend time and energy. Not only do we need to eat, we also need to have sex. Sex is a primary drive, given to us by nature to help ensure the survival of the species. These statements are not idle conjecture, but tangible facts of life. The more we embrace the realities of life, the fewer bruises we sustain.

Whatever leeway we may have within the bounds of natural law, we can count on the following rules:

1. *We get only one body.* We may like it or not, but it's the only thing we are guaranteed to keep for a lifetime.
2. *We will learn lessons.* Since Earth is a full-time school, every person or incident is our teacher.
3. *Lessons often appear as "mistakes" or "failures."* The only real "mistake" is not learning the lesson.
4. *A lesson is repeated until learned.* It will appear in various forms until we learn it. If we are still here, we still have lessons to learn.
5. *If we don't learn the easy lessons, they get harder.* Pain is one way the universe gets our attention.
6. *We'll know we've learned a lesson when our actions change.* Only action turns knowledge into wisdom.
7. *We will tend to forget these rules.*
8. *We can remember any time we wish.*
(I have edited but did not create these "rules." With gratitude, I acknowledge the source, Cherie Carter-Scott.)

There ain't no rules around here!
We're trying to accomplish something.
Thomas Edison

Waking Up

Hunger is real; so is lack of clothing or shelter. Most other troubles we perceive in our lives are generated, in large part, by the illusions of the subjective mind. Our tendency to mistake our thoughts *about* reality for reality itself acts as a fundamental cause of human suffering.

Waking up involves a moment-to-moment recognition of how we perceive reality through the filter of our beliefs, associations, and interpretations. In a sense, when we look at the world or other people, we see our own mind. This recognition allows us to grasp the peaceful, calm, objective reality that lies just beyond the veils of the mind.

Waking up—getting real—involves a process rather than a single event. But even the first glimmer of recognition can change our life forever. To awaken, we have to realize we've been asleep; to break our chains, we have to realize we're bound.

The Game of Let's Pretend

Like most people, I've done my share of playing "let's pretend"—one of humanity's oldest games—pretending I was happy, pretending I liked someone, pretending there wouldn't be any consequences for my actions. I pretended a relationship was working, until I had to face that it wasn't; I pretended I could get away with things, until I didn't. I played pretend for many years, until finally Socrates shook me loose of my most stubborn illusions.

Many criminals play pretend; caught in mental schemes that have little basis in reality, they imagine they are getting away with something if they don't get caught, but ignore the spiritual costs and consequences in their own lives and the lives of others. Those of us who smoke cigarettes, abuse alcohol or other drugs, drive while intoxicated, or act out any other destructive behavior can also get stuck in fantasy worlds. Others of us have built walls of illusion to protect ourselves from memories of childhood abuse, molestation, or other painful or frightening traumas.

Intelligence offers no exemption from the game of self-deception. One very dear woman I know takes pride in her sharp intellect. She excels at mathematics and has a superior vocabulary and an awesome memory. She reasons well and has many assets, among them, a logical, analytical mind.

This same woman has smoked cigarettes for over forty years. Loved ones and friends have urged her to quit; they have shown her the surgeon general's report. Like many of us, she always has a good retort. She *puts the consequences out of her mind, but she can't put them out of her body.* I feel sad when I see her fight for breath as she struggles up some stairs, one slow step at a time. Sometimes she cries with regret. At great cost, she now understands the law of cause and effect.

By paying attention to the feedback in our lives, we can learn our lessons quickly, gracefully, and with relative ease. Even if we pick the hard way, life is a master teacher; sooner or later, one way or the other, we all learn the lessons of reality.

The Hazards of Illusion

Shakespeare reminded us, "This above all: to thine own self be true . . . " Those of us who deny our inner reality and our deepest feelings tend to have higher blood pressure, less flexible bodies, and more headaches, stomach pains, and sore lower backs; all of these symptoms reflect our Basic Self's efforts to get our attention and call us back to reality.

Carl Weisbrod, Ph.D., in a talk to the Honolulu Vegetarian Society, offered examples of some defense mechanisms Basic Selves use to resist change—in this example, related to diet:

Few of us want to die early, but according to statistics from the Center for Disease Control in Atlanta, the majority of U.S. deaths stem from heart disease, stroke, and cancer—nearly all of which we can prevent. In fact, as high as 75 percent of deaths can be linked to alcohol, smoking, other drugs, and dietary abuse.

Populations living on a starch-based diet, as our ancestors did, have little or none of the heart disease and cancer so common in "civilized" countries. And today, a growing weight of undeniable evidence indicates that a low-fat, low animal protein, low-sugar, high natural carbohydrate, primarily vegetarian diet is optimal—for a healthier, more energetic, longer life.

And yet, millions of Americans sicken and die prematurely each year because they resist changing their diets, getting more exercise, or quitting smoking. They avoid a conscious choice based on available facts by using a variety of psychological defense mechanisms:

Denial: *I don't worry about high cholesterol.*
(It remains whether we worry about it or not.)

Discounting: *I like bourbon; I'm entitled to one vice.*
(Nature grants no entitlements.)

Evasion: *Nobody lives forever.*
(True, but we don't have to dig an early grave with our knife, fork, and teeth.)

Procrastination: *Maybe tomorrow I'll quit smoking.*
(Tomorrow never seems to arrive.)

Projection: *It's my mother's fault I never learned to eat right.*
(Now, as adults, we can teach ourselves, and take responsibility for our own lives.)

Rationalization: *Ice cream tastes sooooo good.*
(So do a lot of other things; we acquire taste.)

Regression: *Fatty food is FUN!*
(Heart attacks are not.)

> To compound the denial, nearly anyone can find
> research studies to back up almost any preferred diet.
> As Mark Twain reminded us, "There are three kinds
> of lies: Lies, damned lies, and statistics."

With complete respect for individual choice and process, we each have a right to choose our own lifestyle; the peaceful warrior's way encourages conscious choice. So, after taking a realistic look at the consequences of our actions, we can either make changes or choose not to change and accept the consequences. But let's not pretend the consequences don't exist or that they won't happen to us. Let's make our choices consciously, free of illusions, wishes, or denial—taking the outcomes into account. Maintaining our illusions can be hazardous to our health.

Short-Term and Long-Term Consequences

If everyone who took one drink were to get liver pains; if everyone who smoked a cigarette immediately got lung cancer; if everyone who committed a criminal act were immediately caught and incarcerated, almost no one would drink alcohol, smoke a cigarette, or commit a crime.

Most of us tend to play the odds, however, and focus more on short-term rather than long-term consequences. The long-term problems always seem "somewhere in the possible future," until the possible future becomes probable, then very immediate, then very real.

Those of us who stop smoking cigarettes or any other self-destructive habit usually suffer some relatively short-term discomfort but gain long-term benefits. By helping our Basic

Self "get real," and educating it to appreciate long-term outcomes, both negative and positive, we gain some leverage on breaking old habits.

Many of us display a tendency to go for a quick symptomatic fix, however, and sweep the source of our problems under the rug. Years ago, when Joy and I were dormitory directors at Oberlin College, certain students, ill from too much partying, would occasionally knock on our door and ask for a pill that gave symptomatic relief so they could go back to doing whatever it was that got them sick in the first place. If we relieve symptoms instead of examining the lifestyle that created them, we repeat the same cycles over and over—until we finally accept *how things are.*

Choices and Consequences

1. Sort through your memories and find a significant choice you made several years ago. It might relate to something you did or didn't do. Look back on that choice objectively, without regrets or judgments.
2. Assess the consequences of your decision, asking yourself the following questions:
   - What positive effects did your choice bring?
   - What negative effects did your choice bring?
   - Would you choose differently now?
   - What did you learn that may help you now or in the future?

A number of years ago, I received an important lesson about the consequences of ignoring life's warning signs. After hiking up the narrow Mist Trail at Yosemite National Park to the top of Vernal Falls, I met a park ranger who told me about a woman who climbed out over a low railing near the stream just above the falls. She sat down on the shore's edge, removed her hiking shoes, and put her feet in the calm, shallow water. Twenty yards downstream, those calm waters poured over the edge, hundreds of feet down to a thundering torrent below.

The ranger was about a hundred yards away, walking toward her. He broke into a run as the woman stood and started wading around in the knee-deep water. Suddenly, he saw her slip and fall to a sitting position. A moment later, pulled by the strong current, she began sliding over slippery rocks toward the precipice. He yelled, but it was too late. He said he'd never forget the look in her eyes—not panic, just innocent surprise, as she disappeared over the falls.

He told me he just stood there, joined by a few other people who had seen what happened, stunned by this placid drama, unbelieving as she had been. It would have been easy to deny that anything had happened. But the woman's hiking boots sat alone, next to the stream.

He pointed and I turned to see a prominent sign that read, "*Danger: Strong currents. Do not wade or swim.*" Beneath the calm surface was a powerful undertow, sucking everything toward the falls. The poor woman had either missed the sign or ignored it.

Life can seem like a calm pond, but an undertow may lurk beneath the surface. In the realm of the peaceful warrior, the winds or currents may change at a moment's notice; we do well to stay optimistic but to keep our eyes open for signs that appear. Staying awake has survival value.

Natural laws—the fundamental principles of reality— serve as the warrior's staff and sword. Acknowledging our inner reality helps generate the momentum to begin the work of clearing the emotions and balancing the body. As we do this by making a conscious commitment to express our feelings, improve our diet, and exercise regularly, our health and overall well-being improve naturally; symptoms of repressed emotions disappear over time.

Back to the Body

Our body is naturally attuned to objective reality. If we don't get enough rest, our body grows tired; if we eat too much or too little food, our body lets us know. The Basic Self abides by natural laws unless overruled by the desires of the Conscious Self. The body lives in the present moment; the mind, however, sails between past and future like a ghost ship.

The spiritual domain of inner work can be filled with illusions; for example, we can sit cross-legged, close our eyes in meditation, and imagine ourselves to be "highly evolved" — while turning our back on real-world responsibilities. In the physical domain, we can't escape reality for long. When I used to walk into the gym and leap up to the rings, I couldn't *pretend* to be a gymnast. Neither could the ancient warriors pretend or posture; life would soon call their bluff, and the stakes were high.

Looking back on my life, I've realized that the highest education I received was in the gymnasium. Coming back to the body provides a direct way to reconnect with present reality. We can each benefit, in this manner, from a chosen form of physical training or skill practice (in movement, music, arts, or crafts), appropriate to our interest and level of readiness.

Training and the Laws of Reality

My introduction to the way of the peaceful warrior began by getting *into* the body, where instinct and response replaced abstract thinking. Physical training taught me that while our beliefs help create our reality, reality doesn't care about our beliefs; gravity works whether we believe in it or not! When I soared through the air, I "lost my mind and came to my senses"; when my attention wandered, I found out about it very quickly!

Training taught me to accept the inevitable ups and downs — the peaks, the plateaus, and the failures. The process of physical practice also provided feedback, a reality check, and a measure of wisdom.

I learned that I never had to travel farther down the road than "the next mile," and that if I was willing to go step by step, I could reach any goal no matter how far off it seemed by focusing on immediate, reachable goals. By defining each small step in the right direction as success, I experienced a string of "small successes" that kept me moving, motivated, and on track.

Physical training also taught me difficulty is relative to preparation; the better I prepared myself, the easier anything became.

No one had to lecture me about these principles; the laws of nature branded them onto my psyche. In those magic moments of flow, I found an intimate, kinesthetic connection with life. The larger lessons of training expand, over time, beyond the walls of the gymnasium, out into the arena of daily life, and up the mountain path.

5

Universal Addictions

Nothing so needs reforming
as other people's habits.
Mark Twain

A Universal Problem

A number of my most respected friends regularly attend meetings of Alcoholics Anonymous, Narcotics Anonymous, or other twelve-step programs. Having taken a cold, no-nonsense look at themselves in the mirror of their pain—having seen themselves at their worst and having dealt with the darkness—they have an aura of authenticity about them; they've lost their taste for playing "let's pretend."

This chapter provides a reality check in the form of a clear and compassionate look at our human predicament, specifically, at our habit patterns—the ways we discharge or release blocked energies, which generate the drives, behaviors, and compulsions that can become addictions. This chapter, then, addresses *every* reader—not only those of us dealing with addictions to alcohol, tobacco, or other drugs—because we all have varying kinds and degrees of compulsive or addictive behaviors.

These behaviors devour untold billions of dollars of our resources and account for inestimable self-recrimination and suffering. In order to generate the will to change, both on social and individual levels, we have to see ourselves clearly, in a mirror free of mental distortions. Recognizing our patterns takes courage—a first step on the road to healing, recovery, and transformation.

While this chapter provides a useful means of understanding compulsive and addictive behaviors, such understanding is only a starting point. Most drug, alcohol, food, gambling, and other life-disrupting addictions require an appropriate twelve-step program, residential treatment facility, or the help of a specialist. Group support and feedback are central to the healing process.

Addictions and Compulsions

This chapter outlines the primary *gateways of stress release*. These gateways comprise our everyday means of stress release and when taken to compulsive extremes become classic addictive behaviors. Some of these gateways involve substance abuse based on *physical dependence*, in which the Basic Self develops an escalating tolerance and craving and displays withdrawal symptoms in body, mind, and emotions if deprived of the substance. Thus, alcohol and other drug use can quickly become self-sustaining, compulsive, and addictive rituals. Other gateways involve forms of *psychological dependence* that are just as compelling to the Basic Self.

All true addictive behaviors, however, whether physical or psychological or both, serve to release energy from the body.

Understanding Energy

Energy comes to Earth through the radiant light of our sun, stored most directly in green plants, and then distributed throughout the food chain. In addition to taking in energy from food, we also take in energy from the people around us, and, some say, from breathing charged, or ionized, air.

In the larger sense, we don't just take in energy; we *are* energy. The organs of our body are made of tissues made of cells made of molecules made of atoms made of whirling, pulsating, vibrating fields of energy. Energy not only surrounds us; it interpenetrates the cells of our body. We are energy beings, made of the same stuff as the stars.

We know that energy takes many forms, some of which are visible, like a bolt of lightning. Life energy is more subtle; we usually cannot see it with our physical eyes, but we can certainly feel it.

Since our bodies and the world are filled with energy, our perceptions of feeling high or low energy point *not* to a relative abundance or lack of energy, but to our own openness to feeling it. As an analogy, we're always surrounded by air, but we still have to breathe in order to take it in. When we feel most energetic, we feel fully alive; when we feel very low energy, we feel "dead."

Most of us have noticed how energized we feel after exercise, partly because our circulation and other physiological functions improve, but on a deeper level, because exercise (or good news, or sexual arousal) stimulates our Basic Self to open up the faucet and let the universal energy pour in.

We can learn to sense the energy fields of other people and ourselves as naturally as we see, hear, touch, and smell.

Sensing Energy Fields

1. Feel the energy fields of people around you. In your own mind, rate each person you meet on a scale of one (very low) to ten (very high). You will find yourself rating people without consciously knowing how you do it (all Basic Selves are in contact).
2. Rate your own energy level on the same scale at different points during the day. Notice how your field of energy expands or contracts at various times and in various situations.
3. Hold your arms in front of you as if embracing a large beach ball, with your palms facing you, slightly below chest level, with the fingers of each hand pointing toward one another, about three inches apart. Relax and breathe slowly, and you'll

soon notice, if you gently move your hands closer to one another or farther apart, either a magnetic attraction or repulsion between the fingers – one way to sense your own energy field.

◆

The Body as a Channel of Energy

We function as a conduit of energy, like a large, vertical water hose, receiving energy "from above," and using or spending it in various ways. Picture energy flowing like water down through this hose. Applying a basic principle of fluid dynamics, we see that if that hose (our body/mind) has no obstructions, then the water (energy) flows through us smoothly and easily. If, on the other hand, the water (energy) becomes blocked by lumps or knots in the hose (physical, mental, or emotional obstructions), these obstructions are going to create turbulence – a disturbance in the flow. We experience this turbulence as discomfort or pain, which we call *stress*. The severity of this discomfort will depend upon the amount or force of the energy flowing through us at any given moment, and the degree of acute or chronic obstruction we feel. Therefore, a high level of energy can feel wonderful or terrible, depending upon the degree of obstructions we have at that moment in body, mind, and emotions.

Energy, Obstructions, and Pain

Even though maintaining a high energy level might seem desirable, if obstructions are present when we start to feel a "surplus" of energy (defined as more than we can comfortably handle), we tend to exercise, have sex, smoke a cigarette, or eat something sweet or heavy; in other words, we try to *get rid of our "surplus"* energy. Thus, a high level of life energy is a mixed blessing for most of us. Flowing smoothly, high energy can create art and beauty, but blocked energy creates pain. Most of us experience excess energy as discomfort, and as the level of energy increases, so does the discomfort. Consciously or unconsciously, we seek to release it.

Going back to the analogy of water running through a hose, if the water flows rapidly (high energy) and collides with big obstructions, this creates high turbulence, agitation, and discomfort (or extreme stress). In such cases, we can either lower the amount of water (energy) flowing through, or remove the obstructions.

If we find a way to lower the level of energy flowing through us so that it just trickles, we reduce the turbulence and the discomfort, *but the obstructions remain.* Since the nature of the universe is abundant energy, the energy in our body eventually increases. Therefore, reducing the flow only works to reduce the discomfort *temporarily;* the energy soon builds again, and as long as the obstructions remain, again requires release; over time, this cycle generates a compulsive or addictive behavior pattern.

To make this image more concrete, let's look at what happens in our life when we meet with a typical mental obstruction (concern), an emotional obstruction (anger), and a physical obstruction (such as tension in our neck or back). When these obstructions have *high* energy behind them, they feel *worse:* Concern becomes an obsession or preoccupation; anger can turn to rage or fury; and physical tension can become an acute pain. However, *if we've just lowered our energy level*—if we've released energy through drug use, exercise, orgasm, or one of the other gateways—then the concern, the anger, and the physical tension will not trouble us to the same degree; we will experience temporary relief.

A Universal Formula

Energy plus obstruction equals pain. Unobstructed energy feels blissful; blocked energy feels painful. The greater the energy and/or the greater the obstruction, the greater the pain. Living beings seek pleasure and avoid pain. Therefore, the pain (or stress) creates the need either to release the energy or to remove the obstruction. Since removing obstructions takes commitment, courage, and conscious effort, most people apply the more immediate, if temporary, solution of releasing the energy.

Obstructions

Mental obstructions include worries, concerns, regrets, resistance, judgments, and associations—thought forms that impose tension on the body (Basic Self), blocking the free flow of life energy.

Emotional obstructions center around forms of fear, sorrow, and anger, such as anxiety, envy, jealousy, depression, irritation, frustration, and rage. Though they are generated by the mind, we feel these emotional obstructions in the body as they block the flow of life energy.

Physical obstructions stem from injuries, poor posture, and poor movement habits, and from the mental and emotional obstructions mentioned earlier. The result is the same—turbulence in the flow of life energy.

In our bodies and our lives, we experience both acute and chronic obstructions. *Acute* obstructions usually reflect temporary issues or difficulties. *Chronic* obstructions, most often planted in childhood, tend to lie far deeper—hidden, repressed, and long lasting.

Though painful and dramatic, acute obstructions (upsets) generally have an obvious and visible source: "Damn it! I think I broke my toe!" "Tim and I had a terrible argument." "*What?* A bill for *a thousand dollars?* How are we going to pay for that?"

Acute obstructions are fluid rather than solid, stable "things." They rise and fall, ebb and flow, with the circumstances of our lives. Our relative level of openness (or of obstruction) can change from hour to hour and from day to day.

We can use one or more of the gateways to temporarily release the obstructed, stressful energies until we resolve the issue (clear the obstruction)—until the toe heals, until we make up with our partner, or until we resolve our financial pressures.

In daily life, acute obstructions often create painful symptoms that stimulate us to seek relief through a physician, a chiropractor, a psychotherapist, or a bodyworker. Although our acute obstructions send us seeking help, our chronic obstructions generate a much deeper underlying need for intervention.

Chronic obstructions in body, mind, or emotions reflect deep, unresolved issues; the body is the Basic Self's filing cabinet, where these obstructions fester as physical memories, often in the form of tension or pain. Depending upon our childhood circumstances, some of us have to deal with more of these chronic obstructions than do others. For example, those of us who grew up with violent, absent, or disturbed parents will have more of these underlying issues to clear. Until we clear them, no matter how "happy" or successful our circumstances, they remain with us, and we perceive our lives through a dark glass.

For deep or chronic obstructions that don't seem to have a visible solution, the gateways of release can also become chronic, compulsive rituals or addictions, until we undergo the necessary processing (perhaps through a combination of psychotherapy and bodywork) to clarify and resolve them.

Understanding the gateways and their uses enables us to make conscious choices to discharge energy as needed, deal with obstructions as they arise using the tools available, and apply courage and insight in facing the deeper fears and underlying, chronic obstructions that remain with us. Increased energy and aliveness will reward us for clearing our obstructions.

The Source of Obstructions

As infants, we had few obstructions: Our minds still free of complex thoughts, we gazed into a bright and mysterious world with clear perception. With uninhibited emotions, we expressed whatever feelings arose naturally. Our relaxed, sensitive, and elastic bodies felt fully open to life.

By four to seven years of age, and up through adolescence, our original state of innocence gave way to expectations, disappointments, anxieties, and stress. As our Conscious Self—the sense of separation and individuation—became more defined, we experienced social conflicts, competition, and authority issues; life seemed more complex and problematic than ever before. Adolescence, in particular, involves a time of high ideals and corresponding disillusionment with the adult world. The relatively safe, protected world of childhood has dissolved, as in waking from a pleasant dream into the cold light of reality. Hormones run wild and physical changes create awkwardness and imbalance. Therefore, teenagers are prone to experiencing painful obstructions and are extremely vulnerable to addictive behaviors.

The developments mentioned happen to all of us even in the *best* of circumstances. In the case of dysfunctional families, where children lack affection, nurturing, or self-esteem and suffer from physical or sexual abuse, the levels of stress, anxiety, negative programming, and destructive behaviors rise geometrically.

In addition, we all inherit, from those who raised us, an attic full of subconscious artifacts. Along with their love, their genetic strengths, their wisdom, and their talents, our parents passed along to us their shadows and their fears, their negative patterns and their addictions. Even in the best family circumstances, few of our parents were fully enlightened, happy, secure, or nurturing. Thus, we have all been wounded on the path between birth and the present, and the scar tissues of these wounds have helped form our obstructions in body, mind, and emotions. The results are the same: addictive behaviors.

The Gateways of Stress Release

This chapter aims to generate insight *into* our compulsive patterns. Awareness is the first step toward resolving any problem, but it is only the first step. We also need to generate the will to change (Chapter 6) and use the specific methods for clearing the obstructions in our body, mind, and emotions covered in Part III, Tools for Transformation.

First, however, we need to examine the primary gateways of stress release:

1. Alcohol, tobacco, and other drugs
2. Stress-produced illness or injuries
3. Overexertion
4. Fear and high-risk behaviors
5. Overeating
6. Cruelty
7. Orgasm

I emphasize here that drinking some wine, getting sick or injured, working hard, having a big meal and a sundae, having sex, and so forth aren't *necessarily* compulsive or addictive behaviors. Because they provide the Basic Self with a means to reduce pent-up energy, however, they can *become* compulsive or addictive.

Some of the gateways, such as engaging in high-risk behavior, work through an adrenaline rush, followed by a period of lassitude or "relaxation"; others (such as the use of opiate drugs) lead to an immediate lethargy. Each gateway has benefits and liabilities. (If they didn't have some benefits, no one would use them.) The primary benefit all have in common is that they produce a sense of satisfaction and a reduction of internal stress. The negative aspects of each gateway are obvious to most of us, but moralistic judgments only hold the pattern in place; we are wise to consider the consequences of each gateway and make our choices accordingly.

Alcohol, Tobacco, and Other Drugs

The gateway of drugs includes overuse or misuse of alcohol, drugs such as "uppers" and "downers," or social drugs such as tobacco, coffee, or even soft drinks that contain caffeine. In addition to psychological dependence, they produce a strong physiological compulsion. Even though some stimulant drugs give an initial hit of energy, all have the same eventual effect of releasing energy (for example, someone feels jittery or nervous and smokes a cigarette to settle down).

If Peter has some wine or other alcohol at a dinner party, or if he goes out to a bar on occasion, he is probably not involved in compulsive or addictive behavior. But if he feels he has to have a drink *every* day—if he repeatedly or exclusively uses alcohol to relax when he feels tense or depressed— he may be displaying an addictive pattern.

Physically addictive substances (both legal and illegal) such as alcohol, tobacco, opiates, and amphetamines exert a profound grip on the Basic Self, programming it for dependence and creating a tremendous fear of withdrawal. Therefore, any form of healing and recovery *must* involve physical, mental, and emotional methods for inspiring, educating, and empowering the Basic Self. Exerting self-discipline to stop the use of a particular substance, while essential, is only a beginning. Merely stopping drinking, for example, only creates a more disciplined "dry drunk." True healing requires a new way of life—in combination with insight and profound psychological transformation. Twelve-step programs have proven especially effective in inspiring the Basic Self to change.

While it is a dark and difficult path, overcoming addiction serves, for many, as an important step on the path to spiritual growth and awakening.

Stress-Produced Illness or Injuries

Bacteria, viruses, or even cancer cells are always present in our body. But our immune system, under the direction of our Basic Self, has the natural capacity to control "unfriendly" organisms. However, in the presence of mental, emotional, or physical stress—when we worry or get upset, or when we let our body get toxic or run down—we may become ill because the subconscious tends to lower our shields in response to stress, suppressing our natural immune response.

Just as alcohol and other drugs can temporarily relieve pain, illness often brings a weakness that at least approximates relaxation. Despite the unpleasant symptoms (which we can relieve somewhat with drugs), illness relaxes us by draining off pent-up energy. Injuries also tend to reduce the level of stressful energy as the body uses the energy to heal itself.

Some people use this gateway in more extreme forms by deliberately injuring themselves or engaging in self-mutilation (generally as a result of extreme childhood trauma or abuse). This behavior pattern can become addictive because it entails the cycle of adrenaline buildup followed by energy release and a sense of relaxation.

Those of us who unconsciously use illness or injury as a release usually do it by default—either because we avoid other gateways of release, such as exercise, or because we face such extreme, often repressed, discomfort that our Basic Self uses illness or injury in addition to other gateways.

Not every illness or accident is a deliberate or even subconscious decision to release energy. Virginia may normally take good care of herself, but during the stress of final exams, she gets exposed to a rampant virus. Or Claude, a careful driver, enters the intersection and gets broadsided by a drunk or inattentive driver. Sometimes we just get sick; sometimes we just have a bad day. Random incidents of illness or injury don't necessarily point to addictive behavior, but *patterns* of illness, injury, or any of the other means of releasing energy, reveal the necessity of taking a good look at our lives, and working to achieve new levels of well-being.

Overexertion

Regular, moderate exercise or sports training opens our body to *more* vital energy, and can serve as a healthful, conscious, even joyous form of recreation, social interaction, and personal development. *Overexertion*, on the other hand, tends to be a stress-driven, compulsive, and relatively joyless activity *whose absence makes us feel depressed or frustrated.* Compulsive, stress-produced overexertion tends to generate chronic joint and tissue injuries due to pushing too hard with too little rest. Like alcoholics who come to recognize their addiction as a problem, those of us who can fully acknowledge our dependence on overexertion can, through that act of awareness, begin the healing process and set in motion the forces of change. With insight, attention, and effort, our patterns of overexertion can change, over time, to relaxed, pleasurable exercise as we break free of the compelling nature and driving force of addictive behavior.

Overexertion doesn't only happen in the gym or on the playing field. Those of us who work long hours at jobs we don't really enjoy, or who use immersion in work to avoid intimacy, or who can only get to sleep if exhausted, or who can't enjoy ourselves when we're not working are also displaying compulsive behavior. We can begin rebalancing our lives once we see the problem clearly. Of course, some of us occasionally or even regularly work long hours because we love our work—because it gives us a sense of purpose and meaning; this is not necessarily addictive.

Compulsive, nonstop talking and continual fidgeting both reflect a buildup of stressful energy, and an attempt to reduce the energy by continual chatter or movement, a variant of overexertion.

Fear and High-Risk Behaviors

Fear produces the rush of adrenaline followed by lassitude that characterizes a potentially addictive behavior. We can deliberately use fear as a gateway of stress release, as in attending a horror film, going skydiving, committing a crime, or engaging in another high-risk behavior. Our Basic Self also generates subconscious fears in the form of nightmares, panic attacks, or phobias.

When other gateways aren't as readily available—for

example, in childhood—our Basic Self may create chronic, recurring, or compulsive fears in the form of *phobias, nightmares, or panic attacks.* Phobias are classified as anxiety disorders—persistent, exaggerated, or illogical fears, out of proportion to the actual danger or threat in a given situation. Common phobias include fear of the dark, fear of heights, fear of enclosed (or wide open) spaces, and fear of snakes, rodents, or insects.

Many of us have fears of dark alleys, stinging insects, and so on, but when fears become persistent, chronic, or debilitating—or if they interfere with the normal functioning of our daily life (for example, if we lose control of our car when a moth or bee flies in the window, or if we're unable to ride in an airplane or elevator)—they become full-blown phobias.

Like phobias, nightmares and panic attacks are generated by the Basic Self. Most panic attacks occur in the dream state—as nightmares. The most common nighttime panics are terrifying dreams of insects or rodents; of vague, shapeless creatures or fears (free-floating anxiety); or of frozen panic.

Horror films contain fearful images that hold the audience captive—spellbound with the impact of music and sound effects that create a fear-produced adrenaline rush and the relief that follows. Those of us who have walked out of a good horror film with weak knees can attest to this effect. Those who disdain "dark" or unpleasant films or books of this nature simply choose not to use this gateway, which serves others in a relatively constructive way. This genre offers a side benefit of allowing a safe glimpse into the shadow side of the psyche, and provides a relatively harmless means of venting our own dark side.

Ironically, "side-splitting" *comedies* in which we laugh until we're weak have the same effect as horror films, perhaps accounting for the common wisdom that "laughter is the best medicine." As Norman Cousins discovered, laughter serves as a useful gateway for relieving the pressures that create stress-produced illness. Films or books that evoke *other strong emotions such as sorrow or anger* can also generate a similar effect of tension followed by release; thus, many people become addicted to "tear-jerker" movies and soap operas.

Children and adults can also get addicted to the vicarious "high-risk" activities of *video games* and suspenseful *television shows*, which produce a tension release. While television and even video games can be enjoyable, if they become obsessive or compulsive, they can create conflict in families and supplant or interfere with more productive or constructive activities. As with any other activity, we need to stay aware of the difference between use and abuse.

Thrill seeking is a favorite among those who pursue the gateway of fear with enthusiasm. "Adrenaline junkies" savor their first few parachute or bungee jumps, their high-speed driving, or other thrilling pastimes, because after the adrenaline rush comes the release of tension. *Amusement park rides* offer maximum fear with minimum risk—filling the need for stress release, as any of us have enjoyed such rides can attest. As with the other gateways, people will pay good money to lower their stress level. Not all parachutists or race-car drivers are addicted, however; some quite earnestly seek competitive excellence and, in fact, don't experience fear at all.

Most forms of thrill seeking, excitement, or amusement represent relatively harmless pastimes; only when they become compulsive do we need to consider the debilitating consequences. This seems especially true for *gambling,* the effects of which can range somewhere between an amusement park ride and a horror story. For many of us, an occasional visit to Las Vegas, Atlantic City, or other places with legalized gambling represents nothing more than recreation and a vacation: We win a few dollars, lose a few dollars, see some shows, enjoy the outdoors, go shopping. But for those of us with no immunity to gambling fever, the addiction is as serious and devastating as any other. Compulsive gamblers may first find "easy money" the primary attraction, but they soon become addicted to the excitement/tension followed by the energy release (whether they win or lose). No matter how wealthy, a compulsive gambler will raise the stakes to a point of high risk, sacrificing security, family, home—anything—for the next rush.

Though different from other high-risk behaviors because of its antisocial nature, committing a *crime* also produces a brief period of intense concentration and excitement, followed by a corresponding release of energy. The first time some of us commit crimes, we may do it for money, for excitement, out of passion, for revenge, or even from peer pressure. But once our Basic Self discovers the adrenaline rush followed by a release, then crime takes on a life of its own, independent of the reason it began. Compulsive thieves (kleptomaniacs), for example, often steal things they don't even need and could easily afford to purchase, but they steal because of the tension and release associated with the risk.

Crime is like heroin or other drugs; we may start small, but over time we develop a tolerance; we cease to get the adrenaline rush; we escalate to "bigger" or more risky crimes; we play on the edge and take bigger risks until the game is up. (Those who commit crimes "only for the money" tend to be sociopathic professionals, less likely to be caught than amateurs who do it for the rush.)

Other high-risk behaviors include forbidden or taboo activities such as engaging in sex or nudity in a public place, taking chances walking on the edge of promontories, or doing anything that produces a rush of adrenaline from fear or excitement, for the release it provides. The late author Graham Greene would play Russian roulette when he needed something "exciting" to "wake himself up" after bouts of depression.

Overeating

Overeating serves as one of the most popular and universal gateways for releasing energy. One way of lowering the body's energy level through diet is by eating *sweets and refined carbohydrates,* psychologically linked to feeling a lack of affection from others and therefore "taking care of ourselves" by giving ourselves "treats." Fast-metabolizing refined carbohydrates—candies, pastries, and so on—create a steep rise of blood sugar followed by a corresponding drop. Some people even put themselves to sleep by overloading on carbohydrates and almost literally knocking themselves out.

Other people use this gateway through *heavy protein consumption*—primarily meat and dairy—which draws off the energy required to digest these dense proteins and fats, making the body feel heavier, lethargic, or more relaxed—the grounded feeling after a big protein meal.

Those of us who heavily spice nearly all of our food may be addicted to this; *spices* create an extra demand on the digestive system, and though many have benefits and are even used medicinally to stimulate the body, they also have an effect of lowering available energy.

Not everyone who uses overeating as a means of dissipating energy becomes obese. Some of us overeat and then overexert; those of us with eating disorders such as bulimia binge then purge. Ironically and sadly, the self-imposed starvation of anorexia, the opposite of overeating, also lowers the energy level, leaving a feeling of artificial "lightness" and lassitude—a form of tension relief that can prove seriously debilitating, and eventually fatal if not confronted.

Cruelty

Though cruel behaviors may bring to mind the images of sadistic prison guards, Nazis, or gestapo-type criminals, sociopaths, or villains who take pleasure in causing pain, these represent more extreme and fortunately rare examples of those who use this gateway.

More common examples of cruelty in daily life include hurtful comments we throw at one another when we feel hurt or angry, or the tension-release cycles of "lovers' spats," when couples end up in bed after passionate fights.

Other common forms of cruelty include children teasing

other children, or adults teasing, belittling, verbally criticizing, or abusing children or other adult victims. Children and adults sometimes use the gateway of cruelty by torturing insects or animals, an unfortunate practice that may be more common than we would like to imagine.

Spouse or partner abuse, battering, and child abuse serve as tragic examples of addictions to cruelty as a gateway of stress release. The perpetrator's guilt and pain only serve to create more internal tension that is ultimately released in a cycle of compulsive repetition.

Orgasm

Orgasm serves as a universal and relatively benign method of tension release, through masturbation, sex with a partner, or spontaneously, as in nocturnal emissions ("wet dreams"). As an inherent biological drive to help ensure continuation of the species, orgasm can be distinguished from higher motives of love, affection, and intimacy—we can, and often do, achieve orgasm without any of these higher motives. Mutually consenting adults can and do engage in uncommitted "sport sex"—having their orgasms, then going their separate ways. However, the highest forms of sexual intimacy include both love *and* desire.

As with the other gateways, sexuality only becomes problematic when it becomes compulsive or addictive—when we abuse it rather than use it. Those of us who become addicted to orgasm pursue a variety of means to achieve it and tend to use partners or ourselves as sex objects in order to release tension.

In today's world, indiscriminate, promiscuous, unprotected sexual relations have become a high-risk behavior with serious, even fatal consequences—not to mention the emotional turmoil related to the regret, deceit, and insecurity that sometimes accompany affairs.

For those of us without a partner, I recommend masturbation as a means of managing our sexual-creative energies. A near universal practice, masturbation provides an accessible gateway of release with no emotional strings attached. Masturbation seems preferable to deceitful, loveless, and compulsive sexual encounters that risk disease, pregnancy, or one-sided emotional entanglements. Masturbation also helps resolve, in a simple and harmless way, different levels of sexual desire in a relationship; if our partner is not interested or available when we desire orgasm, we can masturbate to relieve the sexual tension.

By definition, however, masturbation does not involve relationship with anyone else; it involves no circuit of energy exchange, vulnerability, or intimacy. Those of us addicted to this particular gateway even though we have an available partner may want to reexamine the level of openness and communication in our relationship, and to explore deeper levels of sexual intimacy.

The fewer internal obstructions we have, the less compelling our need for orgasm. With less need, we have more to give, which enhances the intimacy of our sexual relationship. Reduced pressure for orgasm is quite different, however, from inhibited drives, sexual blocks or repression, or guilt-driven attempts at celibacy, which may signal a need to seek professional help.

Combining Gateways

As we look more closely at our lives, we can recognize that we often combine different gateways of stress release. We may use overexertion to balance out overeating; we may employ a combination of sex and drugs; or we may combine sex and exercise. On the darker side, we see combinations of drugs, crime, cruelty, and other high-risk behaviors. We all face the human predicament of compulsive behaviors and addictions until we complete the inner work necessary to clear our obstructions in body, mind, and emotions.

An Addiction or Not?

As I've pointed out, not everyone who uses a particular gateway—who takes a drink of wine, or gets sick, or exercises, or commits a crime, or overeats, or hurts a loved one, or has an orgasm—is addicted to that gateway. In fact, we can draw no distinct or clear-cut line that separates addictive or compulsive behavior from nonaddictive activities. We can only say we feel relatively free, or relatively trapped, by compulsive behaviors.

Generally speaking, when a possible gateway *interferes with our lives*—with our relationships, our work, our health, or our well-being—if we think about it a lot when we're not engaged in it, that activity has probably crossed over the line into the domain of compulsions and addictions.

Some of us waver just this side of addiction without seeing it. For those of us who tend to be in denial about our addictions, I'd like to suggest one simple test that helps us determine for ourselves whether or not our behaviors are free choices or compulsive habits: *Refrain from the activity (or activities) for one to two weeks, and notice how that makes you feel.* (In the case of periodic binge behavior, a longer break may be required.) If even the thought of ceasing one of the gateways creates anxiety, we might want to take another look at the challenges and opportunities that await us.

When our use of one or more of the gateways reaches the point of true compulsive or addictive behavior, our Conscious Self loses control of the behavior as our Basic Self succumbs to the pattern and resists any attempt to change it. At first, our Conscious Self may remain in denial, believing we "have it under control and can stop at any time"—that is, until we try to stop. Then a heroic struggle begins, back to dignity and self-worth, back to life. Our best intentions fail and our willpower seems powerless. We may feel helpless or hopeless as we go through repeated attempts—cycles of success and failure: "I want to stop, but I can't." We *can* stop, but it will not be through the good intentions or resolutions of the Conscious Self; we will stop when we grow truly desperate and truly committed—when some force or source of inspiration bigger than our ego takes command, and our Basic

Self surrenders to a higher will. If we wish to ascend the mountain path of the warrior, we need to face the hurdles to self-mastery that lie in our path.

Gateways of Choice

The reasons we use or combine different gateways of stress release remain as complex and varied as personality itself. Factors may include early, random, or even accidental exposure to that form of release, the subconscious modeling of parental behaviors, peer pressure, beliefs, values, and associations, or simply the fact that other gateways aren't available.

Alcohol and other drugs are favored by those of us who seek a relatively passive or easy way to escape the pain of the everyday world, which is really the pain within our psyche. Others of us may use alcohol or other drugs as a means of finding altered states, or seeing a more open, spiritual connection with life. Unfortunately, the long-term results are the opposite.

Illness and injury serve as a common gateway for children who don't have ready access to other means of releasing pent-up energy. Those of us who use this gateway as adults may have found when we were children that illness or injury were among the only ways we got our parents' attention or sympathy or were a means to stay home from school or to avoid other responsibilities that seemed burdensome or threatening.

Overexertion or overwork become a chosen gateway for those of us who feel driven by high achievement, unrealistic standards of fitness, or puritanical work values.

Fear serves as a gateway for many different people for different reasons. Phobias or panic attacks often come to those of us who feel repressed or inhibited and who refrain from using other gateways, or during times of unusual stress when our usual means aren't enough. Those of us who are more extroverted may consciously choose suspenseful, shocking, humorous, or sad movies. Thrill seeking, gambling, or other high-risk behaviors may be motivated by the drive for excitement, getting high, and living on the edge. Crime is often used by those of us who are underskilled, undereducated, or who feel angry at what we perceive as an unfair society.

Overeating may serve as a psychological insulation from life—another form of the kind of body armor used by some bodybuilders—or as a perceived protection against unwanted attention for those who have been sexually abused. It may also result from lack of education about food, familial pressures, or blocked creativity. Our Basic Self may have associations between food, especially sweets and "treats," and a form of love or indulgence; we may be trying to fill a lack that will never be filled until we learn to love ourselves and feel loved.

Cruelty serves those of us feeling tremendous inner pain, self-hatred, and frustration (though it may not show at the surface). Work with a therapist and support group can help us break through the walls of our agonizing childhoods so that we can feel loved and cared for.

Orgasm, like food, serves as a primary biological drive and is readily available to most adults. Those of us who use this as a gateway have plenty of company! We masturbate simply because it's convenient and represents being able to "take care of ourselves." If we have a partner but prefer masturbation, we may have a difficulty with communication and intimacy. Childhood molestation or abuse can create many unfortunate "pictures" and associations that a good therapist can help to clear.

◆

Habit Assessment

1. Consider where you are now. Examine the following list and note, with compassion, when and how your Basic Self has used these gateways of release:
   - Drugs (alcohol, coffee, tobacco, or other)
   - Stress-produced illness or injuries

- Overexertion (compulsive exercise or overwork)
- Fears (phobias, panic, nightmares); thrill-seeking activities (gambling, crime, and other high-risk behaviors); movies that provoke fear, laughter, or tears
- Overeating (not one incident, but a pattern)
- Cruelty (being verbally or physically abusive)
- Orgasm (not just sexual interest, but the compulsive need to release sexual tension)

2. Accept your past (or present) patterns, and yourself, completely, but recognize the power you have to choose differently, and do whatever it is that you need to do to adapt to a different choice, such as exercise or looking into a twelve-step program. Open the space for change.
3. Visualize how *wonderful* you will feel as the obstructions melt away. Imagine what it would feel like to be entirely free of the compulsion. Feel yourself filled with self-respect and a sense of self-mastery and personal power.

------------------------◆------------------------

As we become aware of our gateways of choice, we may tend to catch ourselves: "Here I am, doing it again." I need to emphasize that until we clear our internal blocks, these gateways are necessary and useful. We need to accept them, manage them, and make constructive choices, while we work to clear the blocks that created them.

Managing Our Addictions

The various gateways of energy release work like a Japanese toy I once saw—a wooden box with metal rods sticking into it. You push one rod in, and another comes out. Shut one gateway and another opens.

A friend of mine volunteered for an organization that successfully helped people get off heroin and alcohol. However, virtually all those in the program ended up smoking cigarettes, guzzling gallons of coffee, and biting their fingernails.

The danger of using certain behavior modification, or aversion therapies, or hypnosis in kicking habits is that we may stop one form of addiction to start another, unless we deal with the source of the addictions in the first place.

For this reason, managing our addictions—choosing the least harmful gateways—is at best a temporary solution to the problem. For long-term healing, we need to look deeper.

Accepting Responsibility for Our Actions

The term *addiction* has become a catchall phrase referring to any compulsion that feels beyond our control—implying helplessness and victimization. It may seem that way, even intensely, after numerous attempts at controlling the behavior, but we all have the opportunity to regain control of our lives. Those of us who practice the peaceful warrior's way need to recognize that even though any number of strange, negative, or compelling thoughts and impulses normally pass through our minds, we can still accept responsibility for our actions. *Compelling thoughts do not have to become compulsive actions.* We can each choose what action we will take; even though some choices may appear extremely difficult, beyond our capacity, or even "hopeless," we each have the power to make these choices through skillful work with the Basic Self.

Understanding our addictive patterns—the gateways of stress release—is a first step in a process of empowerment and change to help us transform our lives.

The Power of Choice

Oscar Ichazo, who taught me about these gateways, used to say, "It's better to eat a cookie [overeating] than get a headache [illness]"—indicating that *we can consciously choose how* we are going to compensate for stress rather than get locked into only one or two gateways.

Knowledge is power; understanding offers the freedom of choice. *Overall, exercise, overeating, and orgasm are the three "best" (or least destructive) gateways;* when used judiciously, they can help keep other compulsive behaviors from escalating.

Short of clearing our obstructions, common wisdom suggests that a combination of good aerobic exercise with stretching may serve as our best preventative means to relieve the pressures that create the need to use other gateways of release. Those of us who exercise regularly are *less likely* to develop problems with addictive behaviors. Exercise is not, however, a guaranteed antidote for established addictions—some of us dealing with many painful obstructions may easily use overexertion in addition to drugs. In general, however, the more we engage in balanced exercise, the less we are troubled by stress.

Though eating a sweet or having sex or working out will not eliminate our obstructions, by managing our energies consciously rather than unconsciously, we create breathing space, freedom of choice, and a chance to consider our lives from a place of compassion and understanding rather than self-recrimination. Seeing our patterns in this light, we can take a more objective look at what serves our growth and what does not.

Selective Avoidance

Until we are free of obstructions, a good general principle to follow reads, *If we don't handle something well, we best avoid it altogether.* If any habit or action interferes with our relationships, work, or health, or if we think about it a lot, or if it troubles those who care about us, or if we must repeat it every day or feel uncomfortable, then we are *not* handling it.

Let's not do things the hard way. If we have a problem with sweets, then let's not have them in the house. If we have a problem with drugs, let's not associate with those who take them. If we find sexual fidelity difficult, let's avoid casual flirtations or situations where temptation may become an issue.

As long as stress continues to arise, we will continue to need a means to release or balance our energies. Cravings never go away entirely. For those of us who have a problem area, especially with physically addictive substances such as alcohol, tobacco, or other drugs, I recommend complete abstinence, coupled with *regular* daily exercise and participation in a relevant twelve-step group or other form of therapy. Committing to these choices can help change the course of our life.

Overcoming Addictions

Many of those who speak with experience in the field of addictions say that "it sometimes has to get worse before it gets better," that addicts have to "hit bottom" before they can finally bounce back. I would agree, but what constitutes "bottom" differs from one person to the next, *based on our level of self-worth*. By raising our level of self-worth (Chapter 11), we create a climate inside ourselves where even the milder forms of addiction become intolerable; we reach the time when we have seen enough and *had* enough and are ready to deal with the obstructions—not just the external problems of life, but the internal issues in body, mind, and emotion that have been crying out for healing.

The Energized Being

Though every positive lifestyle change involves a period of discomfort, the rewards are in proportion to the efforts. The rewards of clearing our obstructions are greater than many of us might imagine. As we balance our bodies, clear our minds, and accept our emotions, we open to levels of energy that create an alchemical transmutation down to the atomic structures of our cells.

Spiritual seekers from every culture practice methods to increase available life energy, because they have discovered that *increased energy can, under the right circumstances, enhance every human faculty:* Our mental clarity increases, and our bodies and immune systems become stronger. As conduits for higher levels of energy, we can assist in the healing of others. Our bright energy fields manifest as personal magnetism, presence, charm, and charisma. We experience an expanded field of awareness and focused powers of attention, and the so-called mystical states occur naturally. We attain a more constant experience of radiance, bliss, power, clarity, presence, healing, focus, and strength.

Up the Mountain Path

Addictions can enslave or even kill us, but if we persist beyond them, they offer a painful, difficult, but inevitable path to freedom and self-knowledge. Sometimes we have to pass through hell to get to heaven.

Knowledge is power, and understanding the nature of addictions and compulsive behaviors can provide a powerful impetus and a foundation for change. The promise and the possibility remain before us. As our lives reveal to us both inner darkness and inner light, we find, through our own efforts and courage, a new freedom from compulsive rituals. With growing self-respect and personal power, we can become like the child we once were and the master we will become: mind clear, emotions open, body relaxed, elastic, sensitive—innocent, vulnerable, and real.

With the commitment to see and clear our obstructions, we take a critical step, a quantum leap, up the path of the peaceful warrior.

6

The Will to Change

There's a part of every living thing
that wants to become itself:
the tadpole into the frog,
the chrysalis into the butterfly,
a damaged human being into a whole one.
That is spirituality.

Ellen Bass

A World of Change

Life gives birth to movement: The planets whirl; the rains fall; the rivers flow; the seasons change; seeds take root; forests grow and die, the old making way for the new; winds and tides ebb and flow; and the dance goes on and on.

The urgency of a changing external world demands that we transform our internal world to keep pace. Like surfers, we ride the crest of an accelerating wave; it cannot be stopped, even by our own fears. We can only enjoy the ride. Those who learn to ride the waves of change will soar into the future; those who resist will learn that resistance creates pain.

The urge to change, to grow, to evolve, burns deep within every soul, every cell, as native to us as our hunger to learn. And yet, a part of us holds back—a part that fears the unknown.

Outer Versus Inner Change

In *Way of the Peaceful Warrior*, when I insisted that I was willing to change, Socrates agreed: "You're only too happy to change your clothing, your hairstyle, your partner, your apartment, your job; you seem willing to change everything except yourself."

78

All serious daring starts from within.
Eudora Welty

Socrates was right; I had spent years searching for happiness outside myself, fruitlessly trying to improve the world and other people instead of focusing on the need to change *my* insides— *my* attitudes, beliefs, and approach to life. I was like the man who insisted that he didn't need glasses—that they just weren't printing the newspapers clearly anymore. It took me years to realize that I was the only cause of my difficulties, and that to change my world, I would first have to change myself.

If each of us sweeps in front of our own steps,
the whole world will be clean.
Goethe

We come to maturity as human beings when we take conscious responsibility for our own actions. This responsibility comes the moment we realize that the world we see mirrors our state of awareness, and our conflicts and dissatisfaction originate from a dependence on the outside world to satisfy us and make us happy. We can change our outward life endlessly and not touch the cause of our dissatisfaction. Conscious evolution begins as we take responsibility for clearing our own obstructions. In Chapter 5, we examined some of the primary obstructions and their destructive effects in our everyday lives. In later chapters we will deal with specific methods to clear these obstructions. But before we can make good use of any method or approach, we have to generate the *will* to change.

Knowing Versus Doing

Libraries and bookstores contain information on every conceivable subject—facts, advice, and guidance about improving relationships, work, money, health. *Knowing* what to do is not usually the problem; the elusive goal becomes translating intentions into action and resolutions into results. The gap between *knowing* and *doing* remains a weak link in most of our lives.

We may resolve to improve our diet or exercise habits; we *want* to do it; we *wish* for the results; we even have a pretty good idea how to do it. But we wait for permission from our insides before we act: We wait to feel motivated; we wait until fear, self-doubt, and insecurity dissolve. Nothing changes until we find the will to *follow through.* Our inner adversaries won't go away until we've faced them—until we do what feels right and necessary in spite of the fears or insecurities that may lurk within.

If we want to lose weight, we do brisk aerobic exercise (such as fast walking) for at least one hour every day and stop eating fats or oils for a while. If we want to stop drinking badly enough, we do whatever we need to do in order to stop, whether that means attending a twelve-step meeting or entering a residential treatment facility. All addicts will quit, sooner or later, one way or the other—either through the strength of their own will, through the grace of God, or on the day they die.

When we come to love, understand, and accept ourselves, that love and acceptance will generate in us the heroic efforts and commitment to stop our self-destructive behaviors and become masters of our destiny.

No Easy Ways

Participants in my trainings sometimes ask, "I know what I need to do, but where do I find the discipline? How do I motivate myself?" When people ask me how to do something, I remind them that they already know how; they are really asking, "What's the easy way?"

On planet Earth, "easy" is hard to find. Any accomplishment requires effort, courage, and will; some goals involve more difficulty, others less. If we really go for what we want, we encounter one kind of difficulty; if we give up, we confront another kind. Either way, life is difficult.

> *You know, we can't get out of life alive!*
> *We can either die in the bleachers or die on the field.*
> *We might as well come down on the field and go for it!*
> Les Brown

Positive change of any kind requires that we climb higher, expand our awareness, focus, pay attention, and invest time and energy. Those of us who master change, or at least accept it, recognize the cold, clear realities. Those who haven't yet accepted how the world works still look for the easy way out, that magic formula that produces something for nothing.

> *Every complex problem*
> *has a simple solution*
> *that doesn't work.*
> H. L. Mencken

Rites of Initiation

In ancient cultures, young men and women underwent rites of passage as an initiation into the adult world. To make a strong impression on the Basic Self, such rites involved difficulties, even pain—symbolizing death and rebirth.

Every positive change—every jump to a higher level of energy and awareness—involves a rite of passage. Each time we ascend to a higher rung on the ladder of personal evolution, we must go through a period of discomfort, of initiation. I have never found an exception.

Les Brown, a popular motivational speaker, likens this ascent to an airplane taking off. "The first thing they ask you to do," he reminds us, "is to fasten your seat belt. As you go to a new altitude it gets bumpy for a while before you get comfortable at that height."

Discipline and willpower entail amassing enough psychic energy to cut through old patterns, which involves a distinctly uncomfortable period of adjustment.

Beginning a new exercise program involves discomfort; losing weight involves discomfort; quitting smoking involves discomfort; going into therapy involves discomfort. Life is an uphill climb. It requires commitment, strength, courage, and will.

Basic Selves unaccustomed to going through initiations fear that the discomfort will last forever—so who needs it? Those of us at home with the process of change, who have undergone many rites of passage, know that initiations don't get easier; we just get used to them. We know that eventually the discomfort ends and turns to a feeling of energy and satisfaction. Those of us who have turned back again and again at the doorway of change may find it difficult to break the pattern. The first time is the hardest. The tunnel of transformation does have a light shining at the end. After we get through the darkness once, our Basic Self learns, "I can do it again."

Finding the Discipline

Life rarely lays out a red carpet between us and our goals. More often, we have to struggle through a swamp or a forest of thorns. But if we choose a goal that shines brightly enough for us, it will light our way like a beacon; it will attract us like a magnet, pulling us through the swamp or forest. The power of attraction generates the discipline and will to go on, to persist through difficulties and discomfort.

Very few medical students wake up every morning and say, "I just *love* medical school!" But if these medical students look ahead and see themselves as physicians, working in a hospital or clinic using their skills and knowledge, helping people stay healthy, feeling the success and rewards of their career, they find the will to push on.

The same applies to each of us. Though few of us experience every day of schooling or training or life as fun, if we find goals that shine for us—if we follow our vision—we will find the will to change.

The Three Selves in Conflict and Cooperation

Working together, the three selves can accomplish nearly any goal; separately or in conflict, they can sabotage one another's aims. When the Conscious Self has the support of the Basic Self, change is graceful even when challenging. When our Basic Self and Conscious Self pull in different directions, we hit a wall of resistance.

Qualities of the Three Selves

Each of the three selves has its own area of responsibility: The Basic Self maintains and supports our body and provides the instinctual wisdom and energy for a successful life. The Conscious Self gathers and interprets information, educating and guiding our Basic Self, for example, by taking the Basic Self through experiences that help develop confidence and self-worth. The Higher Self watches over the Conscious Self with loving detachment, uplifting and inspiring it, sending messages of guidance through intuitions and feelings that register in the body (Basic Self). When out of balance, however, the Conscious Self tends to dominate the Basic Self's feelings and intuitions with overbearing logic while dismissing the importance, or even existence, of the Higher Self.

When Communication Breaks Down

Just as adults and children don't always see things eye to eye or understand one another's values, the Conscious Self and Basic Self have different needs and priorities; communication can break down. The Conscious Self and Basic Self often have very little rapport or understanding—like estranged intimates who have had a falling out. The goals of the Conscious Self may overrule or deny the Basic Self's instinctual needs and emotional energies.

The Basic Self may then go into "rebellion," in much the same way an alienated child throws a tantrum or acts out antisocial behavior. This rebellion may take the form of low energy, low motivation, financial difficulties, physical illness or injuries, or, in the most extreme cases, suicide or fatal accidents.

The estrangement between our Conscious Self and Basic Self—reason and feeling—reflects the kind of conflict we see in the outside world between individuals, groups, and nations. The solution, in all cases, depends upon mutual support, appreciation, and cooperation.

Harmony Among the Selves as a Catalyst for Change

We can apply our Conscious Self to train, support, and educate our Basic Self in a spirit of mutual respect—and open channels of cooperation and communication between both selves under the loving dominion of our Higher Self.

The more our Conscious Self understands how our Basic Self (subconscious) operates, the more energy we can generate to achieve desired outcomes. As the three selves open lines of communication and cooperation, we function with more efficiency, energy, and power. By learning to acknowledge, support, and guide our Basic Self, we experience transformations in our health, abundance, and energy.

Willpower Versus "Won't" Power

Lord, make me chaste.
But not just yet.
Attributed to St. Augustine

Most of us believe that we *should* be able to make changes in our lives simply because we have good reasons to do so. We rely on the logic of the Conscious Self to reach our goals. We might as well rely on an airplane to fly us to the moon, for without the cooperation of the Basic Self, the willpower of the Conscious Self doesn't stand a chance. It's like a twenty-watt bulb trying to compete with a lighthouse. Every *will* has a *won't*; if the Conscious Self lacks the support of the Basic Self, it will lose every time.

Reason and logic form only a small part of the magic of motivation. Reasons help define directions, but excitement provides the energy to act. If logic alone had the power to move us, we would see more of it on television commercials! Sophisticated marketing experts design commercials to appeal to the Basic Self; advertisers know that the subconscious generates the impulse to pick up the telephone or go to the store—the will to act, to move, to change.

On the Verge of Change

Before we can find the will to change, we have to find a *willingness*. This willingness can only come from a twofold realization:

1. We realize that our present situation isn't working very well.
2. We realize that the answer lies not in trying to change others or the world, but in changing ourselves.

Before we can awaken, we have to notice we've been asleep. The realization that we've been asleep for most of our life can feel disillusioning, disorienting, and even depressing; we see clearly, perhaps for the first time, how far we have to go.

On the verge of change, things seem to get worse because we finally see our errors clearly. *When we feel stuck, going nowhere—even starting to slip backward—we may actually be backing up to get a running start.*

The Mind of a Child

Those of us who don't seem able to sustain the energy or will to reach our goals sometimes feel like failures, but we have only failed to understand ourselves, and the deep, subconscious source of motivation.

The Basic Self gives us our vital energy for life—the energy to persist in even the most difficult circumstances. It holds the keys to motivation, discipline, and follow-through. It has the values and interests of a young child. When we learn how to motivate young children, we'll also know how to access the vital energy and cooperation of our Basic Self.

Children like *fun* and *pleasure*; they love new toys and excitement. When we feel attracted to or excited about something, the Basic Self gives us the energy we need to overcome any obstacles that stand in our way.

Exciting Memories

1. Recall an incident or event in your life when you felt excited about something and that excitement generated an unusual amount of energy.
2. Ask yourself:
   - What stimulated you?
   - What inspired you?
   - How can you tap into that energy again when you need it?

Our Basic Self rises to the occasion in emergencies or other exciting situations. It has incredible energy; we only need to learn how to call on it. The ability to excite ourselves is as important as the ability to relax. Many psychologists differentiate between what they call "harmful stress" and "beneficial stress" because a little stress—in the moment of truth, when the chips are down, when the deadline approaches and the job's almost done — actually stimulates the Basic Self to give us the energy and inspiration we need. Self-knowledge is critical here. What one Basic Self finds stressful, another may find stimulating.

The Pleasure/Pain Principle

Our Basic Self seeks pleasure and avoids pain. We generate the will to change by

1. understanding the amount of energy that's required;
2. taking into account the Basic Self's natural resistance; and
3. overcoming this resistance by working with the subconscious, which involves
   • visualizing the pain of staying in the same situation, and
   • imagining the pleasures associated with the new pattern.

In a good situation, the Basic Self will choose the greater pleasure; in a bad situation, it will choose the lesser pain. Our Conscious Self also seeks pleasure and avoids pain; logic dictates this. However, these two selves have different definitions of pleasure and pain: An adult who feels ill may get an injection from a physician to help him or her get well. A child may find the illness less painful or fearful than the injection, and so make a different choice. The pleasure/pain principle functions in unique ways for each of us, depending upon our values, fears, and beliefs, but the basic principle applies universally.

---◆---

Pleasure and Pain

1. Quickly write down everything painful you can think of about your present state. As you write, see the *pain* – hear it, touch it, taste it, smell it; use all of your senses. The more vivid and real your scenes, the more powerful your impetus to change.

2. Quickly write down pleasurable ideas about where you want to go, about your goals. As you write, see the *pleasure* – hear it, touch it, taste it, smell it; use all of your senses. Again, the more vivid and real your scenes, the more powerful your impetus to change.

--------------------◆--------------------

Let's say Linda wants to quit smoking. She writes, "stained teeth," and visualizes opening her mouth and looking in the mirror at ugly, blackened teeth. She writes, "bad breath," and sees people stepping away from her and looking at her with distaste. She imagines herself licking and chewing the contents of an ashtray, then breathing into the face of a loved one. She writes, "lung cancer," and sees smoke entering her lungs, turning them dark, and so on—visualizing herself older and wheezing, with wrinkled skin.

Linda follows up that barrage of painful images with positive, pleasurable ones: She sees herself a nonsmoker, writes, "white teeth," and pictures her beautiful smile in the mirror. She writes, "fresh breath," and pictures herself close to a loved one. She writes, "saving money for vacation," and pictures a cookie jar overflowing with green ten-dollar bills, then sees herself in Hawaii and smells the fresh sea breezes. She writes, "vibrant health," and sees herself running and laughing through the waves, with her lungs full of light, healing and strong. She sees herself throwing away cigarettes and feels the power of self-respect that comes with self-mastery. She sees herself laughing at magazine ads associating pleasure with smoking cigarettes.

What We Imagine Becomes Our Reality

Conscious, positive visualizations can help us tap into vast inner resources and Basic Self energies because *the Basic Self does not clearly differentiate between images we see with our physical eyes and pictures we create with our imagination.*

Although I use the word *visualization*, I actually mean using as many inner senses (seeing, hearing, touching, smelling, tasting) as possible to create a fully dimensional experience. By concentrating our complete attention and using all of our senses, we can create inner experiences more vivid than outer ones—because our everyday senses are often dulled as our attention is distracted by thought (for example, when we drive down the highway without noticing what's around us for several miles).

Every Basic Self carries different images, fears, and resources; if we consciously form positive pictures in our mind, we recruit the support of the subconscious, which can give us an almost *unlimited* supply of energy.

Some of our Basic Selves show more strength or courage than others, largely because of the pictures we imagine. For example, if we mention an ocean cruise to Keith, he pictures a swimming pool on the top deck and sumptuous meals. Mention an ocean cruise to Peter, and he pictures the sinking of the *Titanic*.

Many athletes improve their physical skills by visualizing and feeling themselves going through the movements with perfect grace and control, setting up a Basic Self expectation and habit of success. Positive imaging and erasing negative imaging can access strong resources and help to clear old blocks and fears.

Visualization excites the Basic Self, gets it interested in pleasurable possibilities, and fires up its energy reserves. The question becomes, *What* do we visualize that will excite the Basic Self enough to give us the energy we need? How do we motivate ourselves at the subconscious level, which produces the fuel to follow through?

Knowing that our Basic Self seeks pleasure and avoids pain, we can apply the old "carrot-and-stick" principle: "Do this and I will buy you a toy; if you don't do it, I [or consequences] will punish you." For maximum impact, visualize *both* the carrot and the stick to get the point across to your Basic Self.

Again, the more we understand about motivating young children, the more effectively we can generate the subconscious will to change. We know that young children often have perceptions of pain and pleasure different from those of adults; we also know that simple principles appeal to children more than abstract ideas, and that immediate rewards attract children more than long-range ones (as mentioned earlier, children tend to avoid the sting of an injection in spite of our assurances that it will help them later on).

On the other hand, the adult part of us (our Conscious Self) can educate the "child" to help it understand the long-range rewards that we can achieve through short-range discomfort. In this way, we can gain the cooperation—if not necessarily the enthusiastic support—of the Basic Self. The Basic Self doesn't get excited by delayed gratification, abstract concepts, or spiritual ideas, but we can gain its support if we frame the benefits in language and *images* the Basic Self understands.

Back to Basics

The Basic Self is concerned about success in the world; survival, pleasure, and power remain its primary values and motivators.

For example, if we want to find the motivation to meditate every day and come up with reasons such as, "I'll be able to commune with Spirit, clear my mind, open to higher energies, and come closer to illumination," the Higher Self may support such spiritual motives, but it doesn't push or interfere; it only waits, with love. The Conscious Self, with its logic, may feel that meditation would serve a constructive purpose in helping us to relax. But the Basic Self will respond with indignation: "Meditate? You mean just *sit still?* You've got to be kidding. Come on, let's have a pizza instead; let's go play, have fun!"

When we garner the enthusiastic support of the Basic Self, we find we have the energy and will to do *anything* within human limits, and sometimes beyond them! First, however, we have to offer the Basic Self something it really likes: Fun! Glory! Power! Pleasure! Good feelings! So if we want to meditate, we can focus on how it will help us be more relaxed, more fun loving, and more easygoing; on how we'll be more attractive and more effective in life, with better concentration to make more money—to have more, be more, live more! "Now you're talking!" our Basic Self will likely respond. "Let's do it!"

During my college years, I lived in the gymnasium, practicing gymnastics over four sweaty hours, six days a week, every week. I did this whether or not I happened to be in the mood. No matter what else transpired on campus, unless I had a high fever, I knew where I would be from 2:30 until 6:30 every day—working on gut-wrenching, muscle-straining routines. Sometimes I felt so tired at the end of a workout, I could barely walk up the stairs from the locker room.

How did I develop the commitment and motivation to do this? Did I work out so I could train my body, mind, and spirit, or so I could become a "more balanced human being"? No. Did I push through bouts of inertia, fatigue, discouragement, and discomfort so I could someday inspire other people? Not on your life. Perhaps I understood that my training would teach me about myself, and about the laws of reality. Who am I kidding? These goals weren't in my consciousness at the time.

I trained to gain recognition, admiration, and adulation; I believed my gymnastics prowess would make me more attractive to women. These weren't Conscious Self motives; they came straight from my Basic Self. The point is, they *worked*—all the way to the national and world championships.

And while I worked so hard to satisfy the goals of my Basic Self, I also learned about the laws of reality and about myself; in the process, I gained high levels of coordination, flexibility, and balance. Gymnastics helped prepare me for the work I would do later. But none of those "higher" motives were enough to generate the required energy.

The key to motivation and discipline involves achieving rapport with our Basic Self, our subconscious—finding out what *it* wants rather than what our Conscious Self *thinks* it *should* want.

If we decide to achieve something, if we associate that change with a sense of *security* or *fun* or *personal power*, the Basic Self will give us energy to accomplish the task, *because it wants the carrot.* If the goal has little to do with these three things, we probably won't persist.

———————————◆———————————

Three Selves, Three Motives

1. Pick a challenging goal you would like to accomplish someday. Perhaps it involves changing something about yourself, improving your lifestyle, or achieving success in a chosen area. Select something you might actually do – something you would work toward if you felt sufficiently motivated.
2. Write (or state aloud) the three different kinds of motives:
   a. First, write Higher Self motives such as love, service, and spiritual illumination. *Imagine yourself achieving these goals; how does that make you feel?*
   b. Next, write Conscious Self motives: logical, constructive reasons to achieve the goal. *Imagine yourself achieving these goals; how does that make you feel?*
   c. Then write Basic Self motives: safety and security; pleasure and fun; power, recognition, and self-mastery. *Imagine yourself achieving these goals; how does that make you feel?*
3. As you visualize yourself achieving your goals, always *pay special attention to the motives that give you the most excitement.*

———————————◆———————————

The Process of Change

The process of personal transformation ebbs and flows like the tide. It doesn't follow a straight line; we meet hills, valleys, and plateaus as we climb the mountain path.

I've observed many times in the physical realm of skill learning that we suffer the consequences of repeated errors only until we become aware of the error.

At first, we don't see the error; then we begin to see it *after* the event has taken place, and we suffer regrets. Later, we see the error *during* the event: "Oh! I'm doing it again!" Finally, we anticipate the error *before* we make it and so avoid it.

Many of us chastise ourselves because we don't yet accept the natural process of learning and expect ourselves to "get it right" the first time. But life doesn't work that way. The more we understand the process of change, the more patience we display, both with ourselves and with the world.

The following quotation[1] beautifully captures the process of change:

Autobiography in Five Short Chapters

Chapter I: I walk down the street. There is a deep hole in the sidewalk. I fall in. I am lost. . . . I am helpless. It isn't my fault. It takes forever to find a way out.

Chapter II: I walk down the same street. There is a deep hole in the sidewalk. I pretend I don't see it. I fall in again. I can't believe I am in this same place. But it isn't my fault. It still takes a long time to get out.

Chapter III: I walk down the same street. There is a deep hole in the sidewalk. I see it is there. I still fall in . . . it's a habit . . . but, my eyes are open. I know where I am. It is my fault. I get out immediately.

---

1. Copyright © 1977 Portia Nelson, *There's a Hole in My Sidewalk* (Hillsboro, OR: Beyond Words Publishing, Inc.)

*Chapter IV: I walk down the same street. There
is a deep hole in the sidewalk. I walk around it.
Chapter V: I walk down another street.*

Resistance to Change

Most of us believe we want to change—to improve ourselves—but our Basic Self needs boundaries, thrives on limits,
and remains fond of familiar patterns. We carry the weight
of inertia, the resistance to change, within us.

We build our lives around routines: the way we get up
in the morning; what we do before bed; how we get into our
car—habits at work and at home. We can get so locked into
old patterns that we stick with them even though they clearly
don't work anymore. I once asked a battered woman why she
didn't leave her husband; she answered sadly, "At least I'm
used to it."

Change involves a leap from the known into the unknown;
fear of change mirrors the fear of death. How many of us are
really willing to jump out of the frying pan of the familiar
into the fires of transformation?

The less we resist, the more we learn; the more quickly
we adapt, the more easily we ride the crest of change. But
whether we change with relative ease or great difficulty, we
can and will change. We are born with an innate ability and
desire to improve ourselves.

The difficulty of any task relates to preparation. If we
start out overweight, inflexible, and out of shape, for example, it will be harder for us to master a physical skill such as
jumping rope, doing a cartwheel, swinging a golf club or tennis
racket, but we can learn nearly anything once we complete
the necessary preparation and lay a good foundation.

Our Basic Self is not the problem; resistance is. By understanding our Basic Self's fear of change, just as we might
understand the fears of our own children, we develop the patience, insight, and rapport necessary to open channels of

communication with our subconscious. Just as young children can learn to accept change, so can our Basic Self.

We are changing, we have got to change,
and we can no more help it
than leaves can help going yellow
and coming loose in autumn.

D. H. Lawrence

Change gets easier, just as surfing gets easier, with practice. But it remains a challenge. Even the smallest changes in our lives require courage and commitment. Ram Dass, a respected spiritual practitioner and teacher, once said, "After all these years, I still have all the same neuroses." I can certainly relate to his situation; after years of intention, I still chip away at old habits such as driving and eating too fast.

Keys to Transformation

Since it holds the keys to a vast storehouse of transformative energy, let's review what we know about the Basic Self.

1. The Basic Self is responsible for, and controls, the body.
2. It gives us our vital energy for life.
3. Its qualities, drives, motives, logic, interests, and values most closely resemble those of a young child.
4. It only gives energy to activities it values or feels excited about.
   • Like most young children, it gets excited by new toys, fun, surprises, recognition, attention, and appreciation.
   • Like most young children, it likes excitement; it likes to acquire new things, see new places, feel safe, and feel pleasure.
5. The Basic Self is responsible for survival and security, sexual/creative energy, personal power, and discipline. It is concerned with *success in the material world.*

6. Like most young children, the Basic Self fears the unknown and tends to resist any change unless that change appeals to it enough to overcome its resistance. Promising and delivering additional, pleasurable compensation enjoyed by our particular Basic Self can make the difference. (For example, "I'll stop smoking, *and* I'll get a massage every week.")

Most often, when we make a change in our life, we focus on what we have to give up: We "lose" weight; we "give up" smoking, alcohol, or another drug; we "end" a relationship. But the moment we end one thing, we begin another: In losing weight, we *gain* lightness; in giving up smoking or other drugs, we *enhance* our health and vitality and form a new relationship with ourselves and with reality; in ending a relationship, we may *open the space* for a more fulfilling one.

Choice involves giving up something we want for something we want more. Usually, a part of us wants to change, and another part doesn't. No change is all good or all bad. Whether change feels easy or difficult depends upon where we put our focus and energy. Contemplating what we "have to give up," then, puts our Basic Self into strong resistance. Focusing on the benefits will gain the cooperation and energy and support of our Basic Self—if it finds these benefits appealing.

---◆---

Pros and Cons: The Decision to Change

1. Write or say aloud the change you want.
2. Make a list of the main things you will *lose* when you make this change.
3. Make a list of the main things you will *gain* when you make this change.
4. Compare the lists, and decide.

---◆---

If the inherent benefits of a change don't compensate for our perceived loss of something we feel attached to or dependent upon, we can "sweeten the pot" by giving ourselves something extra—a reward for making the change. For example, after losing a certain amount of weight, if we treat ourselves to a soak in a hot tub, buy ourselves something we've wanted, or do something else that excites us—the subconscious will accept that reward as compensation, and will support the change because it associates the change with an even greater pleasure.

Teaching the Basic Self Through the Body

Just as we can educate our children to develop their strong qualities, we can educate our Basic Self to develop less resistance and more spontaneity, less fear and more confidence, less petulance and more understanding.

The Basic Self understands kinesthetic feelings and direct experience better than concepts. We can best teach the Basic Self about determination—about the step-by-step process to accomplishing a goal—through physical movement. For example, if we wish to overcome the Basic Self's inherent resistance to change, we can teach it the art of *nonresistance* using a fundamental principle from the martial arts. This principle teaches, *When pushed, pull; when pulled, push*; in other words, like a tree bending in the wind, go *with* the forces of life, rather than resist them.

Judo and Aikido practitioners employ this principle in the training hall; as their partners begin to push them, they step aside and pull; staying balanced, they use their partners' own weight and force to throw them off balance. If their partners pull them, they quickly step forward and push, adding their own force to their partners', again sending their partners in the direction of this force.

We can use the same approach to verbal confrontations or other situations—getting out of the way, blending with the forces that impinge upon our lives and making use of them.

The Fear of Failure

Let's not confuse the love of success with the fear of failure. The love of success excites us and garners the enthusiastic support of the Basic Self. "Dare to be great!" it cries. "Live with passion! Go for it! Just do it!"

Fear of failure, on the other hand, paralyzes us. Children *hate* to fail, and they feel like failures a lot, when they compare themselves to adults. We adults have developed our abilities through time and experience. But children don't always understand the process; neither does our Basic Self, so we have to teach it.

Though we aren't consciously aware of it, as we grew up and experienced many small, inevitable failures, each time we were teased or criticized, we tensed our muscles. That tension didn't feel good; thus, our Basic Self learned that failure doesn't feel good.

One of the most important lessons we can teach our Basic Self is that when we fail, the sky does not fall. By going through failure, we can show our subconscious the hidden rewards of persistence through the tough times. In the gymnasium I used to fail fifty times a day. Whenever I decided to accomplish a new routine, I knew the process: *I would fail until I succeeded.* Failures can become the stepping-stones between us and our goals.

We often fail many times before we finally reach our goal. Overnight successes often take about ten years. If we persist, we succeed.

> *You must do the thing you think you cannot do.*
> Eleanor Roosevelt

Our past mistakes serve as a university for success, because they teach us what not to do next time; this process is called learning. We learn through mistakes, but intelligence means not repeating the *same* mistake over and over. We can also learn from the mistakes of others.

Using Anger

Most often, our resistance to change comes from fear (paralysis) or sorrow (weakness). Anger manifests at the solar plexus and is stronger than either fear or sorrow, so we can use anger to overcome both.

We can also use anger to fuel our efforts to stop self-destructive habits. As an example, let's look at the smoking habit. Nearly everyone not connected with the tobacco industry acknowledges that smoking has distinct, long-range health liabilities, and yet not everyone stops smoking. Reasons for this include ignorance (ignoring the facts; using denial, rationalization, and other defense mechanisms) and the addictive nature of nicotine. But most people who want to quit yet still smoke simply haven't gotten angry enough.

I heard a story about J. Paul Getty, who was stationed in France during World War II: He woke up one night at about 2:00 in the morning, dying for a cigarette. He got up and looked in his cigarette box: empty. He looked for a butt in the ashtray, in his pant cuffs, in all his pockets. No cigarettes.

So, with a sigh, he got up, got dressed, and walked out into a pouring rainstorm, headed for an all-night market about a mile down the muddy street. Twenty minutes later, about halfway there, sloshing through ankle-deep mud, Jean Paul stopped in his tracks, as if struck by lightning. He looked up into the pouring rain, and yelled over the roar of thunder, "*What am I doing?*"

In that instant, he realized something that had escaped him. Standing in the rain, ankle deep in mud, he realized how smoking had enslaved him. Jean Paul Getty got angry—not perturbed, not irritated, but coldly, fiercely angry. He turned around, walked back home, and never smoked again.

Oh, he had cravings; a part of him wanted a cigarette the next day, and the next. But his anger had turned to a commitment that would not waver. When anger and commitment join forces, you don't have to "try," you just do.

According to the system of astrological archetypes, the planet Mars rules anger, but it also rules energy, motivation, and assertion. Anger works; self-pity doesn't. Logic and reason only point the way; anger moves us to action. Anger at ourselves, however, only compounds the problem and reinforces the self-destructive impulses that maintain our addictions in the first place.

We need to remain aware that our Basic Self wants to continue the habit because it's used to it. If we open lines of communication with this part of ourselves, we discover that it clings to old ways for reasons of its own, coping with issues from childhood that may no longer apply. Ultimately, our fearful Basic Self wants to help us, but it may feel too insecure or afraid. As we seek to understand it, the rapport we achieve can help the Basic Self to learn and grow into new ways of being.

> *True change and higher human adaptation*
> *are not made by resistance to the old habits.*
> *Change is not a matter of not doing something;*
> *it is a matter of doing something else.*
> Da Avabhasa (Da Free John)

Change comes down to a choice—whether to defend our habits while destroying our lives or to commit to the difficult process of transformation.

Misjudging the Road Ahead

Looking back, each of us can probably recall times in our lives when we set out to accomplish something but failed to reach our goals. Most likely, we either *under*estimated the challenge ahead and later gave up, or we *over*estimated the challenge and got scared off.

When we *underestimate* the task, we begin with optimism and high expectations ("This will be a piece of cake!"). We set ourselves up for discouragement when we discover that the challenge looms larger than we had thought, and requires more energy, time, or experience than we had first believed.

Probably nothing in the world
arouses more false hopes
than the first four hours of a diet.
Dan Bennett

By underestimating the difficulty, we start out overconfident, and our Basic Self rations too little energy for the task; we get caught in the common trap of *almost enough* to succeed. Ancient warriors knew that underestimating the enemy meant almost certain death.

On the other hand, if we *overestimate* and start out with underconfidence, we may give up before we've even begun; after all, why take on an "opponent" or tackle a job that appears to be impossible, or out of our league?

Therefore, by realistically assessing the challenges before us, and taking a confident but balanced view of our own capacity, we can strategically gather the support and tools we need to assure completion.

A Time for Every Purpose

We don't plant most crops in autumn or reap the harvest in spring. Everything has its own time and pace. Ramakrishna, the Indian saint, reminded us, "When we try to open a nut when the shell is green, we find it nearly impossible; but when the shell is ripe, it will open with a tap."

Take time to deliberate;
but when the time for action arrives,
stop thinking and go in.
Andrew Jackson

Windows of opportunity open and then close. By staying in the present, handling what's in front of us, and riding the wave of opportunity when it comes, we follow the natural order of things.

The Power of Commitment

Everyone *wants* to change, but not everyone wants it enough to go through the period of initiation and discomfort. We may think we have the *will* to change, but we really only have the *whim* to change.

Fears and paralysis can require that we have to "hit bottom"—lose friends or family, or face a life-threatening illness—before we take stock and realize we are dealing with a serious situation. Finally, in the eleventh hour, something clicks inside of us; we cross a line from *thinking* we want to reach our goal to a *do-or-die commitment.* Maybe we pray and give the situation up to God or a higher power. When we reach the turning point, we also find a "lower power"—the surging energy and indomitable will of our subconscious.

Change doesn't happen until we commit to it. Some of us *think* we feel committed to losing weight, quitting smoking, or changing in the direction of our ideals. We state firmly, "I'm committed," but when heavy obstacles fall in our path, our commitment may waver. "If this were the right goal, everything would fall into place; these difficulties must be signs that I should choose another direction. I was committed, but I've changed my mind."

Commitment means no matter what. When we commit to a relationship, we stop wondering if someone else out there might make an even better partner for us. If we commit to a career, we give it our best and waste no time toying with other possibilities. The feeling of commitment doesn't come naturally. We have to develop it, and earn it.

The moment one commits oneself,
then providence moves, too.
All sorts of things occur to help one
that would never have otherwise occurred.

A whole stream of events;
all manner of unforeseen incidents
and chance meetings and material assistance come forth
which no one could have dreamt would appear.
I have learned a deep respect for
one of Goethe's couplets:
"Whatever you can do, or dream you can, begin it.
Boldness has genius and power and magic in it."
W. H. Murray

Commitment does not, however, require that we stand firm and inflexible even when our heart tells us that a situation isn't working over time. To keep commitment from becoming blind stubbornness, I've applied the following two-part principle to my own life: *If a situation doesn't work, first I do everything I can to make it work*; this may mean exploring new options and choices rather than passively tolerating the situation or merely escaping. The best way to "escape" from a problem often involves solving it. Commitment does not mean beating our heads against a wall for the rest of our lives. The second part of the principle states, *If, after giving it my best effort for a reasonable time (ranging from an hour to a decade or more, depending upon the context), the situation still doesn't work, then I leave it with full confidence that I've done the right thing.*

If we stick with something through the hard times, if we face our troubles, we have the opportunity to learn about ourselves and our reactions. In learning, we evolve. But there is a difference between commitment and masochism; when our innermost feelings inform us that our current direction no longer serves our highest good, we may then in good conscience commit to a new direction.

Forming New Patterns

Since life can seem routine and boring and variety spices it up, part of us welcomes change. In fact, we may welcome it so much that we find it difficult to do anything the same way twice. So what's all this fuss about resistance to change? Changes can be fun!

Few of us resist the *idea* of changing or improving ourselves. We may not even resist beginning to change our diet, or starting a new exercise program, or even practicing new ways of expressing ourselves. But *sticking* to these changes over time presents the challenge.

We've already established that the Basic Self, which can support changes if we motivate it effectively, also tends to resist change *because it gets used to familiar patterns.*

The Basic Self has its own internal rhythms and timing; it takes time for it to begin adjusting to a new pattern. Therefore, until the Basic Self supports a new pattern wholeheartedly, we have to persist on the willpower of our Conscious Self—doing what we think is best. As I've already noted, the Basic Self likes excitement and new things, and may give us immediate support to begin a new pattern if that pattern seems fun or if we've promised it a reward in the future. But our Basic Self can also get bored. Sticking with a new program challenges us most after the newness and fresh enthusiasm have worn off and before it has established itself as a pattern.

> *Great works are performed*
> *not by strength, but by perseverance.*
> Samuel Johnson

Here we find a clue to garnering the support of the Basic Self: *If we can maintain a change for about thirty days, the Basic Self will recognize this as a new pattern.* After thirty days, the Basic Self recognizes the new pattern and will support that pattern in a way it had not supported it before. For example, about thirty days after starting a new exercise routine, if we do it every day, a shift occurs and it becomes a part of our daily routine. We no longer have to exert the same degree of conscious willpower in order to do it. Another jump in additional Basic Self support happens at six months, then a year.

The Basic Self's tendency to stick with established patterns operates, for example, in the arena of body weight. If we have weighed the same for several years, the Basic Self grows accustomed and attached to this sense of itself. Though the Conscious Self may desire to lose weight, gain muscle, or both, we feel a subconscious (and physical) pressure to return to what the Basic Self considers equilibrium.

The will to change, then, must be strong enough not only to persist through the initial start-up phase but to maintain that new pattern in the face of inevitable pressures to revert to old ways, for enough time that what was once new becomes an old pattern. Then the Basic Self will again nestle into that shape as it becomes comfortable, like an old shoe. First, however, we have to break the shoe in.

> *There came a time when the risk*
> *to remain tight in a bud*
> *was more painful*
> *than the risk it took to blossom.*
> Anaïs Nin

Visualizing the Road Ahead

We have already seen that our Basic Self doesn't discriminate between our internal reality and our external one. Therefore, *imagining* ourselves and our lives as we want them to be gives our Basic Self a preview, and allows it to start getting used to the change we wish to generate. If we see and feel ourselves *enjoying* that change, we add additional momentum.

Our Basic Self will then create subtle changes in our behaviors that encourage those in our environment to support that change as well. The process can seem almost magical, but it works. For example, if we want physical change, we

start by clearly imagining the body we want to have and experiencing how good this will feel. Our Basic Self then generates increased energy for us to work for that goal. If we want
to have more money in our life, we start out by visualizing
our purse or wallet bulging with cash as we step into our new
car on the way to buy some gifts for friends, which we can
easily afford. We feel the enjoyment of this—and the warm
glow as we mail generous checks to our favorite charities. Our
Basic Self will get very excited about images like this, and
while we maintain the vision and feeling of pleasure, it will
give us all the energy, will, and inspiration we need to come
up with creative ways to experience the fruits of abundance.

The Paradox of Acceptance and Change

The mechanics and feelings of our Basic Self reveal the
means to change. These means work; they have worked for
many thousands of warriors, like us, throughout history, who
knew how to harness the powers of the subconscious. But
before we go bravely into new territory, let's take a moment
to accept and appreciate ourselves as we are *right now*—to
love, understand, and honor our body, our mind, and our
emotions—our strengths, our weaknesses, our habits, and
our failings. Self-acceptance and compassion provide the support and open the way to change.

Let's examine our motives as well as our goals. If we want
to change because of an underlying lack of self-worth, that
lack will undermine our efforts; even if we get where we're
going, the lack will remain. Beginning from a place of unconditional love for ourselves, with the recognition that we are
good and strong and brave deep inside—a peaceful warrior
now—encourages us to become *even better*, not out of lack,
but out of our longing for a full and meaningful life, for the
challenge of personal evolution and a chance to turn dreams
into reality. Once we develop the will to change, we're ready
to apply the tools for transformation.

Part III
Tools for Transformation

Introduction

We have now taken a clear, compassionate look at our habits and the obstructions that create them. We understand how we can appeal to the powerful capacities of our Basic Self to turn intentions into action, and generate the will to change. Now we're ready to step into the arena, and apply the tools for transformation.

Nearly all the problems we have ever encountered in daily life stem from a weak link in our chain of body, mind, and emotions. Part III focuses on universal tools for strengthening our weak areas and clearing our obstructions as they arise in the moment. Over time, as these obstructions dissolve in the light of awareness and the heat of committed effort, we begin to notice subtle energies as our inner sight and intuition expand; the "ordinary" moments of our daily lives become extraordinary.

The tools presented in Part III are designed to become a natural, pleasurable part of everyday life; changes happen so gracefully we hardly notice them, until one day we look back and realize that we perceive a different world than the one we used to know – a happier, more relaxed, more peaceful, and more loving world. We begin to pass through the adversities that once posed such barriers with a calm focus, the way a master of the martial arts might deal with opponents who once seemed menacing.

The closer we come to achieving a balanced body, a clear mind, and open emotions, the greater ease we have in areas of health, money, relationships and sexuality, and work. As we apply these tools, we open ourselves to higher levels of energy and awareness and to a closer contact with our Higher Self and the uplifting light of Spirit.

7

Balancing the Body

If we don't take good care of our body,
where will we live?
Anonymous

Reowning the Body

Life and spiritual practice begin and end with the body. In this world, we can enjoy life, serve others, learn, and evolve only if we have a body. If the body is the house of the soul, we need to build a strong foundation for that house before we can leap into higher realms of awareness. Our bodies are the roots through which we connect heaven to earth. We can't blossom until these roots run deep.

When our bodies feel ill, sluggish, and out of balance, they can feel like a burden, and a source of pain. Those of us who pursue "out-of-body" travel may wish to wing free of this "mortal coil." When in balance, however, our body is one of the most finely tuned instruments in creation—a self-regulating biological organism that no computer can outthink and no machine can outperform. Our bodies alchemically transform gross foods into refined energy. The moment we appreciate our human body as a miraculous gift and an unfathomable opportunity, we naturally feel moved to take better care of it.

Betrayal of the Body

Four of our five primary senses—sight, hearing, taste, and smell—center around our head, creating the illusion that our awareness emanates from a point behind our eyes; sometimes

109

it seems as if we *live* in our heads. We identify with this "head awareness" and call it *mind.* We also call it *I,* and tend to view the body as a mere vehicle of the mind, as if we sat in a control booth, directing the body below.

We identify with the Conscious Self, which often seeks to control or dominate (rather than guide) our Basic Self (or bodily instincts and gut feelings). Most of us experience a certain alienation or estrangement from our body. This is understandable; after all, the body feels pain, gets ill, and cannot always satisfy the mind's desires. For most of us, body and mind exist in an uneasy partnership; we may view the body as a problem—as a weight our soul must carry.

Many of us resent our bodies because they don't measure up to our programmed values; we perceive them as too short or too tall, too fat or too skinny, or with the wrong-shaped face or wrong type hair, or even wrong skin tone. Most of us heave an existential sigh and make the best of it. But we don't really understand or trust our own bodies. Many of us would trade ours in for another model, if we could, as the growing popularity of cosmetic surgery testifies. And ultimately, the body seems to betray us by wearing out, growing ill, and dying.

We live in a world of judgments and values about our bodies, and the bodies of others, in which we measure ourselves and others against arbitrary, programmed fashions of beauty. Rather than exercise and eat as part of a balanced lifestyle, we tend to pursue erratic regimens to create and sustain self-images dictated by others, based largely upon unexamined values.

Despite what we may have believed for years, consider that while obesity does pose a health risk, *slim bodies have no more inherent attractiveness than rounder bodies; we have just been conditioned to believe this.* Different cultures have considerably different ideals of beauty, as well as diet. We acquire our sense of physical beauty the same way we get our taste for foods, through a complex array of cultural programming and personal associations.

Some of us take good care of our body; others ignore it until problems arise. Those of us who tend to ignore our body—spending more time and money on objects such as our car or home—may have mixed feelings about our physical side. Preoccupied with how we look on the outside but ignoring what we can't see on the inside, we may take our body for granted, mistrust it, or even resent it. To make matters worse, we didn't come with an owner's manual, so we add ignorance to neglect. Habitual use of tobacco, alcohol, other drugs, fatty foods, and refined sugar contributes to premature aging, chronic degenerative diseases, and physical misery.

Until we come to understand, trust, appreciate, and love our own body, we won't take care of it. The often hidden negative feelings we have toward our body constitute an important issue we need to face and resolve. Until the Conscious Self forms a caring relationship with the body and Basic Self, reading about methods to clear physical obstructions and improve health will accomplish little.

We need to get in touch with and express our negative feelings about our body before we can learn to accept and love it.

Forgiving the Body

1. Ask yourself the following questions:
   - How do you feel about your body?
   - What do you like about it?
   - What don't you like about it?
   - What can you change (through diet, exercise, or other means)?
   - What can't you (realistically) change, and what do you therefore need to accept?
2. Specifically, how do you feel about the following:
   - Your skin tone and color?
   - Your height?

- Your shape?
- Your hair?
- Your face?
- Your physical limitations?
- Your strength?
- Your overall health?
- Your energy?

3. Having considered your feelings, both positive and negative, send love and forgiveness to your body, recognizing that it is doing the best it can.

Inside Out

To a significant degree, our body, face, and voice reflect our habits, emotions, thoughts, and lifestyle. Our innermost thoughts, neuromuscular tensions, and habits form, in large part, the shape of our bodies and the topography of our faces. For example, horizontal wrinkles on the forehead can come from chronic self-doubt, confusion, puzzlement, or insecurity.

The tone, volume, and quality of our voices—whether muted or shrill—also mirrors our state of mind. The body cannot lie; our innermost emotions, both positive and negative are literally written all over our face. By changing our thoughts and habits, we set in motion forces that change our outward appearance over time.

We may enjoy looking at people who have classic features and fashionable body types because we find them aesthetically pleasing—the same way we might enjoy looking at a flower, a sunset, or a scenic view. But inner beauty—love and happiness—shines through even the most homely features.

Insomuch as love grows in you,
so in you beauty grows.
St. Augustine

Our Only Real Possession

However our body may look, whether it pleases us or not, we get only *one*, and it lasts a lifetime. To put this another way, our lifetime only lasts as long as our body. And the quality of that lifetime will parallel the quality of our body.

During our life, with all its cycles, we will say good-bye to friends and loved ones; we will lose homes, cars, and money; we may even shift beliefs and values. But our body, loyal to the end, will stick with us for life—guaranteed. When this truth penetrates fully, we begin to take good care of our "best friend."

Master of the Body Shop

Each of us bears sole responsibility for our own body. We were born with inherited *tendencies*; the rest we make up.

> *God gave us faces;*
> *we make our own expressions.*
> Anonymous

Our bodies remain malleable for a lifetime. Apart from height, body type, and other inherited characteristics, we can shape our faces and bodies—inside and out—by our habits of diet and exercise, as well as our mental and emotional states. *By changing our habits, we change our body; by changing our body, we change our life.*

Bob and Sid, fraternal twins, grew up in a typical meat, milk, and potatoes family. As they reached adulthood, their parents died within a year of each other of heart disease. Bob continues eating a diet laden with fat in the form of meat and dairy products. He rarely exercises, is under stress at work, and has trouble expressing his emotions. He will very likely follow the family tradition of "early retirement," and he may even break some records. Sid, on the other hand, rarely eats meat or dairy products; he exercises regularly, does yoga, practices deep breathing, and meditates. He will very likely live longer, despite inherited tendencies very similar to Bob's.

The "work with what you've got" principle applies to positive traits, as well: We each come in with potential; whether we reach it or not depends upon what we do. Inherited traits give us the clay to work with; our habits shape the clay.

Once we get past our negative programming and accept, appreciate, and love the body that Spirit gave us, we open the space for change, because acceptance and love encourage the Basic Self far more than criticism.

Getting Into the Body

The more balanced the body, the more easily we can feel the uplifting, inspiring presence of Spirit. If our body feels weak, toxic, stiff, or aching, we lack the free and focused attention that enables us to tune in to more refined energies or levels of existence.

That doesn't mean we all have to become athletes or engage in intensive, spartan physical regimens in order to travel the peaceful warrior's way; in fact, many athletes, trained to "use" the body like a machine, dissociate from it, ignoring signs of fatigue or pain in order to accomplish competitive goals.

We all have lungs, however, so it makes sense to use them fully, learning to breathe deeply, with ease, and with feeling. We all have muscles; it makes sense to keep them toned and vital. We all have a digestive system; it makes sense to learn about what food nourishes us best. We also benefit from mastering the ability to relax in any situation.

Spending Time in Nature

Accepting ourselves means accepting our body. If we lose touch with our physical nature, with the earthy or lower aspects of ourselves, we also lose touch with our higher aspects—the intuitive feelings that come through the physical body. Reconnecting with the body of earth and with the natural world around us provides a good way to tune into our body.

♦

Back to Nature

1. Every day, make some form of simple, meaningful contact with the natural world: Smell, touch, or gaze at a flower; run your hands down the bark of a tree and feel its energy; tend a flower box; start a small garden in your yard or on your windowsill. These simple actions can help heal frantic spirits. Getting in touch with the earth and growing things can help you reconnect with your own nature.
2. On weekends or vacations, spend a little time walking in the hills, at the beach, or in the park. As you walk, you may find you gain a new appreciation for your own body.

♦

The Body and Natural Laws

The body (Basic Self) functions best when we live in alignment with the natural laws of diet, exercise, breathing, stretching, rest, relaxation, posture, and balance. We cannot bend the rules for long without suffering inevitable consequences, which vary among us due to our individual differences.

We can all benefit from practicing a lifestyle relatively free of toxicity, stress, fatigue, and imbalance. Sometimes, due to the nature of life on planet Earth, we get exposed to a particularly nasty strain of virus or bacteria at a time of lowered immunity. But most often we can trace illness to a period just prior to symptoms when we consciously or subconsciously allowed our shields to drop — through partying too hard, working too hard, eating too much junk food, and so forth.

Toxicity, fatigue, and imbalance lower our immune responses. We *toxify* ourselves by taking in more food than we can process, by eating foods that burden our system, or by eating improperly, too fast, or when upset. We grow *fatigued* from pressure-driven, externally imposed work that gives us no satisfaction or from making demands our body cannot meet. *Imbalance* in our nervous system also sets us up for illness. We throw the nervous system out of balance by strong emotional upsets, *especially* when we hold in our feelings rather than express them, or when we confront unaccustomed or stressful circumstances. These circumstances may also include "good" things, such as winning a lottery, getting married, or experiencing radical changes, which disorient the Basic Self.

The Best Coach

We learn about our heart and lungs, our muscles, our nervous system and our ability to relax, our digestive system, and all the other aspects of ourselves through *paying attention to feedback*—through noticing what we do and how we feel afterward. This sounds very simple, but few of us really pay attention.

If Christopher starts an exercise program on Tuesday and on Wednesday feels like he got run over by a tank, maybe his body is trying to tell him, "Start out easier and progress gradually." *Our body is our best coach.*

If Paul gets headaches by the end of each workday, and recognizes this as a clear signal from his body—rather than as a random thing that happens to him for no reason—he'll learn to slow down, let go of chronic tension, and perhaps do some gentle neck stretches and breathing, and some exercise to release stress before lunch.

If Jane eats in a hurry, under stress, or eats a food she doesn't digest well, her body will give her feedback in the form of gas, stomach cramps, low energy, or other symptoms. If she pays attention, her body teaches her about the best diet and nutrition to meet her unique requirements.

The body knows itself; our Basic Self knows every cell and tissue of the body. Not even the most sophisticated experts in the fields of exercise and nutrition can match the body wisdom of the Basic Self.

Lessons of the Body

Our body lives and moves subject to the same laws as the planets and stars. Our body has direct access to universal wisdom: Through it, we can learn every principle of living we will ever need to know.

For example, my gymnastics training taught me a great deal about life. The teachers and books I've encountered only confirmed the secrets I learned internally and intuitively, at the cell level, through physical training—the laws of balance, acceptance, cooperation, discipline, concentration, motivation, courage, self-trust, and commitment—all qualities that can, when fully developed, change the course of anyone's life.

Finding Natural Balance

In this chapter, I focus on three primary tools in the process of physical transformation—the fundamentals of diet, exercise, and bodywork—because they offer the most obvious and powerful leverage we can exert toward clearing obstructions and balancing our bodies.

Through a simple and direct application of the principles and practices that follow, we can rejuvenate our bodies without exaggerated effort or temporary heroics.

A Warrior's Approach to Diet

Two primary issues stand between us and optimal diet: *knowing* and *doing*. We have to know before we can do. We can know indirectly, through our minds, or directly, through our body's instincts.

Developing an optimal diet is largely a matter of teamwork between our Conscious Self (mind) and our Basic Self (body). When we were an infant, our Basic Self instinctively knew just what foods served our needs, day to day. It guided us by hunger and taste. Since then, however, programming from television, parents, peers, and advertising—plus the overwhelming effects of refined sweets and processed foods—has confused our instincts.

Thus, "trusting our instincts" may not be the best course until we *tune up* our Basic Self and refine our instincts. We can do this in small increments, with the guidance of our Conscious Self. In other words, we might read some good books on diet and begin making some small dietary changes, gradually adding more foods that are wholesome, and eating less foods that don't serve us. For every food we give up, we can find a substitute we like. For example, when I gave up refined sugar, I started eating homemade desserts with natural sweeteners such as baked cinnamon apples cooked in their own juices. We don't have to suffer!

We can learn and study about current research and guidelines for healthful eating. We may even explore nutritional therapies to clear a variety of physical problems brought on by imbalanced diet in the first place. While the Basic Self can check out the food by tasting it, smelling it, and feeling its effects on the body, our Conscious Self can read the labels.

As we change our diet, our instincts sharpen; we notice more, which, in turn, helps generate more changes. Our pace has to suit our Basic Self. Once we have sharpened our instincts, then we can trust them to guide us, but only if our Conscious Self is also paying attention to these messages from the body. We can smell foods, taste them carefully, and sense, as best we can, the life energy they have (we can do this without knowing how). Then, we can trust the process of change.

Systematic Undereating

The most important dietary rule for longevity and health is *systematic undereating*. Study after study of both animals and human cultures has shown that those who eat less and tend toward healthy leanness live longer and stay healthier than those who overeat. Overeating taxes the body and digestive organs, and can overburden our ability to assimilate and eliminate waste. Of course, the advice to undereat does not apply to those of us who are already *below* our ideal body weight. As with any principle, we do well to consider our unique situation before putting systematic undereating into practice.

The Basics

In general, we need to eat *more* fresh vegetables, fruits, and complex carbohydrates (whole grains, whole breads, pastas, yams, and potatoes). We also need to eat more raw and unprocessed foods. Cooking destroys many of the natural enzymes that help us assimilate and make use of the nutrients in the food. Our bodies consist mostly of water; regularly drinking purified water as well as fresh fruit and vegetable juices serves us well.

We need to eat *fewer* fats, fewer simple sugars, and fewer refined and processed foods. Just eliminating most fats and refined sugars from our diet can make a huge difference in our energy level and long-range health.

Eating as a Sacred Activity

From early childhood, many of our Basic Selves have developed an anxiety about taking in food, and so we tend to eat unconsciously—while reading, for example—hardly noticing the food we consume. Rather than treating a meal simply as a means to get food into our stomach as quickly as possible, we can approach our meals as a *sacred activity,* much like the Japanese tea ceremony. We can learn to eat with patience, ease, and real attention, taking small bites and chewing well. After swallowing, we can take one deep breath and smell the aroma of the food before taking another bite. We can express gratitude to Spirit for providing us with the food that nourishes us.

How and when we eat is nearly as important as what we eat. We can benefit from avoiding food when we feel tense or upset as well as refraining from eating just before bedtime.

◆

Conscious Eating

Right now, or at your next meal, take several minutes to practice conscious eating.

1. Look at the color of the food.
2. Take a deep breath and smell its aroma.
3. Relax your body, and take a small bite of food.
4. Chew slowly, staying conscious of the flavor and aroma.
5. After swallowing, take one deep breath before taking another bite.
6. Take a moment to give thanks for the nourishment this food provides.
7. Consider how pleasurable it might be to eat most meals in this way.

◆

Finding Out What Works for Us

Though all our bodies function in similar ways, each of us has unique needs; no one diet works exactly the same for everyone. The minimum recommended allowance (M.R.A.) of vitamins and minerals represents a statistical average; it does not apply exactly to every one of us. Besides, our dietary needs change from day to day, depending upon our level of activity, stress, and other variables.

Many of us take high doses of supplements out of fear, believing they will make up for our dietary deficiencies. Though supplements have their uses for specific purposes, it seems wiser to center our attention on the conscious eating of healthful foods. We can learn to let our instincts guide us, occasionally taking a multivitamin and mineral supplement, but not every day—only when we feel like it.

We don't necessarily have to eat "three square meals" every day; we can eat more, or less, depending upon what our body seems to want. Different body types thrive on slightly different diets to balance out their qualities. By paying attention to our body, day to day, we can reconnect with our instinctual wisdom as to what works best for us.

The Conscious Self tends to impose theories or systems over the body's instincts. Theories or systems may look good on paper, but they may not work as well for us as individuals. For this reason, check with both the Basic Self and the Conscious Self and reach a compromise. When in doubt, listen to the body; it knows. For example, many of us naturally eat more carbohydrates in cold weather and put on five or ten pounds through the coldest winter months. Though our Conscious Self may not like the idea of gaining weight, the additional pounds need cause no concern; with our instincts in balance, we lose the weight again as the weather warms and our appetites decrease.

Adapting to a New Dietary Lifestyle

We already know that real and lasting change doesn't come easily, so we won't take it for granted. Since simplicity has power, and a little bit of something is better than a lot of nothing, rather than going for a sudden or dramatic change, we're better off scaling the mountain of nutrition in small steps.

Like most of us, I grew up with relatively little dietary awareness; in spite of my parent's advice to eat fewer sweets, I ate anything and everything—including plenty of meat and dairy products, every kind of candy, pastry, and processed "junk" food. I also had tonsillitis, allergies, acne, a chronic stuffy nose, a mouth full of dental fillings, dandruff, and everything else that goes with such a diet—conditions that many Americans consider "normal" and seek to remedy with medicines that cause their own side effects. If I hadn't been so active, I probably would have had a weight problem, too.

Over the years, I began to study more about nutrition, and as my knowledge grew, I made gradual changes in what

I ate and began to exercise more; my tastes began to change in favor of the foods that had more "life energy." I went on several short fasts, drinking only juice. These fasts helped to detoxify my system and to awaken my instincts. Since tastes are acquired, I began to enjoy foods that had previously tasted strange. I ate less meat, less fat, and less candy and pastry. I ate more salads and fresh, wholesome foods. As my diet changed, my instincts sharpened. I started to notice the positive and negative effects of some foods I had never noticed before. Along with the new habits, my health and vitality improved vastly. I feel better today than ever before; diet really does make a difference.

In order to adapt to an optimal diet, we do not have to become an ascetic or puritan. We can eat simple, healthful, and delicious meals that leave us feeling light, strong, and balanced.

The main principle of optimal diet is to remain aware of what we eat and how we feel afterward. By stretching ourselves just outside our dietary comfort zone, we gradually move in the direction of eating more foods that feel healthful, light, and energizing, and less of those that don't serve us. We can return to old habits briefly, then push forward again, then cut back again. Each time we do this, we never go back quite as far as we were before, so we continue to make gradual but real and lasting progress.

Dietary change works best if we recognize it doesn't have to happen all at once. It takes some time and adjustments for our Basic Self to get used to a new diet—even a healthful one. Reading good books on diet, such as *Diet for a New America* by John Robbins, can be very helpful in expanding our awareness and inspiring change.

Before we adapt to a new diet, it's useful to distinguish between a *therapeutic* diet and a *lifestyle* diet. Therapeutic diets are temporary, even emergency, methods of correcting specific health problems or excesses, such as high cholesterol or obesity. The Pritikin nonfat diet serves as an excellent example; in conjunction with exercise, it helps reverse the effects of certain types of heart disease. While eliminating virtually all fats and oils from the diet is excellent for therapy, it's generally too restrictive for a permanent dietary lifestyle.

Many specialized diets work for a little while, but no special or extreme diet is intended as a lifetime discipline. The best *lifestyle* diet is one we can live with and learn to enjoy *for the rest of our lives.* Only lasting dietary habits can bring lasting physical change.

The basics of good diet are relatively simple. The challenge, of course, remains the doing—adapting to a more and more vital, fresh, light, healthful diet. Ironically, one of the most important aids to a healthful diet has little to do with food: As we find more meaning and purpose in our lives, we experience a renewed energy and sense of fulfillment and we no longer use food as a consolation. We eat to live rather than live to eat.

Fasting: One Key to Dietary Change

Classically, *fasting* refers to refraining from food for a period of time. All ancient spiritual traditions recommended fasting. We all fast each night, and break fast in the morning. There's more to a prolonged fast than just not eating. Most people do well to drink plenty of fresh water, and diluted fresh fruit and vegetable juices during a fast.

Our body naturally loses its appetite—our Basic Self's way of telling us to go on a fast—during periods of illness. This releases considerable energy normally used for digestion to aid in the healing and detoxification process. Fasting is not for everyone, but most people benefit from an occasional fast, either during certain bouts of illness or as a means of detoxification.

Fasting offers several important benefits:

1. It helps clear general food anxiety and the fear of not eating. Going on a fast generates confidence and security that we can go three, five, or seven days or more quite easily without eating.

2. It serves to sharpen and refine our instincts; with each fast, our body's tastes begin to change in favor of what it *needs* rather than what it desires.
3. As mentioned, fasting tends to detoxify the body through a self-cleansing mechanism generated after the first three days of the fast.

Anyone fasting for more than one or two days should definitely consult with a book; anyone fasting for more than five days would do well to check with a physician or other health professional.

Diet and Expanded Awareness

As we clear old, stressful beliefs and repressed emotional issues, and begin opening up to a sense of our interconnectedness with the world and other people, our diet naturally starts to change. And as our diet changes, other areas of our life also begin to expand. Our diet and our state of consciousness constantly interact. Thus, any improvement we make in our diet, *no matter how small,* represents a very real form of spiritual progress.

By mentally assessing our current diet, we can select one small change we can begin to make today in our dietary lifestyle. Since the greatest overall dietary problem in America involves eating too much of what we don't need and not enough of what we do need, a good next step might involve choosing one food to eat less often, and another food to eat more often.

---◆---

Diet: Taking the Next Step

1. Quickly review your typical daily meals.
2. Select one food you would do well to eat less often.
3. Select one food you would do well to eat more often.
4. Now you know the next step. All you have to do is take it.

---◆---

Physical Exercise:
The Moving Experience

Diet ranks high in order of importance for good health, but exercise ranks even higher. Paavo Airola, a recognized authority who made the study of diet and nutrition his life's work, once stated that it would be preferable to "eat a typical, junk food diet and to exercise than to eat a natural, organic diet without exercise." In fact, trying to improve our health through diet without exercise is like trying to start a car without an engine.

Exercise strengthens muscles, including the heart; it expands our lung volume, increasing oxygen supply to our brain, other organs, and all our cells; and it stimulates our nervous system. In addition to these well-known physiological benefits, exercise clears blocked emotional energies and also raises our metabolic "fire," developing an artificial "fever" that helps purify the body of toxins, making it less hospitable to invading bacteria and viruses.

The Nature of Movement

Over the years, I've practiced and taught most fitness activities, Eastern and Western, including martial arts, dance, hatha yoga, almost every traditional sport and game, as well as other mind-body disciplines. I won a world trampoline championship, coached at Stanford University and U.C. Berkeley, and served as a professor of physical education at Oberlin College. I've worked extensively with both children and adults.

I never liked to "exercise" as a child; few children do. But I loved to *move*—to play, to dance, to run, to jump, to *feel* what my body could do. Movement comes naturally to all of us in the beginning, before inhibitions set in. Like cats, we thrive on moving and stretching and staying active. We all know this, but for a variety of reasons, not all of us put it into practice.

Many of us became discouraged from pursuing physical exercise when it took the form of competitive games that didn't suit us, or when someone either unskilled or impatient led us to believe we weren't "good at it." Like many children, some of us got caught in a vicious cycle of inactivity—watching television, playing video games, or even reading. Living a sedentary lifestyle, combined with eating devitalizing foods that left us with unnaturally low energy, we just didn't feel like getting up and running.

Those of us who do move regularly know the secret: Physical activity can *expand* our energy field and can often invigorate us far more than a nap or a rest. Physical exercise also stimulates endorphins, the body's natural painkillers and relaxants. It sharpens our instincts, since as our body becomes more finely tuned we get more particular about the kinds of foods we give it.

Not everyone has to compete in athletics or even pursue intense fitness activities to enjoy the benefits of physical training. Appropriate kinds of training exist for every body, every age, and every level of condition. Even those who are ill or otherwise limited in some way can do a variety of focused, slow-motion movements combined with deep breathing.

New Frontiers of Fitness

Fitness and vitality used to refer to brute power, size, or muscularity. In recent years, however, our concepts of fitness have grown more sophisticated and internalized. Now, cardiovascular efficiency and aerobic capacity have replaced body armor as the touchstones of fitness. Even this more meaningful measure may soon give way to a new paradigm, defining fitness in terms of a supple, relaxed, balanced body; a calm, clear, focused mind; and open, expressive emotional energies. In other words, we may soon define fitness in the holistic sense of *freedom from internal obstructions.*

Conscious Exercise

Distinct from most sports, games, and athletics, *conscious exercise* is a form of balanced, integrated movement *specifically designed for the overall health of body, mind, and emotions.* Conscious exercise includes and incorporates all the basic qualities of physical talent: strength, suppleness, stamina, and sensitivity (including balance, rhythm, timing, coordination, and reflex speed). Any kind of exercise develops some of these qualities, but most sports do so in a random, haphazard, or piecemeal manner.

In today's world, examples of conscious exercise include noncompetitive gymnastics, modern aerobic dance, certain martial arts, and various forms of yoga. I created *The Peaceful Warrior Exercise Series* (available on video tape), which I enjoy every day, as a routine of conscious exercise anyone can complete in under five minutes a day. Following the principles in this chapter, readers can develop similar forms of conscious exercise that fit easily into daily life.

The Principles of Training

No matter what our needs or interests, the following principles will help us achieve optimal enjoyment and benefits from conscious exercise.

A little bit of something is better than a lot of nothing. One of the greatest stumbling blocks to adopting a new and stable pattern of exercise stems from all-or-nothing thinking: "I've got to go 100 percent or why bother?" Those of us caught in the all-or-nothing trap may not feel up to a "good workout" so we skip it and do nothing at all. But a little of something goes a long way.

We already understand that the Basic Self has a tendency to look for patterns of behavior and support these patterns, especially after we've passed the thirty-day threshold. If we do only *five jumping jacks* a day, or one minute of moving to music, but we do it *every* day, no matter what, our Basic

Self will recognize that pattern and give it energy, so that it soon becomes a natural part of our daily life.

Strengthen the weakest link. Those of us who have special difficulty with a particular challenge in life stand to benefit the most from overcoming it. This principle clearly applies to exercise: We all have different strengths and weaknesses, and the movements that seem the most difficult for us will, when mastered, do us the most good—because these movements strengthen our weakest link.

Simplicity has power. When Socrates took me under his wing and guided me through intense practices and harrowing experiences, I was a young athlete; his demands suited my temperament. My teaching, however, involves finding ways to generate real and lasting change without demanding the same heroics of everyone.

We come in all shapes, sizes, temperaments, and levels of condition. To be workable, any approach to exercise (or diet, or anything else) must be *realistic,* which means *practical, convenient, accessible, and enjoyable* enough to appeal to the Basic Self over time. Such an approach will generate real and lasting results.

Many of us have purchased one of the many excellent exercise videos on the market, but few of us stick with them over time. I once purchased a pair of "inversion boots," a brilliant and useful device invented by Robert Martin, M.D., that enables one to hang and exercise upside down, giving the body a healthy stretch and increasing circulation to the brain and upper body, as well as other benefits. But I stopped using them because they weren't convenient enough, and I'm a pretty disciplined guy!

Instead of chastising ourselves for not sticking with things we think we *should* do, let's get real and get going: Whether training the body, mind, emotions, or spirit, let's choose practices that integrate easily with daily life; feel convenient, accessible, and enjoyable; and match our values and motivation. That way, *we will continue to do them.* Simplicity has power.

What we maintain depends on what we sustain. Perhaps it's human nature to start out with enthusiasm and heroic intentions: "I'm going to run two miles every day." Maybe that will work for some of us, but if we want results over the long haul, we may find that a brisk walk, combined with deep breathing—perhaps while listening to an informative audio program or enjoyable music—is far easier to sustain. Temporary heroic efforts may get results—if we don't injure ourselves—but we won't keep those results unless we maintain the same heroic efforts forever. So consider what kind and level of exercise you can enjoy and sustain over time.

Balance between pleasure and pain. Sooner or later, we all have to confront our inner drill sergeant who says, "Don't be a sissy! That's not tough enough. Exercise has to hurt!" If discomfort becomes the measure of a "good workout," what happens when we can run our mile and it no longer hurts? Then our drill sergeant says, "A mile and a half!" This soon becomes two miles, then three, then five. Soon we end up paying a visit to our local podiatrist or orthopedic surgeon.

Similarly, when we practice a regular stretching program, we can stretch so easily that it's completely comfortable but we don't increase our flexibility, we can stretch so hard that it feels like agony, or we can remember to balance between pleasure and pain, making a gentle, progressive push that allows our body, and Basic Self, to bend but not break.

Accept where you are and progress gradually. A man I'll call Mac once hired me as a personal fitness coach. Mac weighed 340 pounds, about 120 pounds over his trim weight; his body appeared tense and inflexible, with little muscle tone. Not only that, but he had grown depressed after an automobile accident had injured his shoulder. He had really let himself go and lived like a recluse. I later found out that he used numerous drugs, drank too much, and favored a diet high in fats and sweets. His cholesterol was up in the stratosphere. In other words, Mac was a mess; we both had a terrific challenge ahead.

We started where Mac was, based on what he could do — which wasn't much — and progressed gradually. The first day, I showed him how to bounce gently on a small trampoline; that was about all he could do. Later I added some gentle stretches, strength exercises, and aerobic elements.

A year and a half later, Mac had lost 120 pounds. His shoulder had healed, and his cholesterol was within normal range. His diet had changed; he rarely drank; and he was off all drugs. Mac looked and felt far better than he had in years. We had accepted where he was, and he had gotten to where he wanted to go.

Stay realistic. Short-term goals ("I'd like to accomplish ten push-ups right now") will keep us focused and motivated more than far-off and idealistic resolutions ("I want to win the Olympic Games in six years"). If we only look to the distant goal, we fail every day to reach it, but if our goal is the next small step in the right direction, we succeed every day again and again.

We earn results in proportion to the efforts we invest. We get out what we put in. Nevertheless, we're wiser to start with too little rather than too much. Many of us who haven't stuck with an exercise program started with enthusiasm, took on too much, then hurt, and then stopped. A good general rule: We can pick our immediate goal and cut it in half — or take twice as long to reach our goal as we expect. This pace leaves the Basic Self and body feeling good and ready for more.

The key to any exercise program involves doing what we find relatively enjoyable, convenient, and accessible — what really works for us — because we only benefit from what we actually do.

Pay attention. Arnold Schwarzenegger once said that when he performed a strength-building exercise concentrating fully on the muscles being worked, he got faster results than if he just went through the motions without real attention. That statement, based on the wisdom of direct experience by a trainer observer, fits with what we know about the Basic Self.

Whether we happen to be relaxing an area of the body, stretching it, or strengthening it, if we focus our attention *on the feeling we desire* (release, flexibility, or strength), the Basic Self will give us accelerated change.

Avoid extremes. Anything—including exercise—can be done to extremes. Any choice or action has benefits and liabilities. Sometimes an activity has few liabilities; other times it has many. When we overdo anything—when we lose our natural sense of proportion—the liabilities begin to outweigh the benefits.

The principle of diminishing returns applies to eating, sexuality, exercise, and any other activity. For example, lifting weights can build strength, but if we lose our sense of proportion and it becomes an end in itself, we end up building more muscle than we need for anything but lifting more weights. Muscles weigh more than fat, so we end up carrying around extra weight that serves no useful function.

What constitutes "extremes," of course, differs for each of us, depending upon our body type and strengths. We all need to stay aware of where the line exists for us, or we won't realize we've crossed it until symptoms appear. Many of us even ignore the symptoms until life gets our attention with its trump card: physical, emotional, or mental pain.

Trust the process of training. Progress takes time. Those who make it look easy have worked hard over time. A favorite Zen story illustrates this point:

> *A rich man, fond of felines, asked a famous Zen ink painter to draw him a cat. The master agreed and asked the man to come back in three months. When the man returned, he was put off, again and again, until a year had passed. Finally, at the man's request, the master drew out a brush, and, with grace and ease, in a single fluid motion, drew a picture of a cat—the*

most marvelous image the man had ever seen. He was astonished; then he grew angry. "That drawing took you only thirty seconds! Why did you make me wait a year?" he demanded. Without a word, the master opened up a cabinet, and out fell thousands of drawings—of cats.

Excellence is a function of time and *practice*. Don't rush: Those of us who are always pushing hard, running up the mountain, may reach the top first only to realize we forgot to enjoy the climb.

Variety is the spice of life. Use *cross-training* methods. Doing different kinds of conditioning activities each day has psychological as well as physical benefits. Cross training appeals to our Basic Self, which can get bored doing the same exercises every day. By alternating different kinds of workouts, we also avoid chronic overuse injuries, and give muscles and ligaments a chance to rest and rejuvenate. By experimenting, each of us can determine what training pattern works best for us.

There are no free lunches. Change always involves some discomfort—*temporary* discomfort. We can all get through this period of initiation if we clearly understand that the rewards are inevitable, waiting for us just on the other side of the swamp. Within a mere six weeks after starting a balanced exercise program, we experience less fatigue and more energy, less discomfort and more pleasure; we reach a point where exercise feels *terrific*.

Walking: The Master Exercise

Though many of us have become aware of its benefits, I'd like to add a few words on behalf of walking. It is the most accessible, natural exercise for the human body. We're designed to do it. Brisk walking uses more muscles than running. It avoids the jarring of running on concrete, which even the best running shoes only partially soften.

Striding along with arms swinging, and deep, rhythmic breathing develops a strong cardiovascular system, improved muscle tone in legs, arms, and upper body, and stimulates the "exercise fever" that helps the immune system. Walking improves lymph circulation, expands the energy field around the body, and can be done outdoors on nearly any terrain, or indoors on a treadmill.

A vigorous walk will do more good
for an unhappy, but otherwise healthy, adult
than all the medicine and psychology in the world.
Paul Dudley White, M.D.

For those of us who want to lose weight, an hour of brisk walking will, like running, increase our resting metabolic rate for a significant period after we've finished the exercise, continuing to burn off fat at an accelerated rate.

Walking costs no more than a good pair of shoes. For many of us, the ideal way to stick with a walking program involves finding a partner or small group to walk with. Sometimes the conversations get so interesting that the miles pass before we realize it. And as with noncompetitive running, if we go too fast and are too winded to talk, we're pushing too hard.

Bodywork

Many forms of therapy work with the mind by changing or clearing outmoded or destructive beliefs, memories, and associations. But memories aren't just stored in what we call "the mind"; subconscious memories are stored in the body as neuromuscular tension. Therefore, whenever we work with the body, we also work with the mind and the emotions. Long-forgotten memories often surface for people undergoing deep-tissue massage, as the therapist kneads into tense, painful, or blocked areas of the body. Bodywork physically triggers these stored memories, resulting in both physical and psychological release. Follow-up sessions with a psychotherapist can help in such cases, just as psychotherapists may refer certain clients to qualified bodyworkers as an adjunct to working with mind and emotions.

Bodywork offers an effective and direct way to work with all three selves simultaneously, especially if the practitioner has skilled hands, clear energy, and an open heart.

Numerous approaches and methods of release, rejuvenation, relaxation, balance, and healing comprise the field we call bodywork. Here I will not be evaluating the relative merits of the particular schools of bodywork but rather encouraging you to explore bodywork as one primary means to clear obstructions from the body.

The principles behind various kinds of bodywork may differ, but the underlying intention remains the same: bringing awareness to our body through touch, which sets in motion a process of healing. Massage itself stems from our most primal instincts—the way we rub or knead painful or injured areas.

When we gently touch or put pressure on a muscle and then release that pressure, we induce the muscle to release, relax, and let go of stored tension, as well as unconscious and unnecessary contraction.

While receiving a bodywork session from a friend or professional provides clear benefits in terms of our sense of well-being, we can also put principles of tension release into practice on our own, through systematically tensing, then relaxing, our muscles.

◆

One-Minute Tension Release

1. Focus on any area of your body where you hold chronic tension – the neck, forehead or eyes, jaw, shoulders and upper back, stomach, thighs, or lower back. Scan your body, and select a tense area.

2. As you slowly *inhale*, gradually tense that area to whatever level of intensity feels right; then, as you slowly *exhale* with an audible "ahhhhh" sound, gradually relax that area *completely*.
3. Follow this deep breath with three more relaxed, effortless belly breaths. Then, breathing normally and easily, staying aware of that area, gently shake your whole body, feeling loose, like a rag doll.
4. Repeat as desired. The entire process takes a minute or less – a little bit of something that can make a big difference.

Massage by Self and Others

Getting bodywork from someone else has several advantages:

1. We can stay completely relaxed and receptive – similar to relaxing on a train or bus while someone else takes responsibility for driving.
2. A trained bodyworker has the skills and experience to get results.
3. A bodyworker can reach areas we can't reach as well, or at all.

Self-massage, however, has its own unique benefits:

1. We are experts on our own body; we get direct and instant feedback as to what feels best.
2. Self-massage enables us to take direct and conscious responsibility for clearing our own tensions, providing a caring link between the Conscious Self and Basic Self.
3. We need no appointment; we can do self-massage almost anywhere, anytime, as we need it.
4. It costs nothing.

Principles of Self-Massage

Any form of massage involves stroking, kneading, and applying some kind of pressure.

1. Start with a light, caring touch to bring your awareness to the area you're massaging, then gradually go deeper.
2. Use as much pressure as you can. As a general guideline, *go as deeply as you can, but not so deeply that the muscles tense defensively out of discomfort* because that adds tension and fear rather than releasing them.
3. Work *slowly*, with care; sudden pressure shocks the Basic Self and increases fear.
4. The willingness to trust your hands, *let go*, and let your hands (or knuckles) in deeply is as important as mere mechanical pressure.
5. Breathe slowly, deeply, and consciously as you work.
6. Over time, the body opens to deeper and deeper layers of release.

A One-Minute Self-Massage

1. Bearing in mind that a little of something is better than a lot of nothing, scan your body and select any part you feel might benefit from some massage. Common areas that need attention include
   - hands (between thumb and first finger);
   - shoulders, upper back, and neck;
   - face (around the eyes, jaws, forehead);
   - abdomen (including solar plexus);
   - upper chest and underarm;
   - lower back (reach back with closed fists);
   - thighs, feet, or anywhere you choose.
2. Trust your hands to know just what to do; they will discover where to work and how much pressure to apply for the best outcome.

3. Find the point of discomfort and work into that point, knowing you are consciously relaxing and releasing stored tension. Even one minute of applied self-massage can help you prevent tension headaches and other symptoms of stress.

◆

Stretching Ourselves

We can learn a lot by watching cats. For one thing, cats often stretch—especially when waking from a nap with a wide yawn and a radical curve of the spine. Maybe that's one reason their bodies often stay flexible even into old age. Potentially, we, too, can have an elastic, vital body that feels good all of our life. It may seem "normal" for us humans to become less supple as we age, but no evidence exists to prove that we have to lose flexibility with age.

Stiffness and chronic neuromuscular discomfort stem in part from unexpressed emotions stored as tension, as well as from injuries, stored fears, adhesions, scar tissue, and other stressors. Few of us completely escape these factors, so our bodies tend to tighten, contract, and grow less flexible over time; older people simply have had more time to store unexpressed emotions.

Along with massage and conscious relaxation, stretching can actively slow the aging process. I stretch as often as I can— a little in the morning, a little in the evening, a little whenever I feel like it. Following the example of the cat, we can all stretch and remain supple.

Keys to a Good Stretch

There are two kinds of stretching: *cat stretching* (like a cat waking from a nap) and *intensive stretching* (with the intention of increasing flexibility). Cat stretching is always comfortable and feels good. Intensive stretching involves some discomfort—balancing between pleasure and pain.

When we feel tense or anxious, one slow, deep breath and an instinctive stretch, reaching up in the air, arching our back, or gently moving our head or shoulders can wake us up and get our circulation going again. In addition to relaxing us, gentle, conscious stretching exercises practiced consistently can also improve our flexibility. (If we are not consistent in our practice, our Basic Self never recognizes a pattern or a demand, and changes little, or not at all.)

A key principle to bear in mind: Flexibility comes with practice as surely as strength. Many of us who feel stiff avoid stretching because it only reminds us (through discomfort) about our limited range of motion. But by making a very gentle but *regular* practice of stretching—even one minute a day—we can increase our range of motion and reduce both tension and discomfort in the body—a vital step in clearing our obstructions and achieving balance.

------------------------◆------------------------

Stretching Your Body

1. Choose a part of your body you'd like to stretch.
2. As in massage, balance between pleasure and pain; if you push too hard, the pain creates tension and your Basic Self ends up fighting the stretch. Go only as far as you can while staying relatively relaxed.
3. If your body wants to hold some tension, let it do so, and then allow it to relax of its own accord.
4. In the stretch position, take one to three slow, deep breaths. As you inhale, feel the sense of the stretch increase; as you exhale, relax a little more into the stretch. Breathing in this manner during a stretch is important; holding the breath during any kind of exercise tenses the body.

------------------------◆------------------------

Breathing for Life

Breathing may appear to be a purely mechanical process—we take in oxygen, nitrogen, and other trace gases, and breathe out carbon dioxide. But breathing can also involve the conscious recognition that we take in energy, spirit, life.

If our breathing remained as open, relaxed, and natural as that of a young child, our self-regulating Basic Self would take care of it the same way it handles pumping our heart or digesting our food. But due to both acute and chronic stress, most of us tend toward constricted, shallow breathing in daily life.

As we develop the ability to breathe deeply, as if down to the soles of our feet, we utilize one of the keys to cardiovascular health and help to prepare ourselves for any emergency situation we may encounter. By expanding our lung capacity, we actually breathe easier.

---◆---

Breathing Easy

1. Notice your breathing right now.
2. Now, consciously take three deep breaths, feeling your inhalation expand your belly and lower back, then your chest. Make the breaths very slow and deep, but not to the point of strain. Remember to do this at random moments in your day.
3. As you inhale, feel your body filled with vitality. As you exhale, feel your shoulders, chest, belly, and entire body relax and let go of tension.

---◆---

Expanding Our Vital Capacity

The following exercise increases our ability to breathe slower and deeper, expands our vital capacity, and turns any rhythmic activity into a meditation. It may also help us live longer.

This exercise can be done while walking, bicycling, bouncing on a small trampoline, riding a stationary bike, or engaging in any other rhythmic activity. It can even be done as a sitting meditation, to the rhythm of a ticking clock. Doing the exercise while walking seems one of the best and most natural ways to apply the exercise, so I use walking as an example.

◆

Breathing to a Count

1. As you walk in place, inhale for a count of two steps, then exhale for a count of two ("Inhale, two, exhale, two . . . ").
2. Once you get the idea of breathing in rhythm to your steps, begin a regular, increasing progression:
   • Inhale for a count of three steps and then exhale for three steps.
   • Inhale for a count of four steps and then exhale for four steps, and so on.
3. Continue, in this manner, increasing the number of steps, until you reach your *comfortable* limit, then work your way back down. If you got as high as inhaling and exhaling to a count of twelve steps, go back to eleven, then ten, and so on, until you reach a very comfortable pace (say, four steps), and maintain that pace.
4. For shorter walks, you can go up and back down by twos. Within one or two weeks, you will notice measurable results.

◆

Conscious Breathing

Conscious breathing doesn't depend upon physical exertion. In fact, we can do it anywhere, anytime—standing in line at the post office, stuck in traffic, waiting for an appointment. It has the added bonus of calming the mind and the emotions.

Someone once reminded me that "patience is having something else to do in the meantime." Focusing on slow, deep breathing may serve as one of the most conscious and constructive ways to pass the time; it is a key element in clearing obstructions in the body. We can also use the breath as a means to relax and unwind.

Another Look at Alignment

For many of us, "proper posture" means sitting up straight. There's truth to this, but there's also more to the picture. The phrase *good posture* actually refers to our body's natural relationship with the force of gravity. Our body's skeletal structure is designed to balance vertically, like building blocks placed directly over each other. If we move one or two of those blocks out of alignment and push down from the top, the structure is liable to fall apart. This can happen more slowly to our body, over time, in the field of gravity.

If we observe babies, we'll note superb posture, because they do what comes naturally. Our attitudes, emotions, past injuries, and movement habits have all affected our postural alignment in stillness and movement. Poor posture wastes energy and imposes undue strain on the muscles because they have to tense chronically to hold up parts of the body (such as the head) that are out of alignment. Misaligned posture contributes to many chronic headaches, neck aches, backaches, and so forth.

Trying to sit or stand straight does little good if we have shortened tissues that tilt our pelvis, make our head protrude forward, hold our shoulders back, or hunch them forward. Exercise is only as beneficial as the posture in which we perform it. Two people can do the same exercise and get different results, depending upon their body positions and structural integrity.

_____◆_____

Posture Perfect

1. Sit hunched over, and try to take a deep breath; now sit up straight but relaxed, take a deep breath, and feel the difference.
2. When you sit, stand, and walk, imagine a string attached to the top rear of your head, pulling skyward; do this in a relaxed way, feeling your entire spine lengthen.
3. When you sit or stand for more than a few minutes, shift your position regularly.
4. When you sit and bend forward, at a desk, for example, bend forward from the hips, with a straight back, rather than hunching over.
5. In general, notice your posture at least once each day, and in a relaxed way, make friends with gravity.

_____◆_____

The Right Leverage

As our habits and lifestyles change—as our diets grow more refined and our bodies grow stronger, lighter, and more supple through exercise and stretching—we free our attention from gross problems and start to perceive the more subtle energies and intuitions available to us all the time. Pain changes to pleasure, and we see, feel, smell, taste, and touch in new ways. We tune in to different channels of energy and ˙ spirit, and realize, even in the midst of daily life, the magic in every moment.

8

Liberating the Mind

In combat, as in life,
when we start thinking too much, we're dead.
Michael Bookbinder

Opening Paradox

As we begin to open up and break through the blocked, numbed places in our bodies and our lives, we begin to notice pain where before we felt nothing at all. As we uncover previously latent symptoms, we may experience a kind of "healing crisis," including bouts of illness, as the body purifies itself. In general, life often seems to get worse before it gets better; this appears to be part of the process of change.

Pain as Awakener

We can view pain in the body, mind, or emotions as a potential blessing. When the pain gets bad enough, we wake from our slumber and seek the source of the pain. Out of necessity, the hunted becomes the hunter, the victim becomes the warrior. Pain points the way to healing: No longer able to afford the luxury of comforting illusions, we begin to shift our focus of attention. We begin to notice that the pain does not really emanate from "out there" (from our boss or job or partner); it arises from our own mind—from our assumptions, beliefs, and interpretations.

The moment we achieve the conscious recognition that we create our own pain, we gain the power to stop it. Thus, pain contains the seeds of its own undoing.

The phenomenon we call *mind* is the primary source of

143

tension in our body, our emotions, and our daily lives. The mind forms a veil, an obscured lens, through which we see reality. We tend to accept these distorted perceptions as true and real, until we realize that the mind itself is the mischief maker, the trickster, and the magician who weaves illusions while hiding in the home of our own psyche, whispering in our innermost ear, masquerading as friend and trusted adviser.

The mind is the warrior's greatest adversary. From the position of the compassionate witness (the Higher Self), we can cut through the mind by *noticing* our thoughts rather than *believing* or *identifying* with them.

A Choice Between Two Worlds

During the course of a single day, our awareness bounces between two worlds. Only one of these worlds has a tangible reality.

The first we can call the *objective* world—what *is* or what happens, without anything extra: We open a door and walk into a room full of people sitting around a table.

The second is our *subjective,* inner world—the veil of our beliefs, values, perceptions, and thoughts *about* what is, or what happens, and through which we interpret reality: I wonder if I look okay. They're probably wondering why I'm late. Well, too bad! I hope this meeting goes well . . . The subjective realm also includes Basic Self (subconscious) associations stored in the body.

Slings and Arrows of the Mind

Ted, a client of mine, related to me a painful incident in which his fiancée broke up with him. "One night I was in my apartment, reading, waiting for Sally to come over. We were going to spend the weekend together. The doorbell rang; since Sally had a key, I assumed it was a delivery, and was surprised to see her. I remember being happy. 'Did you lose your key?' I asked.

"'No,' she said. Right away I could feel something was wrong. Her expression was serious; she looked upset.

"'Well, come on in,' I said, but she stayed right there, and hit me with a bombshell.

"'Ted,' she told me, holding out my key and the engagement ring I'd given her, 'I have to return these.'

"I just stood there. I couldn't believe it was happening; we'd had a great time the weekend before. My stomach felt queasy; I don't think I was breathing. All I could say was, 'What?'

"Teary eyed, Sally said in a rush of words, 'Bob—you know, my friend who has been living in Europe—he came back to visit. We just met over coffee, but . . . Ted, I'm going to marry him. I'm leaving for Europe. I'm very sorry . . . '

"She didn't look sorry. Yeah, she was crying, but her face looked excited! She said some other things after that, but I hardly heard them. Her words had hit me like a punch in my belly; I was numb. I mean, some guy drops in and the love of my life—someone I trusted and counted on—says sayonara, and my whole life falls apart! How could she do this to me? I wanted to tell her not to go, how hurt I was. But I couldn't say anything. I guess I said something stupid like, 'If that's what you want, Sally.' She looked relieved, but I don't think she believed me. Hell, *I* didn't believe me.

"She was obviously glad to go. Damn her! After she left, I felt more alone than I had in years. Like a part of my life had been cut away. Later, I got angry—I had worked overtime for six months to buy that ring . . . what was I going to do with it? I wanted to get drunk, or get laid, or both.

"I thought about calling her. A lot. But it would just open the wound. She obviously loved this guy a lot more than me. I saw a picture of him once; he's taller than I am, better looking, too. Wears expensive clothes. Sometimes life's just not fair. What's with me, anyway? Every woman I fall in love with falls out of love with me. I feel sick."

Things happen, but nothing ultimately *means* anything; therefore, we make up our own meanings. Ted had related his *subjective interpretation* of what had occurred—all the associated feelings and meanings and pain. Of course we need to accept and understand these feelings, but, at the same time, we can begin to recognize that unless objective, physical pain or injury is involved, psychological damage is rarely a function of the event itself but rather results from the mind's reaction to that event. *Stress happens when the mind resists what is.*

I asked Ted to relate the event again—this time as simply, briefly, and objectively as he could—*without his beliefs, interpretations, assumptions, and meanings.* I suggested that Sally's decision to marry someone else had more to do with her than it did with Ted.

Ted remained convinced, however, that if he had been taller, more handsome, or wealthier he would have "won" Sally. I agreed that if we could turn into a different kind of person we would naturally attract people who liked that kind of person, but that perhaps we're better off finding someone who is attracted to who we are, now. "Let's call Sally's present husband an apple and say you are an orange," I said. "You can understand that some women may prefer apples and others prefer oranges, can't you?"

"Yeah, sure."

"Then you see the possibility that her choosing to go to Europe and marry Bob doesn't necessarily reflect on your worth as a human being?"

"Yeah, I guess so," Ted smiled. "But next time I'm going to find someone who loves oranges."

I told Ted that many years ago, during my college years, I noticed that I had different taste in women than some of my friends. One friend liked short women; another, taller ones. One liked women with petite, almost boyish figures; another, more curvy. One of my closest friends liked women who he felt weren't as smart as he was; I liked really intelligent women. This went on and on, as we compared our various tastes.

One friend noticed, a little embarrassed, that the women

he liked were similar to his mother; another liked women who were the opposite of his mother. And on it went.

It struck me that varying tastes worked both ways—that there were going to be some women who would tend to like me no matter what, and other women who were *not* going to be attracted to me no matter what. And *I didn't need to take it that personally*; their choices were about them, not me.

Ted and I kept talking for a while, and he looked at his hurts and came to understand some of the meanings and beliefs he had about what had happened, and how they related to his level of self-worth.

Self-analysis can be useful to clarify the mind's influence. Many of us, however, end up analyzing our problems for half the day and dramatizing them for the other half. Nothing really changes, *because we only analyze what happens on the outside.* By recognizing the mind's responsibility in creating our perceptions and pain, we stop blaming the world and others and start cleaning up our own house.

Analysis, however, is not the final step; it is only a means for the Conscious Self to learn from the incident. The Conscious Self may long ago have analyzed, "understood," and resolved the incident. In order to help the Basic Self to clear the emotional charge that remains despite our mental acceptance, we need to revision the incident—to see and reexperience it objectively. *When we take a charged incident and "boil off" the subjective part—the mind's associations, meanings, and beliefs—what remains is the objective event itself, free of pain.*

The value of doing this is not just to feel better. By clearing the charge, we also minimize the likelihood that we will repeat the same pattern in the future because we have both consciously learned and subconsciously cleared the event.

The Real Story

I asked Ted to relate what *actually happened*, without his subjective input—simply, briefly, and from a sensory-based perspective.

"Sally, my fiancée, came to my apartment but declined to enter. She returned a key and ring I had given to her and told me she intended to marry a man named Bob, and live with him in Europe. We spoke briefly. Then she left."

Though Ted related this event simply and "objectively," it was clear to me as I observed him that some charge remained, because, as I would have expected, the associations and feelings still affected him. Sometimes we have to tell a story many times before we release the emotional charge. But Ted had at least gained awareness of the source of the charge—the beliefs that hooked him.

He related the incident again and appeared a bit more relaxed. He told it a number of times more. On his final telling, he actually smiled as he recognized that what he was saying described what had actually occurred, and that *the rest he made up.* As Ted realized this, he experienced a simultaneous relief and elation.

An interesting belief that forms the subtext for resistance to this exercise is that objective statements seem "cold"—devoid of "real emotion." That, of course, depends upon how one defines *emotion.* Actually, the less our emotions interfere with our perception of an event, the more heartfelt *feeling* we are able to experience.

Ted discovered that nothing Sally did was inherently hurtful. After all, if he had wanted to break up with her but didn't know how to tell her, he would have welcomed her news with delight and relief. The state of his own mind—his desires and beliefs—created his hurt, not Sally.

Sally didn't hit or kick Ted, or even take his ring. She didn't sue him or ridicule him. Ted suffered the effects of his own mind.

Ted came to see the value of this event in teaching him something about himself. He engaged in the peaceful warrior's practice of using the issues of daily life to grow, to transmute pain into wisdom.

Though this first great awakening to objective reality may

seem fundamentally simple, it is not easy. Cutting through the mind's illusions is like hiking through a forest of thorns. For some of us, the process can take years of conscious effort. On the other hand, we sometimes get in touch with reality suddenly, and quite by accident.

Back to Reality

One day I awoke from a sound nap and opened my eyes, but I didn't know where I was, or what anything was. Nothing made any sense at *all*. I looked at the ceiling and I *didn't understand*. I stared at the clock and saw the numbers, but I didn't know what they meant. I looked out the window and I *didn't understand*. I looked at the floor and I *didn't understand*.

In this confused state, hoping it would help, I found the bathroom, turned on the bathtub faucet marked "hot," but forgot to turn on the cold. As the tub filled, I managed to get my clothes off, but then lost my balance and fell backward, buttocks first, into the scalding water. And, suddenly, I *understood*.

Physical pain puts us back in touch with objective reality, and reminds us of priorities, but I don't recommend seeking it out.

Two Kinds of Knowledge

Each reality—objective and subjective—has a different kind of knowledge associated with it. The objective realm involves practical knowledge we can apply to life—how to fix a leaky faucet, remembering to look both ways before crossing the street. Objective information also includes practical principles that apply to daily life to expand our perspectives and humor, to increase our value to others, and to help our lives work better.

The subjective realm is associated with "pure knowledge" and abstract ideas. I've learned to apply the following internal questions to incoming information: How can I use this?

Does knowing this help my life? Does it add to my happiness? Does it serve anyone? Can it help improve my relationships, or help me support my family? What difference does knowing this make in my life?

Rather than manipulate abstract concepts that have little bearing on everyday reality, I like to ask, What is in my mind right now? What is in my heart? These questions develop mindful awareness and self-understanding. They fend off the trap of mistaking abstractions for reality as the mind weaves its web of illusions.

A Glimpse of the Possible

Most of us can recall rare and happy occasions when we experienced a quiet, simple, happy moment of clarity, when the storms of thought stilled and the world seemed peaceful and silent and bright. Whatever our circumstances, everything can feel so simple, so beautiful, and so right when we no longer pay attention to the mind's incessant chatter.

Those of us who see *through* the mind rather than *with* it, and who have clarified the windows of perception, no longer perceive life through obscured veils of thought, belief, association, and interpretation. We still have thoughts; we still have beliefs and associations; we still interpret and discriminate and compare and make value judgments. *But we don't mistake these thoughts for reality.*

Defining the Mind

We know that our brain has two hemispheres that perform different functions: a linear, rational left brain, and a more holistic, imaginative right brain. The specialized cells of the brain allow us to store data, to compare and discriminate, and to perform an almost miraculous number of the processes we call *thinking*.

We can consciously will ourselves to think about something—to remember an incident from the past, work a math problem, write a letter to a friend, or compose a poem for a loved one. However, *unintentional* thoughts also arise within and just below our field of awareness; often, these thoughts carry negative emotional charge—anxieties or old images we'd rather not think about—thoughts that seem to have the power to lift us up or bring us down, turn us right or left, and jerk us around like puppets on a string. These random thoughts, like dreams, reflect a natural discharge of stressful impressions and memories.

Our Basic Self tends to mistake these internal impressions as real, and reacts by creating physical tension and imbalance. The Conscious Self, too, by interpreting our world through the filter of our thoughts, misreads or misinterprets the meanings of events, making life far more problematic and complex than necessary.

The Larger View

From the most transcendental view, the entire universe and everything in it are made of Consciousness. I use the term *Consciousness* with a capital "C" as synonymous with God or Spirit—the primal force of life and love that animates all things, from the tiniest subatomic particle to the vastness of creation. In the human being, Consciousness manifests as pure *awareness.* When we sleep, we appear unconscious of the world around us; when we awaken, we appear relatively conscious of the outer world.

Attention refers to the degree to which we are able to *focus* our awareness, much like focusing the sun's rays with a lens. And like a lens, the sharper we can focus, the more deeply and powerfully our mind can pierce. Our ability to focus attention—what we call *concentration*—can improve with practice.

We have a brain; with the help of our senses, that brain splits Consciousness as a prism splits white light, and channels various kinds of awareness. Our *mind,* however, as I've already expressed, is comprised of random background noise of arbitrary images, words, meanings, interpretations, associations, and beliefs that separate us from a clear, simple, and direct perception of the world. The world, in other words, is not what we *think*.

For example, if we walk into a local park or town square, we can think about what we see—internally criticizing the woman who lets her dog run wild, wondering if the homeless man heading our way will ask us for money and rehearsing what we'll say, feeling irritation at the teenagers playing music for the whole park to hear—or we can sit on the park bench and mindlessly commune with nature, feel the energy, and enjoy the sights and the variety of people who pass by.

Taming the Runaway Mind

The mind is like a radio that plays constantly (except in deep sleep), tuning itself from one station to the next. This phenomenon of mind probably serves a useful purpose—providing a kind of discharge for the nervous system—and our random thought forms may be unavoidable byproducts of the brain. Taming our mind doesn't necessarily mean turning off the mind noise. Rather it entails recognizing the noise as separate from us, so that when "heavy metal" plays we don't become crazy, and when violins play we don't automatically become sad; and recognizing that once we *notice* what station the radio plays, we have the *power to choose* what station we select.

Socrates once used another image when he told me, "The mind resembles a barking dog. You don't have to get rid of the dog; after all, dogs naturally bark. But you need to train it so it doesn't get out of hand; keep it on a leash."

By accepting the radio/mind for what it is, we can deal with it, learn to control the stations, and eventually, turn down the blaring volume so we can hear the song of the birds, and find ourselves, in the silence.

Mind and Meaning

Life emerges out of mystery. While we can know an almost infinite variety of facts *about* nearly everything, we can never actually know what anything *is*—not ultimately. As we come to realize that *nothing means anything*, and that *we make up our meanings*, we experience the first great awakening.

While most of what we see or hear or touch or taste or smell exists, what we say or think or believe *about* it reflects our mind. Understanding this provides a larger context, or platform, from which to witness the workings of the mind, rather than getting caught up in them—a kind of constant "meditation." Upon close examination, we recognize that anytime we have had a problem, something has *meant* something else. We interpreted, remembered, compared, and judged.

Let me offer an example of how we create our meanings and our realities: Two families—the Bakers and the Johnsons—live next door to one another; both of the fathers go on the road all week and come home on the weekends.

As it happens, Mrs. Baker often complains in front of her children, "Your father is never home for you when you need him because he has to be on the road all the time; he only gets to see you on weekends." These children grow up remembering their "absentee father" who "never had time for them" except on weekends.

Mrs. Johnson's remarks in front of her children differ considerably: "You have the most dedicated father, children. Though he'd love to be with us all the time, he works hard to support us during the week so he can spend his *best time* with you every weekend. You're so lucky!" These children will be far more likely to grow up remembering their "dedicated, loving father who came home *every weekend* to be with them."

It's the old choice between perceiving the glass "half full" or "half empty." We see things not as *they* are, but as *we* are.

We do experience real, objective, physical pain in life, and some external objects do indeed threaten our well-being, but the *mind*, not the body, creates most of the fear, stress, and dissatisfaction we experience in life. The fearful mind even aggravates objective physical pain because *the mind imposes tension on the body*; tension increases pain, and pain *with* fear hurts far more than pain *without* fear.

Mind as Source of Stress

Psychological stress occurs when the mind resists what is. For example, if our longtime partner leaves us, we experience a change: We were living together in the same place, and now we are separating. If we had wished for such an event, or felt fully prepared and willing for it to happen, we would not perceive it as a problem. But the resistance—and the meanings— associated with the change can create ripples and waves of emotional turmoil: "I failed. I was dumped. After all I've done, look how I'm treated. It's not fair. There's someone else—I know it—someone more attractive than me, someone better in bed, someone sexier. I'm not good enough." And so it goes, down into a dark hole of depression.

Those who initiate leaving a relationship may feel mostly good about it, because they associate more positive meanings with the relationship ending. Those who feel left may feel terribly stressed to the extent they resist the event. The same event—a separation—happens to both of the partners, but the meanings each attaches to the event determine that partner's moods.

What feels stressful or frightening to one person may not be for another person who doesn't resist it. For example, Patrick leaps out of airplanes because he enjoys skydiving but feels terrified to speak in front of a group of people. Jane feels just the opposite. Mary finds parties and large groups of people stressful, while Roberta thrives on them; but Roberta goes into overwhelm when facing a deadline at work, and Mary loves the "excitement" and "challenge" of getting the work in on time.

In *Way of the Peaceful Warrior,* I related an incident in the park when I became very upset by a rained-out picnic. "Rain is not the problem," Socrates pointed out. "It waters the flowers." My own resistance to the rain created the problem, though I didn't see it at the time. The *no resistance, no stress* principle applies to any situation, no matter how difficult. Resisting anything—even fear or pain—only aggravates the discomfort.

We have a choice, then: We can wish for "sunny weather" all of the time and spend some of the time disappointed and upset, or we can stop resisting the storms. Whenever we notice ourselves resisting what is, we can ask, "What makes me think this is a problem?" As Socrates observed when we walked past some tennis courts, "Every shot makes *somebody* happy."

Recognizing Distorted Beliefs

If we don't like the way we feel, we can change the way we think. Thinking is a lot like talking to ourselves, but so quietly we might not notice it. We say to ourselves what our parents said to or about us—or what we perceived they truly felt. These messages, stored by our subconscious, create negative physical and emotional reactions.

If someone cuts us off as we drive to work, we can tell ourselves, "What a jerk!" or "Poor guy—must be having a tough day." These thoughts evoke very different physical and emotional responses.

A variety of negative beliefs create and sustain stress; here are some examples:

- When someone seems to disapprove of us, it means we are wrong or bad (and therefore, we must get everyone to like and approve of us).
- Our value depends upon how much we achieve and produce (and, therefore, we must achieve and produce or we will be worthless).
- We need an ideal love and a constantly enjoyable relationship to be happy.

- We must do everything well (and so must everyone else).
- Our view of the world is the correct one (and, therefore, those who disagree with us are wrong).

Various other distorted, absolutist beliefs can entrap us:

- *Either/Or:* Either we did it completely right, or we did it completely wrong. (Antidote: We can accept the shades of life rather than see everything in black or white.)
- *Totally Responsible:* If someone else is in a bad mood, we feel personally responsible for cheering them up. (Antidote: We can resign as general manager of the universe and study a good book on codependence.)
- *Putting Ourselves in a Box:* If we make a mistake, instead of acknowledging it and learning from it, we call ourselves "a dunce." (Antidote: We can notice how our parents labeled us and ask ourselves if we want to continue the job for them.)
- *Sorting for the Negative:* Out of twelve tasks, we do ten very well; we focus our attention on the two tasks we didn't do as well. (Antidote: We can remember to praise ourselves every time we do something well.)
- *Self-Defeating Thoughts:* We're ready to set ourselves up to lose—"You don't want to go out with me, do you?" (Antidote: As difficult or strange as it may feel, we can learn to state things in the most positive way, and assume positive outcomes.)

Though our Conscious Self recognizes these kinds of absolutist thinking as illogical, our parents or other influences in our childhood may have programmed our Basic Self to accept these self-defeating ideas, so we still experience the effects. Awareness of our own tendencies, coupled with positive visualizations to reprogram our ways of thinking, helps to reeducate our Basic Self; over time, we notice fewer and fewer stressful problems and upsets "out there."

Interpretations of Reality

Events are just events; take a birthday party, for example. We can all feel, and probably have felt, happy at some birthday parties and miserable at other ones—depending upon what was happening *inside* us, and whether we believed our mind's interpretations.

Through its mistaken interpretations or distorted meanings, the mind creates emotional storms. Once, when I was driving on a curving road, a car going in the opposite direction passed me, and the driver yelled out her window at me, "Pig!" I felt very upset at being called a pig by a complete stranger. "She probably has a problem with men," I thought, as I rounded the curve—and nearly ran over a pig in the middle of the road.

Health, Stress, and the Resistant Mind

Most illness begins with stress-producing thinking as the mind imposes tension on the body. Every thought has a corresponding effect on the body. Recent studies in the growing field of psychosomatic medicine demonstrate that our body's finely tuned immune system responds almost immediately to both positive and negative thoughts and attitudes.

Resistance is like a stone dropped into a calm pond; the emotions are the ripples. Chronic stress, begun in the mind, creates emotional turbulence and imposes itself upon the body as stored tension. The tension translates to painful symptoms: headaches or pain in the stomach, lower back, or elsewhere. We have all experienced some or all of these symptoms with no apparent physical cause.

The Mind and Emotions

If our bodies remain relaxed, our breathing even, and our minds clear, our emotions stay open. Not a single one of us ever becomes emotionally upset unless our mind first creates it. This realization is not new, even in the West. William

James, one of the founders of modern-day psychology, found that we all experience fear, sorrow, or anger the same way — as a tension or contraction in the abdomen or chest; our mind then *interprets* that feeling as anger, fear, or sorrow, depending upon what thoughts or meanings are going through our head.

Whenever we become upset, our inner turmoil stems from the beliefs and meanings playing in our minds, just below conscious awareness. Fleeting images, inner dialogue, rules, associations, and stored memories generate the emotional contraction.

I recall an incident some years ago when I was standing in line at the bank, holding my daughter, who was then two years old, by the hand. I'd been waiting for some time and finally reached the front of the line when a man entered the bank, looked at the long line, walked to the front, and stepped in front of me! "I'm in a hurry," he said. First I was shocked at his nerve, then angry. My little daughter, however, wasn't bothered at all, because she hadn't yet formed beliefs or meanings about the incident; she hadn't yet learned the *rule* "People should wait their turn in line," or the more subtle "If someone picks you to butt in front of, you must look like a wimp." Not having learned any of this, she had no resistance, no stress.

That isn't to imply we should remain calm and let people walk all over us, but as we clear our beliefs and the resulting emotional contractions, we can act with assertiveness and compassion, and more effectively achieve our desired outcomes. In the incident at the bank, for example, I did nothing but mutter to myself—I didn't want to make a "big deal" of it in front of my daughter. Today, I would smile, walk calmly up to the man and the teller, and let the teller know he had not waited in line and ask her to wait on me next. Or I might let it go—whatever felt appropriate.

The Empty Boat

A favorite story of mine, if taken to heart, offers a key to emotional calm, a means to short-circuit the mind's near-constant domination.

A man rowed a small boat upstream, heading toward home, when he felt another small boat, heading downstream, collide with his boat. Since he had the right of way, he felt angry. Turning, he yelled at the other boatman, "Watch where you're going! Be more careful!"

The other man apologized, and passed by without further incident. But an hour later, as the man continued upstream, he felt another boat collide with his. Furious, he turned to yell at the reckless person. His anger vanished when he saw that the boat was empty—it must have come loose from its moorings. Calmly, he pushed it aside and continued on his journey.

He never lost his temper again, because from then on, he treated everyone like an empty boat.

The Gift of Meditation

Now that we've seen the problem of mind—something about how it works and the turbulence it creates—we can turn to solutions, ways to liberate the mind and realize the truth that there are no ordinary moments.

Meditation represents one of humanity's most wonderful methods of *freeing the Basic Self* from mind noise—*teaching* it the difference between reality and random thoughts. With enough practice, we learn to distinguish between objectivity and subjectivity. Thought noise still arises, but the Basic Self doesn't hold onto it; the body stays relaxed, and the emotions, calm.

Meditation Defined

When we meditate by sitting quietly and comfortably with spine straight and eyes half-closed or fully closed, thoughts come up—angry thoughts, happy thoughts, troubling thoughts, pleasant thoughts—but we do nothing about them. We don't tense, react, resist, or give them any attention.

We just sit. Through this practice, we discover that thoughts arise, then pass, like clouds in the sky or waves in the ocean. As we recognize the passing nature of thought, we see our own true essence in the silence, beyond words, beyond thought.

The most basic or fundamental kind of meditation involves pure *mindfulness*; we watch without clinging, attachment, or judgment—from the viewpoint not of the Conscious Self but of awareness itself. We observe physical sensations, emotions, concerns, images, and inner dialogues come and go.

In order to aid our concentration, we may decide to use an object of attention such as observing or counting our breaths, using a repetitive sound (a mantra), or concentrating on an image (such as a candle flame); when we notice our attention wandering, following the stream of thought, we simply return our awareness, without concern, judgment, or effort, to the object of attention.

We can choose between many forms of meditation, as well as seek out schools and books that teach the basic principles and practices. My purpose here is to point to the heart of meditation—the practice of clear observation without attachment.

The Purpose of Meditation

Every few moments, a vast array of thoughts forms, images, sounds, and feelings passes just below our conscious recognition. Each has the power of subliminal persuasion: An angry thought arises just below the threshold of our conscious recognition, and so, without exactly knowing why, we feel angry; a sad thought arises, and we feel moody; a fearful image comes up, and we feel insecure or anxious.

Advertisers have made use of the power of subliminal persuasion for years, bypassing the discriminating abilities of our Conscious Self and going straight for the suggestible Basic Self, creating appealing images that can motivate us to buy products from paper towels to automobiles.

Meditation serves to turn up the volume of our thoughts and to slow down the subliminal messages of our own mind, so that we can see these thoughts rather than becoming the victim of them. Meditation returns to us the power to choose whether or not to act on our thoughts.

A Map of the Process

When we sit down to meditate, we first notice what's going on at the physical level. Perhaps we're not quite comfortable; we feel an ache, we feel fidgety, or we want to scratch an itch. If we remember to let all that go and return our attention to our breathing, our mantra, or an image we've chosen—or to simple, mindful awareness—and let whatever arises pass, our attention tunes in to a deeper level of our psyche.

We then become aware of the emotional/mental level: We start feeling bored, wondering how long we've been sitting. An old upset comes into our awareness, or some emotionally charged unfinished business—a concern, a regret, a problem. We start thinking about events we anticipate will happen, or we engage in pleasant fantasies. We can get drawn in and forget the purpose of the meditation—insight without attachment—seeing and letting go. But if we remember to let these thoughts and feelings pass and to return our attention to the meditative object or to simple awareness, our attention reaches an even deeper level.

Our meditation then gets much more interesting; at this level, the Basic Self sends us messages in its own symbolic codes, as in dreams. We start to notice passing images, hallucinatory sights or sounds, a face we haven't seen in years, creative ideas or inspirations. We have a real challenge letting go of *this* level, but if we return our attention to the meditative process, our attention can then touch the Void: nothingness, pure, transcendental Being, the great and selfless quiet.

Of course, the moment the Conscious Self jumps back in—"Wow! I'm experiencing the Void!"—it's gone, and we get pulled back to the emotional/mental level.

When we are experiencing the Void, our attention continues to fine-tune, and just on the other side of that quiet place resides the deep underground stream of consciousness that connects all things. In that place, we can know anything or everything, but we won't care. Once we've contacted that place, it becomes easier to return at will, because our psyche "knows where it is," a process parallel to the body learning to relax.

The full development of this process can take many months or many years, depending upon our readiness. Our commitment to stay detached, as pure awareness, also applies to the deepest or highest levels of insight, experience, and phenomena.

Paying Attention

We can all sit still, close our eyes for a few minutes, and breathe. This may look like meditation, but we may actually be engaging in a "vertical nap" or unfocused daydream. Sitting still and going inside can open the space for creative ideas but doesn't necessarily constitute real meditation.

Meditation is born of the twofold commitment to gain insight into thought, and let it go without attachment. This requires clear intent as to the purpose of "just sitting."

On the other hand, meditation practice doesn't always involve sitting down at all; we can meditate standing up, lying flat, or moving around—as long as we stay mindful and maintain the witness position, allowing our attention to focus on something other than our thoughts.

As we walk, or engage in a sport or other form of movement, we can practice dynamic, moving meditation; we can also do this by *paying attention* to what we are doing as we drive a car—especially on a race course where our attention is less likely to wander—or play a video game, for example. In fact, any action we make in the course of daily life, from lacing our shoes to eating breakfast, can become a form of meditation if we give it our full and conscious attention rather than letting our attention drift off into the realm of random thought.

Guidelines for Practice

If we choose the deliberate, conscious, and committed practice of meditation, the following principles, based on an understanding of the Basic Self, may be useful:

1. Form a commitment to meditate *every* day, no matter what, if only for a few minutes. Twenty minutes every day works far better than an hour once or twice a week. Ten minutes — or five minutes, or even *one* minute — is far better than none at all.
2. Whenever possible, meditate at about the same time and place each day. The Basic Self, comfortable with set patterns, will allow your attention to go deeper faster and more easily once you establish a routine.
3. Stop the world. Make sure no one disturbs you: Take the phone off the hook, lock the door, put up a "do not disturb" sign. Unless you "step off the world," your subconscious won't let you go as deep.
4. Make your meditation period a special occasion, a sacred time; the more special you make it, the more energy and focus the Basic Self will allow.
5. Make sure your body is comfortable. Don't be too full or too hungry. Empty your bladder. Avoid physical distractions that bind you to physical consciousness.
6. Don't "try." Meditate without judgments or attachment to results. Stay relaxed, with an effortless attitude, an "inner smile."
7. Adopt the best posture for you; no posture works best for everyone. You can sit on the floor, on a pillow, or on a chair, or you can lie down (but stay awake!).
8. Keep your spine straight, your belly relaxed, and the back of your head pulled upward; breathe easily, with your tongue on the roof of your mouth, and your jaws, shoulders, and the rest of your body relaxed.

Some Encouraging Words

Many of us have tried meditating at some point but stopped because we didn't think we were "good" at it (much the same way children stop playing basketball or swimming if they don't feel very successful at first).

Some of us didn't think we were meditating right because we thought we were supposed to make our mind like a serene pond, but we just got bored or had a lot of thoughts and didn't seem to be able to stop them. The thoughts roll on, and that is precisely what is *supposed* to happen! Just let your thoughts arise and pass without letting them hold your attention, go back to your object of attention when you notice you've drifted.

Beginning meditation is not about stopping thoughts; it is about seeing the mind. Instead of wasting time and energy trying to stop your thoughts—which can be like trying to stop a river with your hand—come back to your object of attention, and let the river of thought run on without getting attached to the flotsam that drifts by.

We get attached anyway, of course; something grabs our attention. That's why we need to continue practicing. Eventually, though, even as thoughts continue to arise, we get better at noticing them and letting them go.

Like running or walking or any other forms of exercise, meditation feels more natural after we break through the initial thirty-day period of initiation and gain a little proficiency. With practice, meditation becomes a natural, healthful, and pleasurable way to discover our own depths.

> The only way out, is in.
> Anonymous

Benefits of Meditation

Meditation serves us on many levels, from simple stress release—offering healthful relaxation, rest, and rejuvenation—

on beginners' levels, to more profound forms of liberation from thought. Regular practice also offers the following benefits in the midst of daily life.

1. We become less reactive, more centered, and more responsive to our environment, because we think less and feel more. By "thinking less," I mean we find ourselves less distracted by random thoughts, and thus can focus better and make more effective use of the brain's natural abilities.
2. Our awareness expands to include more subtle aspects of life; we gain a deeper sense of energy and intuition, where before we noticed mostly the gross material elements.
3. The wall between dreams and waking grows less dense, so that we remember our dreams more easily, receiving useful messages from the Basic Self.
4. We experience a deeper connection to the presence of Spirit, and begin to perceive a more unified, holistic world. The practice of meditation opens us up to our own spiritual nature, where we find more heart and truth in the essence of whatever spiritual or religious path we choose to follow.
5. Careful research studies have documented numerous other benefits, including enhanced creativity, greater longevity, fewer illnesses, and far less tension and stress; in other words, meditation serves as an antidote for nearly every problem created by the discursive mind.

Meditation as a Map Beyond Death

Meditation can serve as a preparation to go through the transformative process of death with greater awareness, clarity, and grace. Firsthand reports of near-death experiences have revealed that the practice of meditation and the process of death have qualities in common; in both, our consciousness gradually lets go, or dissociates, from its objects. In meditation, as in the process of death, we first let go of bodily awareness, then let go of emotions and mind, then let go of the deeper levels of the personal psyche—the subconscious and unconscious; then we experience the Void, touch upon the One Consciousness, and finally merge with the Light.

The very essence of meditation involves *the practice of pure awareness.* In order to do this, we need to develop the ability to let go of the roles we play. We let go of being a man or a woman; we let go of our roles as parents, workers, artists; we let go of our problems, talents, and ideas; we let go of our responsibilities and our beliefs; we let go of our fear, our sorrow, our anger; we let go of past and future; we let go of living, being, and doing; we forget the world, forget the self, forget *everything.* During the sacred period of meditation, we can take a complete time out; we can stop the world. We can assume, for the moment, that we have died to all that we know and all that we are.

Paradoxically, the more we practice this process of "dying while alive," the more we can *live* our dying and enjoy our living. For many of us, dying and releasing the body will be the most transcendental experience of our lives. I look forward to my own death, but I will live as long as I can, because the more we have clarified consciousness during our life, the more consciously we can go through the process of death like peaceful warriors.

In meditation, when the session is complete, we open our eyes and begin anew; perhaps this, too, echoes the process of death and rebirth.

The Heart of Meditation

Meditation remains a paradox, however, because even though it provides a number of practical benefits, these benefits do not represent the significance of meditation. Ultimately, the purest "reason" to meditate has nothing to do with getting anywhere or achieving anything. We do it because it forms a natural part of the peaceful warrior's approach to daily life.

When we lose our mind, we come to our senses. Instead

of acting upon what *we think,* we act instead on deeper intuitions; our actions become spontaneous and beautifully timed — we are in touch with what's going on and who we're with. An angry thought no longer makes us angry; a sad thought no longer makes us sad; a fearful thought no longer makes us afraid. We choose our state of being; we choose love; and we can play any role in the theater of the moment. We realize there are no ordinary moments, and we are free.

A Simple Practice

I recognize that not all readers will choose to incorporate a daily meditation practice into their lives. Therefore, I'd like to describe a simple meditation anyone can do once in a while, for the specific purpose of clearing negative thoughts out of awareness.

When a troubling thought arises within our field of awareness, it exists as a thought form, a manifestation of congealed energy floating within our energy field. The issue we feel concerned about may remain in spite of our meditation, but issues don't create thought forms — we do. Some people get more concerned than others about the same challenge or issue because they create different thought forms.

By gazing into a candle flame, we can clear a negative thought form so that even though we may still need to deal with that issue in a practical way, we no longer feel as troubled by our thoughts about it.

---◆---

The Flame Meditation

The next time you have a concern or worry or any thought that troubles you, go through this simple yet powerful meditation.
1. Get a candle with a good-sized flame.
2. Set it down on a table, away from flammable objects such as curtains. Sit nearby, so that the flame is twelve to eighteen inches away from your face.

3. Take a deep breath, center yourself, and imagine yourself surrounded by the loving light of Spirit.
4. Gaze into the flame; keep blinking to a minimum. As you gaze, imagine that the flame is like a vacuum cleaner, sucking the negative thought forms out of your energy field, into the flame, and up into the ethers.
5. Do this meditation for about one to three minutes, until you feel a relief and release from the concern.

◆

I like the flame meditation because it takes only a few minutes and yet can be extremely effective. In fact, *we have all done this meditation many times* when we've gazed into a fireplace or camp fire and experienced the warm, relaxed feeling that comes as the purifying fire clears the troubles from our awareness.

Liberating the Mind – Here and Now

I will now outline what I consider a *master method* for liberating the mind—a method so simple and so powerful that it can help heal the body of many symptoms and change the course of our life. Best of all, we can completely integrate this method within the normal course of our daily life— anywhere, anytime. It doesn't require even one second of "extra" time investment.

This key to unlocking the mind entails *remembering to bring our awareness back into the present moment.* Many of us think we already know about living in the here and now; the phrase has become part of popular culture. I had a lot to say about it in *Way of the Peaceful Warrior;* Ram Dass wrote the classic *Be Here Now;* and countless other authors and teachers have highly recommended the present moment. So we *know* about it, but how many of us *act* on that knowledge? How many of us remember to practice focusing our attention back to the present moment in the midst of our daily lives?

How, exactly, do we practice it? As an example, let me tell you about the time I had a dental appointment coming up in two weeks to get four fillings replaced. I was about seventeen years old and had a history of tooth decay; I didn't look forward to dental visits. I knew my dentist was going to pull out that big needle. But, hey, I told myself, it's not for two weeks. Why think about it now?

The next day, I drove past my dentist's office and suddenly remembered our appointment. I imagined myself lying back in the chair, saw a fleeting image of the overhead light, and felt a sinking sensation as my hands gripped the armrests and my stomach tightened—that helpless feeling . . . Then I snapped out of it as I realized where I was: Hey, I'll have plenty of time to suffer in two weeks. Why do it now? I'm here now, just driving home.

A week later, while in line at the supermarket, I turned around and saw my dentist just behind me. The clerk took my money and put my bags in the cart, but I hardly noticed. As I walked out to the parking lot, I could visualize the procedure and feel the needle . . . Then, snap! I quickly tuned back into the present as a distracted driver backed out without looking and nearly ran over me, the shopping cart, and fifty dollars' worth of groceries. The driver apologized, saying he was distracted. Back to the present: Why worry about the dentist now? I can feel helpless in a week. No need to worry now. I forgot about the dentist.

Another week passed. I woke up to a beautiful morning. Then it hit me: *Today is the day.* The sound of the drill in my mind blocked the birdsong outside my window. A dark cloud settled over my psyche. Then I remembered, Hey, just look at that sky outside! No problem now; I can suffer all I want at two o'clock. Back in the present, I stretched and enjoyed the rays of warming sun.

Just before 2:00 P.M., I sat in the waiting room, trying

to concentrate on a magazine article, my hands trembling only slightly as I heard, in the background, the drill—the real drill. I felt myself tense, then realized, What am I tensing for? I feel no pain. I'm just sitting here now, reading a good article. Then the dental assistant stepped into the room and said, *"We're ready for you."*

"Now?" I said, feeling a little like the man on death row when the warden opens the bars and invites him for a walk down the long corridor. I rose. My stomach dropped.

I found myself lying back in the chair, helpless. My dentist smiled, making some joke, but I didn't really hear him. I was too busy watching the syringe, poised above me. The moment had arrived. My arms gripped the armrests. I prepared myself.

Then the nurse asked my dentist something and he turned toward her, giving me a brief reprieve. That's when I realized that nothing was happening—*in that moment.* Still no pain—just me, leaning back in a very expensive chair. I might as well enjoy it. So I relaxed.

Then I felt a very brief, almost painless little sting, and it was over. All that worry. As I thanked my dentist and walked toward the front door, the old saying played in my memory: "A coward dies a thousand deaths. . . ."

This story illustrates how we can practice bringing attention back into the present moment in daily life: As in meditation, when we realize our attention has drifted out of the present—usually signaled by some troubling thoughts—we can gently bring it back; we can remember to be here now. Like anything, over time it gets easier and easier. Practicing this simple act of returning to the present moment has immeasurably enhanced the quality of my life.

The Power of the Present Moment

How can the simple act of returning our attention to the here and now solve the problems of mind outlined in this chapter—the tension, illness, and stress?

First of all, mind noise can only relate to the past or the future. *We cannot possibly think "about" anything in the present moment.* We can only think *about* something that has already happened — whether one second ago, five days ago, or ten years ago — or in the immediate or distant future. Isn't this obvious? Consider it: Anytime we have ever thought or reflected about anything, we were thinking about a past or future event. Past or future, that's where the discursive mind lives, where it gets its power — where, like a demon, it draws our attention, out of the peace and sanity of the present moment.

We may be dealing with a variety of challenges in our life — real, even painful issues that have to be faced. But we almost never *experience* a problem in *this* moment. For example, perhaps yesterday our landlord rudely handed us an eviction notice, and we get angry when we think about it, but that was yesterday. Next week we may get evicted, but that's next week. Maybe last night we had a terrible argument with our partner, and we're both moving out later today. Three days ago we got laid off work; tomorrow we have to go look for a new job.

Real issues, but, in spite of all that, I ask: Do we have a problem right *now* — in this moment? Or do we just have a problem in our minds? When the landlord comes to evict us, we don't have a problem; we don't have meanings or interpretations. He will say something; we will respond. We will put one foot in front of the other, carrying boxes downstairs — and so it goes.

Let me clarify further: While doing a life-purpose reading for a friend, I noticed his brow wrinkling with lines of worry. Then tears came to his eyes as he told me that he had lost his job, that his wife was going to leave him, that he had so many problems.

"Burt, tell me, what's your body doing right now?" I interrupted.

"What?" He stopped talking and looked up at me, coming back to the present from those dark places in his mind.

"What's my *body* doing right now? My body's just—it's just sitting here."

"*Right*," I said. "How very enlightened of it."

The fact is, however, that Burt's body was also tensing, probably in pain, and likely experiencing lowered immune response because his Basic Self believed all the pictures he was making as he spoke, bringing all his past or future problems into his present. With a little practice, he came to see that he only had to handle the present moment—that it was all that existed.

Though Burt still had issues to deal with in his life, in that moment, in my office, he wasn't facing a problem; we just sat quietly. I pointed out that if he had *wanted* all these events to happen, he would feel terrific right now. His own resistance caused the pain. Though Burt, like most of us, faced challenges, the major problem in his life resided in his own mind.

The Simple Life

Life is very simple for the body. The body lives in linear time, in the present moment; although it handles many internal functions at once, it can only be here now. But for the mind, it's a different story. When we're caught in rush-hour traffic, for example, our body just sits there behind the wheel, but our mind is standing on the front bumper, pushing the car in front, yelling, "Come *on!* Come *on!*"

How many of us wake up in the morning with our mind like an "In" box piled with a stack of "Things to Do." But consider: When we awaken, we only need to do one thing at a time: First we sit up, then we put our feet on the floor, then we stand.

For the mind, life seems very rushed, frantic, and complex. For the body, life seems very simple: one thing at a time. No matter how "busy" our day is, it still has only one thing to do—the next thing.

We would all like peace and simplicity in our lives, but peace seems more of an *internal* quality than an external one.

Those who seek simplicity by living in a cabin in the woods may feel peace in those quiet and beautiful circumstances for a little while. But soon enough, the mind noise chimes in: "Damn! Gotta find a way to get the raccoons out of the garden. And those deer! Gee, I'm lonely. Joe and Susie aren't carrying their share of the work load!" And so it goes.

For some of us, inner peace remains a distant and fleeting goal; however we chase it, it remains forever ahead and, yet, right in front of our nose.

> *One thing about the rat race;*
> *even if you win it, you're still a rat.*
>
> Lily Tomlin

The Body's Secret

Only when the present moment becomes more compelling than all the junkets of the mind does our life become peaceful. The body holds the secret and the key. *Come back to the body; let go of the mind.*

We have the power in any moment, by a simple act of attention, to release the illusions of the past and future, and simply handle what is in front of us — now, and now, and now.

The peaceful warrior's method for returning attention instantly to the present moment is coming back to the body. This method involves paying attention, whenever it occurs to us, to these three questions: *Am I relaxed? Am I breathing easily? Am I moving with grace?*

My emphasis on paying attention to the present moment may sound like an almost obsessive discipline, based on some kind of dogma that "we should always pay attention to here and now no matter what." I want to correct that impression. It's only natural to project our awareness into a probable future in order to plan our day (we just don't want to get too attached to the plans, because life involves surprises). We may also want to project our awareness into the past, to use our gift of memory to review and learn and heal.

But when we feel troubled by fear, anxiety, or regret, these concerns signal us to take a breath and ask: *Where am I?* Here. *What time is it?* Now. When the mind is creating troubles, it's time to come back to the body and the serenity of the present moment.

Making Decisions

Even when we practice meditation and living in the present moment, we still face the decisions of daily life. Even in the present moment, we sometimes have to make choices that will affect the future we envision. When the time comes for Jeanine to fill out her college applications, she can't afford to say, "In the present, I'm still in high school, so why worry about college now?," any more than a squirrel can afford to wait for the dead of winter to start storing nuts. Jeanine's present task, right now, involves choosing what college she wants to attend in the future.

Let's say that two fine schools accept her. Now she has to make a decision. It's driving her crazy; she just doesn't know how to make a choice: College A has the best reputation and was so beautiful when she visited, but her best friend, Sally, has chosen College B and they could be roommates.

This kind of decision-making dilemma feels familiar to most of us. At one time or another, we have all had difficulties making important decisions. I know one fellow who used to consult the I-Ching every time he went to the supermarket!

Common Causes of Decision Dilemmas

Most of us have trouble making important decisions for two reasons: First, *we try to make decisions before we need to.* We try to decide what fork in the road we'll take long before we get there and see what it looks like, which is like deciding what foot we'll use to step off the curb when we're only halfway down the block. So we end up going back and forth in our minds, weighing criteria, sorting for values, wanting to be assured that we're making the absolute right choice. But the only way we truly make a decision is by *acting*. We don't act until the moment arrives; that's the time to decide— not before. Then we are in the moment; we grasp what's in front of us. It's real. At that point, the decision usually clarifies itself.

Second, we have trouble making decisions because *we fear that we might make the wrong decision*. Let's say we reach the fork in the road and choose the left fork over the right one. As it turns out, trees fall in our path, we hit detours, we run from wild animals, we face landslides, and all kinds of difficulties arise. Does this mean we made the wrong choice? Of course not. These very difficulties may be precisely what we needed to deal with for our highest good and learning.

If our heart tells us at some point that things have changed and this no longer feels like the right path for us, we can almost always backtrack and take the other path. Few decisions in life are irreversible.

Accessing the Wisdom of the Basic Self

If a time machine could take us into our future and from that vantage point we could see the results of each option before us, we would have no trouble making decisions. The good news is we do have such a time machine; it's called our *imagination*.

◆

Time Lining

In order to achieve the best possible perspective before making an important decision, travel a time line into the future.
1. Consider your options: Let's say you want to choose between A and B.
2. Assume, for the moment, that you have made a definite choice in favor of A. Having chosen A, *feel* in your body and *visualize* in your mind what you will look like, feel like, and be doing

- *one month* from now;
- *one year* from now; and
- *ten years* from now.

Take no more than three minutes to do this.
3. Next, clear your mind, take a deep breath, and go through the same three-minute process for choice B. In under ten minutes, you will have a much better sense of the best choice for you.

---◆---

Trusting Intuition

Our brains are like a library with a main floor and a basement; our conscious mind generally has access only to the main floor, so it's working with incomplete data. The Conscious Self can do many things, but it isn't well suited to make decisions—at least not without the guidance of intuition.

> *Good instincts usually tell you what to do*
> *long before your head has figured it out.*
> Michael Burke

The loving guidance of the Higher Self, relayed to our conscious mind through the dreams, gut feelings, and intuitions of the Basic Self, enables us to make faster, clearer, and more comprehensive decisions because our subconscious can access more variables than our conscious mind. As we come to trust and open channels of communication and cooperation between our Basic Self, our Conscious Self, and our Higher Self, we see that our lives have a balance and an order. As we transcend the limits of the conscious mind, we experience a rising energy, stronger faith, and growing intimacy with Spirit.

9

Accepting Emotions

I am here to live out loud.
Émile Zola

The Importance of Feeling

I have a deep intuition that you, who now hold this book in your hands, are one of a growing number of humans preparing to make an evolutionary leap of consciousness—a leap of faith, of illumination, of waking up and coming alive. The times demand it.

Reconnecting with our deepest and truest feelings comprises an important part of this process. If we remain cut off from our Basic Selves like islands of ego, floating in a sea of isolation, we'll stay cut off from the Earth itself, and we won't survive long as a species.

On close analysis, we grasp the possibility that many of the world's political, economic, and ecological problems are the symptoms of a root cause—a fundamental denial of our feelings. As children, we inherit this denial from our parents. Now is the time to break the cycle and let the children of our generation reap the rich inheritance of emotional freedom.

Until politicians awaken, how can we have awakened politics? It comes back to this: To change the world, we first have to change ourselves.

Healing Relationships

Most of us automatically associate the word *emotion* with relationships, because relationships are the primary arena where we learn about our feelings. Relationships, in

177

fact, may offer the greatest spiritual challenge we will ever encounter.

Men and women tend to have different ways of communicating, even of seeing the world. If that weren't enough, Conscious Selves, due to their separate and competitive nature, don't tend to get along very well; Basic Selves, like most children, compare and compete with one another. After the courtship and honeymoon phase, the theater of relationship represents a constant demand to go beyond the Conscious and Basic Selves—a wonderful opportunity to learn about ourselves.

Even the relationships we form in the larger society fall within the context and backdrop of a competitive social world ringing with the constant clash of egos. Competition, an us-versus-them mentality, dominates our governments, our legal systems, and our sports. We still have much to learn.

Clarifying Emotions

Before we can accept our emotions, we have to understand them in the context of the peaceful warrior's way. To most of us, the word *emotion* refers to feelings or sentiments: positive ones like happiness, joy, and excitement, or negative ones like anger, sorrow, envy, depression, and so forth.

Some of us fear our own emotions and the emotions of others, because we associate them with discomfort or weakness—with the opposite of reason. We want to stay "objective" and cool, and "be reasonable," unlike people who are "too emotional." That's the extent of our popular understanding of the feeling dimension. Few of us learned much more from our parents or our teachers.

We do know from experience, however, that emotions come and go, passing like clouds through the sky. We'd prefer to feel happiness and other positive feelings more often, and negative ones less often. So we seek experiences that stimulate good feelings—looking forward to a good television program, going out on Friday night, or meeting someone we love and who loves us.

Nevertheless, our daily experience includes fears, sorrow, disappointment, and anger, even though these are sometimes hidden or suppressed. Though we understand that the mind gives birth to physical tension and emotional upsets, when we feel afraid, sad, or angry, it does little good to dismiss our feelings as creations of the mind. We have to deal with them.

Emotions Defined

We can use the power and clarity of reason to understand emotions in a way that enables us to work with them, and at the same time fully validate, clear, and accept them.

I'd like to propose that *bliss is our native and natural state*—the only real emotion. We often associate the word *bliss* with extraordinary or exalted spiritual states or religious transcendence, yet we could feel bliss right *now* if we cut through the layers of emotional static that surround and obscure it.

To understand how to reclaim the state of bliss, we have to return to childhood, when we were still open, before the programming began. As children, we cried when we felt hungry or tired, but just after a nap—after our mother had fed us, burped us, and cuddled us—we lay on our tummy or our back and gazed into the world in bliss and awe. Our big eyes took in the Mystery. We didn't know what anything was, but it sure looked interesting! We can look into any baby's eyes when it isn't wet or hungry or tired, and we'll see the same eyes of wonder and bliss—the relaxed, open eyes of a tiny peaceful warrior.

Emotion isn't a particular *kind* of feeling; *emotion is free-flowing feeling itself.* Emotion is pure energy moving through us without obstruction—not the vital energy that allows us to lift weights, work hard, or run long distances, but the *feeling* energy that *moves* us to pursue these activities.

As infants with unobstructed emotional energies, we felt naturally motivated to explore, move, learn, act, and discover.

When I say we had unobstructed emotions, I don't mean to imply that we always felt happy, but that when we felt angry, sad, or afraid, we "let it flow, and let it go," quickly and naturally returning to a state of happiness and bliss.

So what happened to us? Why don't we adults let our emotions flow? Why do we feel shame when we show fear; why do we feel embarrassed or "weak" when we show sorrow; why are we afraid to show anger? Why are some of us so out of touch with our emotions we don't even know *what* we feel anymore? Why can't we just experience our feelings completely and naturally, then return to a state of happiness instead of holding in our feelings, suppressing them, and then enduring the physical symptoms that arise as a result of ignoring the cries of the Basic Self?

We've seen how the Conscious Self, with its reason and logic, tends to devalue and suppress shows of emotion and feeling. Our values and priorities, our schools and science, have placed our conscious mind—the intellect—on a lofty pedestal. How much of our education dealt with developing the mind, and how much with the body? Did any of it deal with developing, accepting, and opening our emotions? As children and teenagers, were our emotions encouraged or were they suppressed?

For many of us, dealing with emotions remains a weak link in our lives. Most of us have felt life in shades of gray for so long that we have forgotten what it might be like to feel life in vivid color.

In order to reexperience the aliveness, the excitement, and the incredible motivation we felt as infants, we need to clear the obstructions that block the free flow of feeling energy.

The Three Contractions

All the words we use to express the many shades and hues of negative feelings, including jealousy, rage, hate, depression, anxiety, envy, irritation, worry, and frustration, are derived from *three primary states: fear, sorrow, and anger*. Like the three primary color pigments—yellow, blue, and red—fear, sorrow, and anger blend to form all the subtle colors of emotional upset.

Actually, fear, sorrow, and anger aren't *emotions* at all; rather, they manifest as three primary obstructions to, or *contractions* in, the free-flowing energy we call bliss. Fear, sorrow, and anger name our three fundamental kinds of emotional pain.

Earlier, in discussing the *gateways of release*, I referred to the universal problem of stress created when energy collides with internal obstructions. We've looked at *physical* obstructions and imbalances resulting from poor diet, poor posture, lack of exercise, injuries, shallow breathing, and stress-produced tension, all of which reflect or create inner turbulence.

We've examined *mental* obstructions such as unexamined beliefs, associations, meanings, and interpretations, as well as rigid, obsolete, or contradictory thoughts, which lie at the source of both physical and emotional obstructions.

Now we can learn how to clear *emotional* obstructions to free-flowing energy and open the way for escalating joy and rising bliss, even in the midst of daily life.

Physically, we experience fear, sorrow, and anger in the same way: as a contraction, cramp, tension, or pain in our vital areas—our chest and abdomen. We then interpret this contraction through the mind and feel angry (irritated, put off, frustrated, enraged), sad (depressed, melancholy, blue), or afraid (anxious, worried, nervous) depending on our interpretations.

Most of us can readily understand how the feeling of fear arises from issues of personal survival, safety, and security. We also understand how anger and frustration can manifest around issues of power and discipline. The association of sorrow with sexuality and pleasure may seem more subtle, but is no less real. When most of us first fell in love but didn't know if the object of our desire cared about us, we probably lost our appetite, sighed a lot, and felt something akin to sorrow. Sexual attachment and desire involve inevitable loss, or the risk of loss. Even on the most subtle energetic levels, orgasm itself represents a kind of bodily sacrifice, the release or loss of life energy.

Fear, sorrow, and anger all reside below the heart level that we associate with love and happiness.

The Hierarchy of Emotional Blocks

Fear, the most debilitating emotional obstruction, has the power to paralyze us. When terrified, we tend to stop breathing and freeze, just when we need to act decisively. Fear lies at the root of all emotional contraction—beneath both sorrow and anger. When Todd appears or acts angry (feeling frustrated or powerless), just beneath that anger lies sorrow (he's actually feeling hurt or painfully sad); beneath his sorrow, buried much deeper, lies fear—of being worthless, of abandonment, of death. This same mechanism operates universally, in each of us, as deep introspection will reveal.

Sorrow cannot paralyze us—no one is "frozen with sorrow"—but sorrow does weaken us. Less severe than the implosive contraction of fear, sorrow drains our energy and makes us collapse. Our head drops; our shoulders slump. Severely depressed people can't even get out of bed.

Anger is stronger than fear or sorrow. We can *use* anger in order to act. Anger overcomes both fear and sorrow. For example, when I was training in gymnastics, attempting a risky new somersaulting sequence, I often felt great fear, and my heart raced as adrenaline shot through my bloodstream. Instinctively, however, I had learned to generate a kind of anger or fierceness to overcome the fear. The fear didn't go away; the anger just pushed through it.

When we find out we've been fired from a job or a long-time partner suddenly leaves us, we may experience energy rising up through the hierarchy of feelings, including, though not necessarily in this order, shock or numbness, panic and fear, hurt and pain, and finally, as the process of healing continues, anger. Anger can be a sign of healing, as energies rise higher, but it is not the last stop on the elevator. Anger, too, while stronger and more useful than fear or sorrow, still lies below the heart. A form of emotional pain, anger obstructs the free flow of the rising energies of life, and so, like fear and sorrow, it needs to be cleared in order to find our way back to an open heart and happiness.

Emotions and the Breath

Within this model of understanding, we've established that fear, sorrow, and anger are the three primary kinds of emotional contraction. I'd now like to offer a simple, practical method for clearing these obstructions and releasing the cramp that blocks our natural states of equanimity and bliss.

I base this method on the observation that *our breath and our emotional state mirror each other.* Our breathing both reflects and influences our emotional state. When we feel calm and open, we breathe evenly, slowly, and with ease. When we feel upset, we throw our breathing pattern out of balance.

When we feel afraid, we tend to inhibit or curtail our breathing altogether.

When we feel sad, we inhale forcefully, but our exhalation is weak, as in the case of fitful sobbing or gasping for air, reflecting our need to be consoled, to feed on others' energy and attention (strong inhalation). Chronic sorrow can aggravate certain physical conditions such as emphysema. When held in the grip of sorrow, we function as an energy vacuum and have trouble giving energy out (weak exhalation).

When we feel angry, the opposite pattern of breathing applies; *we exhale more forcefully than we inhale.* Our breath reflects our psychophysical state: When we feel angry, we push away or strike out (strong exhalation); we temporarily or chronically lose our ability to receive, open, accept, or feel vulnerable to incoming information (weak inhalation). Chronic anger can aggravate many cases of asthma.

Clearing Emotional Obstructions

The most direct method for clearing emotional obstructions involves bringing our pattern of breathing back into balance.

---◆---

A Recipe for Equanimity

1. If you feel afraid, just remember to breathe! The only difference between fear and excitement is whether you are breathing.
2. If you feel sad, pay special attention to strong, full *exhalations* until you bring the breath back into balance. Allow yourself to feel strong; as you exhale, project energy into life.
3. If you feel angry, pay special attention to full, deep *inhalations* until you bring the breath back into balance. Allow yourself to feel vulnerable – to receive.

---◆---

Bringing our breath back into balance will not, of course, disintegrate the thought forms that generated the upset, nor will it solve the external issue that triggered the thoughts. But it does serve as an effective means to short-circuit the emotional contraction – the obstruction of emotional energy – and allow us to open up again. In other words, balancing our breathing helps to clear the paralysis (fear), weakness (sorrow), or tension (anger) so we can more effectively deal with the issue before us.

A Ritual of Purification

Another tool we can use in the midst of daily life to release negative energies and feelings from the body, mind, or emotions involves combining breath, feeling, and attention in a ritual of purification.

When we exhale, we breathe out not only carbon dioxide but other waste products such as mental and emotional toxins, including concerns, worries, sorrow, anger, and fear.

When we inhale, we take in not just oxygen but life energy, light, love, happiness, and inspiration (or Spirit). Consciously focusing on this truth as we breathe increases the significance and conscious quality of our breath—a useful image for the Basic Self.

◆

The Cleansing Breath

For a few cycles of the breath, create a conscious ceremony of self-cleansing. I can't overstate the utility of this simple exercise.

1. As you exhale fully, feel as if you're exhaling any negative states or feelings in your field of awareness. You may imagine this as a darker energy. If you have a worry, breathe it out. If you're sad, breathe it out. If you feel angry, breathe it out.

2. As you inhale, feel that you take in light, healing energy, love, and Spirit. Feel your body, especially any areas that may need healing or nourishment, fill with tingling, sparkling light and love.

◆

Sometimes when I remember to take a few cleansing breaths in response to a concern, it works so well I can't seem to remember what I was upset about.

There's Always a Catch

As simple as the practice of breathing to clear emotional obstructions appears—what could be simpler than paying attention to our inhalations and exhalations? — one major problem exists in applying it: When we feel afraid, sad, or angry, *we may not have the free attention to notice*, Ah, yes, my breathing seems out of balance; I'll just take a moment to fix it. It's tough enough just remembering to count to ten, another useful practice when dealing with charged emotions (and while we count, let's breathe!).

One day, several years ago, I came home about twenty minutes late. I hadn't called to let Joy know. And it was the third day I'd come home later than I'd said I would. And I didn't have a good reason — I had just spaced out, browsing through a bookstore. And we only had one car. *And* I had promised I'd be home in time for Joy to go to an important appointment. *And* I had made her late. *And* instead of apologizing I was both arrogant and defensive. I arrived home to find Joy quite angry.

At that point, I made a major tactical error — like trying to put out a fire with gasoline. I suggested, "Joy, now remember your breathing." I'll leave her response to your imagination.

When we feel upset, it may seem simple to remember to breathe evenly, but it isn't always easy. However, easy or not, at least we have the option.

Relaxation and Release

Because emotional obstructions of fear, sorrow, and anger represent a form of tension/contraction, one effective way to release the cramp involves consciously *remembering to relax*.

We'll find it nearly impossible to *feel* as afraid or sad or angry as our body becomes relaxed. By relaxing, our breath comes more easily and begins to balance itself — another way to short-circuit the obstruction and open the body/mind once again.

◆

Dissolving Contractions in the Body

You may not now be feeling especially afraid, sad, or angry, but you can apply this simple exercise to any future incidents you may experience.

1. Recall the last time you felt very fearful, sad, or angry; the stronger the emotional charge, the better for the sake of this exercise.
2. How did your body feel? As you remember the incident, feel your body right now. Do you notice a tension in the abdomen or chest?
3. Take a breath, relax, and let go of any tension in the belly, chest, shoulders, neck, or thighs as you continue to remember the incident.
4. Notice the difference; notice how even when the mind is filled with dissonance, the body lets go of the emotional contraction as you relax and release.

◆

Emotional Payoffs

Before we can release emotional obstructions and contractions, whether through the breath or another means, we have to *want* to do so. Our Basic Self, however, may feel attached to chronic upsets, because many of us, as children, got a payoff for being upset.

For example, the only time some of us attracted our parents' undivided attention was when we were sad—crying, injured, or ill—so sure enough, we regularly got sad, injured, or ill. Sorrow may have felt safer to express than anger. For others of us, getting into an anxious or panicked state was the only way to elicit our parents' support and concern.

Holding onto anger can also have a payoff. Sometimes we *want* to stay angry as a means of punishing another person for a real or imagined offense. "All right, that's it; you've done it this time. I'm not going to talk to you for a week!"

Some of us attend workshops, get in touch with our feelings, and find we feel so good expressing them that we make a compulsive habit of it, and our lives for a time become like soap operas—one catharsis after another.

Children observe their parents closely and experiment with behaviors that achieve the desired results. As children, we may have learned to use emotional melodrama to influence or control others with the threat or use of fear (panic), sorrow, or anger. With dramatic shows of emotion, we manipulated the adults around us, who, because of their own inhibitions and fears, were uncomfortable with unbridled emotions and free expression. So the adults caved in: "Okay, okay, whatever you say. Just stop crying." This unfortunate misuse of emotion bound us to a repetitive cycle of dramatics, and blocked the possibility of honest—rather than strategic—expression and eventual transcendence.

Those of us who have learned to misuse emotional energies can change, grow, and break free when we realize that our old strategies only continue a self-defeating cycle. Before we can clear the obstructions of fear, sorrow, or anger from our bodies and our lives, we have to find new and positive methods of expressing what we want or need directly, and commit ourselves to the process of cleaning up our emotional lives. Knowledge is power; to have personal power over ourselves, we first need to examine our own patterns.

◆

Payoffs and Emotional Habits

1. Of fear, sorrow, and anger, which do you feel most inclined to express? Ask yourself the following questions:
   - Do you ever show fear to create a response in other people?
   - Do you ever show sorrow to create a response in other people?

- Do you ever show anger to create a response in other people?
- How might you ask for and get the desired response without having to use contracted states?

---◆---

Reasons to Rebalance

Fear, sorrow, and anger are neither bad nor good in themselves, but they all have effects and consequences. We have a strong, inherent motivation for clearing the obstructions, because acute emotional upsets, *especially when unexpressed,* throw the body out of balance and lower our resistance to illness or infection. Long ago, when I was separated from my first wife—experiencing deep emotional upset but not really acknowledging it—even a small hangnail or paper cut would quickly become infected.

Long-term or chronic obstructions can have more devastating effects on the immune system, contributing to heart disease, cancer, and many other ills. Our desire to stay healthy gives us an excellent reason for paying attention to our breathing and for clearing the obstructions related to fear, sorrow, and anger. If we don't clear the obstructions, we have to face the consequences.

Clear the Knots
and Express the Feelings

Those of us just learning to accept, rather than deny, our feelings, may take offense at all this talk about clearing the obstructions of fear, sorrow, or anger. The point in balancing our breathing has nothing to do with *suppressing* emotional expression, but instead aims to *clear the obstructions* so we don't get all choked up. In this way, we can *express* ourselves more effectively, with even greater passion and clarity.

Besides, fear, sorrow, and anger are sometimes fully justified! If we see a mugger lurking in the shadows, we're not going to stop and engage the mugger in conversation; we will express the fear fully and run. Not contracting in such a moment will keep us from freezing. If we are attending a friend's funeral, feelings of sorrow will naturally arise. If we breathe deeply, we can let the feelings flow and experience a sense of peace after the tears. If we are confronting a bureaucratic drone who throws meaningless drivel like "company policy" in our face, anger is both understandable and effective. If we stay clear rather than contract, we may get some real results.

When Joy and I were looking for a house to rent for ourselves and our little daughters, I went to speak with the realtor who owned the house we especially liked. It turned out she had an aloof and rather cold air about her. I had filled out a long application form and went up to her desk to hand it to her. She never even gave me the courtesy of glancing up. She just said, pointing to a stack of papers, "We have forty applications; leave yours here—*I'm busy.*" Not wanting to disturb her or invoke ill favor, I placed the application on the pile and started to tiptoe out the door, when a feeling came over me. Was I wimping out here? I strode back to her desk and said in a loud voice, *"Excuse me!"* She looked up, startled. "I know what 'busy' is," I said, referring to her earlier remark. "I've been busy myself; *that* was called '*rude.*'" I definitely had her attention, now. The house be damned; I was on a roll and waxing eloquent! "I'd just like a few moments of your time and attention," I said courteously, pointing to the stack of applications. "About half the time it took me to fill out that form."

"What is it?" she asked.

"I just wanted you to know that my wife, my daughters, and I all *love* the house, and we would take care of it as if it were our own." I explained a few more things about us, wished her a good day, thanked her for listening, and left.

Two days later, we got a call; it was the realtor. She

informed me that out of the forty applicants, she had picked us. Yes, I had gotten angry, and I had let her know it; but she knew she had been out of line, and we had a real, human, interaction. The sky doesn't necessarily fall when we're honest and get angry; sometimes the sky opens.

Achieving Emotional Health

We operate on one of two levels of emotional health. The first level most of us are dealing with entails some form of *denial*, even if we believe we've "gotten past that." The second level, leading to improved health and relationships, entails *expression*.

Denial happens when our Conscious Self tunes out the signals and emotional needs of our Basic Self, resulting in numerous symptoms of discomfort. When we learn and begin to practice acknowledging our feelings—saying how we feel, acting our feelings out—in constructive ways—our Basic Self shows us its gratitude by releasing new levels of energy.

Denial

For the sake of our understanding here, I will use the term *denial* to include suppression and repression—anything less than full recognition and expression of emotions. For example, I knew a man named Kirby who insisted he never got upset because it "made no sense," but his level of tension and his physical symptoms, addictions, and other behaviors seemed evidence to the contrary. Denial, in its various forms, represents the lowest level of emotional health.

Denial originates in childhood as a conscious practice to avoid blame, responsibility, or punishment: "I didn't do it!" Later, as the structure of our Conscious Self develops, we lose touch with or deny the feelings that seem illogical or "childish" to our conscious mind. Because of the Conscious Self's tendency to devalue and dominate the Basic Self's feelings and needs, most of us still have to break through walls of denial in order to get in touch with our genuine feelings and values.

In deeper cases of denial, we selectively forget incidents and feelings in an attempt to protect the psyche from traumatic experiences it may perceive as overwhelming or unacceptable, such as physical, emotional, or sexual abuse. As a means of protection, however, forgetting offers a permanent solution no more than sweeping dirt under the carpet keeps the room clean.

Contacting Emotions

1. Whenever you find yourself in a situation where your mind doesn't yet know what you're feeling, ask yourself, *What if I knew?* Fill in the blank: "If I knew, what I was feeling right now, I'd say I felt _____."
2. If you are still stuck, ask yourself, *Is the feeling closer to fear, sorrow, or anger?*

While our Conscious Self *thinks,* our Basic Self *feels.* Getting in touch with our feelings means opening channels between our Conscious Self and Basic Self, which also amplifies our intuitive abilities.

For those of us just learning to connect with our feelings, discovering how we actually feel rather than what we think may at first seem like a guessing game, but within a short time, we start to tune in and make a shift from "What if I knew?" to "I know very clearly how I feel." Only when we come to know, validate, and trust our feelings can we find the courage to express them.

Expression

Expression—the next level of emotional health—entails a leap into the unknown, requiring great courage. We find the courage to take that leap when our denied emotions so frustrate our Basic Self that it "misbehaves" to get our attention, creating physical problems.

Eventually, these symptoms of denial get bad enough that we recognize we need to question old assumptions—to do something different. Then, perhaps with the aid of a therapist, a counselor, a friend, a seminar, or a book, we begin to contact long-denied feelings; we discover that how we feel has a lot to do with who we are. Over time, we come to release old beliefs and judgments—to accept ourselves and our emotions. We come to express how we feel at any given moment, whether or not it seems "nice."

> *What you bring forth*
> *out of yourself from the inside*
> *will save you.*
> *What you do not bring forth*
> *out of yourself from the inside*
> *will destroy you.*
> Gospel of Thomas

While expressing feelings sounds like a simple, straightforward process, as we know, simple doesn't mean easy. Strong forces within us, as well as outside us, conspire to fight our freedom to know and express how we feel.

Why Express?

Our Basic Self, like a young child, feels emotions intensely. If our Conscious Self denies those emotions because they are "not reasonable," our Basic Self will eventually throw a tantrum that will beat us bloody.

The body weeps the tears
that the eyes refuse to shed.
Proverb

Wilhelm Reich reminds us that "unexpressed emotion is stored as tension in the muscles of the body." Expression, then, holds the key to emotional and physical health. By releasing the pressure cooker of suppressed, repressed, and denied feelings, we make peace with our Basic Self.

Blocks to Free Expression

In addition to our personal blocks to free expression, a large and unaware segment of our culture reinforces, encourages, values, and even rewards the suppression of feelings, calling this "being cool" or "in control," and associating "emotionality" with children. Outside of progressive schools of psychology, not a single professional school, to my knowledge, considers emotional vulnerability, openness, or ability to express one's feelings as relevant to either admission or graduation.

Another element that blocks our free expression of feelings is that such expression can bring up similar feelings in others. Those of us who begin to act out fear, sorrow, or anger may soon discover that friends or relatives who don't deal well with their own emotions feel uncomfortable; they may suggest that we seek "professional help" with our "problem" or try to stifle us in other ways. Expressing our feelings in the face of these cultural and social pressures takes real courage— the courage of a peaceful warrior.

Dealing With Fear

We already know that emotional contractions begin in the mind. Fear rarely happens in the present moment. We usually fear not the event itself, but a negative fantasy of what might happen—the worst-case scenario.

An important step when dealing with a future event we fear is to deliberately play out the worst possible scenario, including death. Painful, tragic things can happen to any of us in mortal bodies. Dan Greenberg's humorous book, *How to Make Yourself Miserable*, strikes close to home. For many of us who constantly picture the worst, the idea of a future camping trip brings up bears, drowning, dirt, snakebite, and bugs. The idea of traveling abroad evokes terrorist bombs, and stolen or lost money, not to mention deadly diseases.

Those of us who "die a thousand deaths" see a different world from those who stay positive but realistic. I used to remind students in my martial arts class, "If your car breaks down and you're walking on a lonely street at night and you think a mugger stands behind every corner, you're paranoid; if you think the streets are safe, you're stupid; if you think there *might* be some danger and stay wary but stay positive, you're smart."

Mike, a friend I met some years ago, related to me a brief conversation he had with his sergeant while in the jungles of Vietnam. Morale was low, and the next day Mike expected to encounter his first combat. "Sarge," he said, "I guess somewhere out there is a bullet with my name on it."

"I wouldn't worry about that," the sergeant replied. "It's the bullets that say, 'To whom it may concern' that bother me."

Mike told me that during the night he lay half-awake and faced his own mortality—the possibility that he would be wounded, maimed, crippled, or killed just after dawn. He saw himself in a hospital, a wheelchair, and a hearse; he saw his loved ones crying, and he cried, too. He sat up and wrote a letter to his family, in case the worst happened. He told them that he loved them and shared his thoughts. It was all he could do. Having faced the worst case, he never again felt as afraid, and he was able to focus on the most positive outcome—getting through that day, and the next, without getting shot or having to shoot anyone else.

With the next exercise, we take conscious charge of imagining the worst-case scenario (quite different from the many times we may have unconsciously rehearsed the worst case); then we let it go, shifting our focus to positive outcomes.

◆

Facing the Worst-Case Scenario

1. Look ahead to any situation that might make you feel afraid, nervous, worried, or anxious.
2. Consider the worst-case scenario.
3. Plan how you would respond if it occurred.
4. Accept that as a possible consequence, then let it go, and *focus your attention on the most positive outcome.*

◆

If fear comes from a negative fantasy of what might happen, we also have the option of bringing our focus back to the present moment—a core practice of the peaceful warrior in daily life.

When I used to attempt a new and risky dismount from the horizontal bar, I would prepare carefully, to avoid the realistic possibilities of injury. I knew very well the worst-case scenario—that the nature of the stunt involved possible catastrophic injuries—and so I took care. But after I completed the necessary physical, emotional, and mental preparation, I virtually never gave injury another thought. Just before I began the movement, I focused on how beautifully I could do it—not whether I would survive. Some of us have formed the habit of obsessing on the worst case; our lives seem full of danger because our minds are full of fear. Others of us have formed the habit of picturing the best; our lives are filled with energy, opportunity, and excitement.

Dealing With Sorrow

As in all emotional issues, the first step in dealing with sorrow involves complete acceptance of it. Embrace your sorrow the way you would a small child. Hold it, feel it, go completely into it. The ability to cry is one of God's gifts, and can make us feel as good afterward as a wonderful laugh; in fact, laughter and crying mirror each other. Have you noticed that crying and laughing look and sound almost identical?

Remain aware, at the same time, that sorrow comes from our attachment, based on a perception of loss that at more expanded states of awareness becomes an illusion. Higher wisdom dictates that life holds no ultimate gain or loss—only deeper understanding.

We do not need to resist or avoid sorrow. Sorrow is a contraction of energy, but it is also a normal response to loss. The problem with sorrow lies not so much in having it or feeling it as in fighting it, denying it, and trying to get rid of it, which only gives the contraction more energy. If we let it be, sorrow, will, in time, burn itself out like a candle flame. It only becomes chronic when we don't allow it expression and release.

The Fine Art of Expressing Anger

There are many ways to express anger: An unsophisticated way might be to take a stick and beat someone else over the head with it. That certainly gets the message across, but it may be counterproductive. We live in a violent society filled with confused beliefs and repressed rage, and many of us, feeling frustrated, act out our anger in violent ways. Those of us without the verbal skills to speak our mind may batter others. Those of us with verbal skills may also batter others, but we use our voices, which can sometimes do more damage than a stick.

A more sophisticated way to express anger might be, "Listen, I'm not trying to make you wrong by saying this, but I feel a lot of anger right now; it seems directed at you. Could we talk about it?" This message may produce positive results. We express ourselves, the person remains open to listening, and we work something out.

There's a difference between expressing ourselves and "dumping" on someone. I used to think I was expressing my feelings when I yelled and told someone off: "And you do this, and you're that way, and I think it stinks, you so and so!" This may have felt satisfying, but it rarely healed anything, because all the "you-you-you" accusations revealed nothing about how I felt; I had only revealed my thoughts and judgments.

---◆---

"I" Statements

1. When you want to express how you feel, begin with the word "I." Try saying these sentences out loud, just for practice:
   - I feel afraid.
   - I feel sad.
   - I feel angry.
2. This exercise may appear simple, but using these three sentences, when appropriate, instead of launching into the usual recriminations and fault-finding expeditions, can make a significant and positive difference in our relationships with others.

---◆---

We can deliver any message if it's in the right "envelope," and if we package it in such a way that the other person will accept it. All the better if we include a "return address," and remain open to accepting the other person's feelings back.

Whether or Not

If we express ourselves and the other person feels receptive to listening, we may come to a better understanding and feel closer afterward; it may benefit our relationship—personal or professional. But whether or not that person feels receptive, we can derive great benefit from expressing ourselves anyway, because doing so acknowledges and honors our Basic Self and its feelings. Our subconscious will thank us with a feeling of relief, a release of tension, and a reduction or elimination of chronic symptoms.

Even if the situation that generated the feelings has

passed—even if the person to whom we want to express our feelings is no longer present, or is even deceased—we can benefit from expressing ourselves fully.

Much of the emotional charge that stays locked into our body and psyche after an unpleasant incident stems from something we would have liked to have said or done, but held in. Therefore, even if the incident happened long ago, if it remains a blown-up image in the museum of our mind, we would do well to express ourselves.

A Second Chance to Express

1. When a negatively charged incident comes up for you, in a private moment, close your eyes and visualize the scene in your mind's eye, *with real feeling.*
2. Say or do what you would have liked to have said or done in that moment.
3. You might want to write a letter to the person involved. Then you can choose to send it, if appropriate, or otherwise burn it.

The above exercise helps resolve and release the charge of negative incidents. Though our Conscious Self may "know" we didn't confront the other person face to face, our Basic Self finds the expression satisfying, and can close the books on the incident. Holding onto resentments against someone just keeps the stressful memory alive in our mind and our body.

The exercise is not meant as a substitute for face-to-face confrontation; where that's appropriate, it's usually the best choice, although it takes courage. This exercise can be used as a "dress rehearsal" when we want to prepare for a needed confrontation.

The Courage to Express

Contrary to our fears and conditioning, the world will probably not laugh at us, hate us, or think us foolish for expressing what we feel. And even if someone does react that way, so what? The only people who don't understand are those who have not dealt with their own emotions. The people around us who appear completely under control may have far more turmoil in their inner lives than we imagine. We owe it to ourselves to feel, and to express what we feel, in spite of other people's views and opinions—because if we do not, we let their attitudes control our behavior and limit our well-being.

The Power of Passion

As a culture, we are only now beginning to progress beyond our puritan heritage. Conventional society may still consider an honest show of feelings "in poor taste" and expect us to remain "calm and reasonable" no matter what the situation.

Joy and I probably raise our voices at our daughters every day, and they yell back! We have a passionate family, and a very close and loving one. We express our feelings in the moment and move on, releasing pent-up energies; nobody in our family takes raised voices too seriously. Our daughters have learned to be assertive and up-front with their feelings. No one will ever be able to manipulate our daughters with some piddly show of anger!

Perhaps the time has come to reexamine old assumptions of what is civilized, right, and proper—to edit the hidden denial out of the etiquette books and bring more passion back into our lives. After all, how can couples have real passion in the bedroom if they repress their emotions the rest of the time?

One Step at a Time

Sometimes we feel in an expansive mood and don't react with fear, sadness, or anger to something that might trouble another person. But how do we know we're not just denying our feelings? After all, it's easy to delude ourselves into believing that if we smile and pretend to be happy and serene, then we are above getting upset.

When our Conscious Self is displaying a calm surface, our subconscious may be sending clear messages in the form of sleep disturbances, rashes, pains, and other symptoms. Our Basic Self can be very capable, very powerful, and very fierce. It has much to offer, but it also holds our shadow side — the disowned and denied parts of ourselves we've come to see as negative. We each need to recognize, accept, and work with all sides of ourselves before we can rise above emotional upsets or reactivity.

---◆---

Denial or Transcendence?

1. When a difficult situation arises, to determine whether you are genuinely calm or whether a pattern of denial is operating, ask yourself the following questions, which serve as a reality check:
   - How does my body feel right now?
   - Am I relaxed?
   - Is my breath flowing evenly?
   - If I were feeling upset, could I express it easily?
2. If your body feels centered, and you can answer yes to the last three questions, you are probably not upset; if your body is agitated and you answered no to any of the questions, you may be in denial; you would benefit from some continued work to get in touch with your feelings.

---◆---

While many methods exist to exert leverage for change, one of the most profound and maturing involves accepting and expressing our emotional natures. Once we overcome external pressure and internal programming, we can open the channel between our Conscious Self and Basic Self and reconnect with our innermost emotions. The mutual support and cooperation between Conscious Self and Basic Self generates an alchemical transformation that opens us to the love and energy of our Higher Self. But before we make the great leap into the heart, we have to get within leaping distance — one step at a time — and face the hurdles within our own psyche.

Part IV
The Battle Within

Introduction

As we have seen, the peaceful warrior's greatest battles don't lie in the external world, but within us. These *inner hurdles* generate most of the obstacles and difficulties we encounter in daily life. They carry greater danger than outer problems, because they slip, unseen and unnoticed, into our every endeavor. Like saboteurs working on the inside, they disguise themselves as "lack of initiative" or "low motivation."

We do well to remember that it's what we *don't* see that can control us. By making our inner hurdles visible, we reduce their power to influence and inhibit our lives. We have already explored a variety of inner hurdles such as resistance to change, misjudging the adversary, and denial. In Part IV, we'll uncover three of the most powerful inner hurdles: distorted self-concept, low self-worth, and good excuses.

These inner hurdles comprise a variety of negative and distorted beliefs about self and world – beliefs that underlie the very structure of our personality and undermine our actions in daily life. If we take an honest look at ourselves, we will find elements of recurring insecurity about our capacities and our self-worth. We sometimes doubt whether people love or even like us; we harshly judge our own negative thoughts. Our accomplishments often don't meet our hopes or expectations. We feel uncertain about our capacity to deal with people and to meet life's challenges; we may subconsciously doubt we deserve success. Our most subtle actions and behaviors reflect this distrust of ourselves.

As we come to understand and accept ourselves *as we are,* we discover that what we perceive as other people's coolness toward us only reflects the harsh judgments we make about our

204

own actions. When we come to *accept and respect* others' rights to their own feelings for their own reasons, we find that the coolness we once perceived from them dissolves. An aura of warmth and authenticity surrounds us, because we act from our own center rather than depending upon or seeking to control the feelings or opinions of others.

As we assume greater responsibility for our own feelings and perceptions, no longer blaming others or the external world for our difficulties, we arrive at the conscious recognition that we cause most of our own difficulties. When we discover with equal force that only we can change our lives, we gain the capacity to face life head-on and to follow the peaceful warrior's way.

To overcome our negative beliefs we need to recognize them as arbitrary illusions, with no more substance than a ghost.

> *An elderly Japanese man whose wife had recently died was considering remarriage, but this thought made him feel guilty. Soon after, his wife's ghost began to appear to him every night. In misery after losing much sleep, he visited a local Zen monk he believed might help him.*
>
> *"She knows everything in my mind," he lamented to the monk. "She knows all about the woman I've been thinking of; her ghost knows everything!"*
>
> *"I see," said the monk. "So if this ghost is genuine, it would surely be able to tell you anything."*
>
> *"Yes!" said the man.*
>
> *"Then tonight, before you go to sleep, fill up a jar with beans. When this ghost appears, ask it how many beans are in the jar."*
>
> *That night, when the ghost appeared, the man asked it, "How many beans are in this jar?"*
>
> *The ghost vanished, and never reappeared.*

In the same way, by shining the light of awareness on the hurdles within, we can uncover and cut away false assumptions we might have previously taken for granted, and, in doing so, our "ghosts" vanish. We open up new possibilities; our daily lives change from a series of tasks to a series of adventures and possibilities. Just as we learn to treat every moment as special, we learn to treat ourselves with the same deep compassion and respect.

10

Self-Concept

As they traveled in the Land of Oz,
the quick-witted scarecrow thought he had no brains;
the loving tin woodsman felt he needed a heart;
and the heroic lion believed he lacked courage.
Based on the stories of Frank L. Baum

Prisoners of Self-Concept

Those of us who believe we *can* and those of us who believe we *can't* both prove ourselves right. Energy follows thought; no matter how hard we work or how much we know, we tend to rise to our assumed limits, and no higher. Most of us labor under the burden of false and arbitrary beliefs about our abilities—beliefs that have held us captive for most of our lives.

We rise to our own level of expectation—itself based upon the expectations and confidence we felt from others, especially in our childhood: Supportive environments engender strong, confident Basic Selves; environments filled with criticism, belittling, and negative expectations create insecure Basic Selves with little sense of their own capacities.

To be a champion,
you have to believe in yourself
when nobody else will.
Sugar Ray Robinson

Basing our self-concept on the opinions of others seems both tragic and wrong. Many of those who have carved a place

207

in history were thought by others to have little talent or aptitude in their early years. Albert Einstein failed mathematics in grade school and was considered to have "no talent" in that area. The early teachers of Edgar Cayce, the "sleeping prophet," mistakenly labeled him "dull." As quickly as others label and limit us, we learn to limit ourselves.

Our self-concept embraces an entire constellation of assumptions, such as: I'm good at English but a dunce at mathematics. I have no mechanical aptitude. I'm naturally coordinated. I have two left feet. I'm attractive to men/women. I can't carry a tune. I have a good/bad memory. I'm good in bed. *These beliefs may not have any basis in reality.*

How do these kinds of beliefs develop? Do they accurately reflect our actual strengths and weaknesses, or is something else going on?

Assumed Limits: A Reality Check

Most of us immediately recognize that our beliefs about our "talent" or lack of talent will influence what we choose to do and how well we do it. Few of us, however, appreciate just how deeply these beliefs affect us.

Our mind, which deals in the realm of concepts and ideas, has ambitions, grandiose notions, and illusions about what it can or cannot do. On the one hand, our mind may believe in its own infinite power to move mountains, but on the other hand, it tells us we can't replace a light switch, cook a good meal, solve a math problem, sustain a relationship, or hook up a video recorder.

Our body, however, knows its own limits and is endowed with a natural humility based upon experience, if left to test and explore without interference from the ambitions or beliefs of the Conscious Self.

When our awareness expands to the point of enlightenment, or complete and total *realization* that only One Consciousness exists, and no separate self, "we" can then know everything and do everything, because "we" *are* everything.

Short of that, however—while we still identify with a point of awareness within a physical body—we remain subject to physical laws. We can fly in an airplane; we can submerge in deep water with diving gear or in a submarine, but we don't float into the air or breathe underwater like a fish.

Many of us have heard or read about psychics, saints, or spiritual masters who could levitate, appear in two places at once, and so on, but unless we experience such things directly, or have personally seen these things, we might relegate them to the realm of the "possible but improbable," and base our beliefs on something closer to home—*our own experience.*

The Limitations of Experience

Our self-concept and self-confidence stem almost wholly from our childhood impressions and experiences, and, as children, we sometimes drew conclusions from false or insufficient data.

For example, as a child, I entered kindergarten at midyear. My first day, I saw children standing by big easels and painting trees. I picked up a brush and tried to draw a tree, too, but it didn't come out the way I'd seen it in my mind. It looked like a green lollipop. I looked around at the other children's drawings; their trees looked more real.

I didn't understand that the other children had been drawing trees, and other things, almost every day for several months. I just compared myself to them and drew the conclusion, based on insufficient data, that I couldn't draw trees very well. I very nearly decided I had less artistic abilities, rather than merely less experience, than my peers.

Perhaps the main function of a teacher in the earlier grades is to help us to understand the process of learning—to grasp the simple but profound truth that we *can do almost anything* if we practice it over time, and *the odds are we can do more than we think.*

Since my kindergarten experience, I've learned that talent

is less important than applied work. But childhood impressions linger—hidden hurdles for which we need to remain vigilant, because we all meet them along the path. The first step in breaking down false and limiting beliefs about ourselves involves going to the source of self-concept—and observing how it developed in the first place.

Though I've already given one example, I'd like to share another—a sad story I saw unfold as I was visiting a junior high school campus some years ago. Early for an appointment, I stopped by the gymnasium, peeked inside, and found a young physical education teacher in the midst of what appeared to be his first session teaching gymnastics. He was attempting to teach cartwheels to a group of young boys.

"Okay," he said to them. "Watch me." He then demonstrated an average cartwheel he had probably learned while taking a beginning gymnastics course in college. "Do it like that," he urged them. "Just hold your arms straight like this, and kick over."

A few of the boys looked eager to try; they had either taken gymnastics at a local club or had played around with handstands and so forth. Other boys looked far less confident; they had probably never tried a cartwheel or a handstand before; some of them were overweight.

As I expected, when the boys attempted their cartwheels, some performed well and others fell down, embarrassed and awkward.

The teacher, who clearly didn't have much experience, said to the ones who had fallen down, "You just have to keep your arms straight, and hold your head up—like this!" And he showed them another cartwheel that he had probably tried and missed many times before he had mastered it. They tried again, and fell again.

I could see the beliefs forming—written all over their faces: "I'm not good at cartwheels . . . at gymnastics . . . at athletics . . . I'm a klutz." And thus, a distorted self-concept took form.

I've never seen a poor student *or* a poor teacher—only

inexperienced ones. But this teacher's inexperience hurt some of those children that day. He missed his chance to explain to the students that we learn through a step-by-step *process,* that some of them had practiced cartwheels many times before, that others, even if they were overweight right now, could lose that weight and get more strength in their arms. What happened that day didn't have to close the book on those boys; their past and present didn't have to become their future. Just as those children formed concepts about their abilities based on limited experience and misinterpretation, we have each formed concepts about ourselves just as false, just as limiting, and just as arbitrary.

Maybe these concepts involve our lack of talent for algebra, sports, art, or another area, perhaps because someone demanded that we learn them a few months or even a few weeks before we were ready to grasp them. Maybe our parents seemed disappointed in us because of their own frustrated ambitions or unrealistic expectations. We can know all that now, *but we didn't back then,* when the concept was formed. So we need more than our Conscious Self's understanding of all this; we need to reeducate our Basic Self if we are to overcome the hurdle of distorted self-concept.

---◆---

Visualizing the Positive

1. Recall an incident or incidents that helped shape your beliefs about something you don't feel very capable of.
2. Replay that incident in your mind's eye, but this time make it come out differently. See, feel, and hear yourself doing very well at that task or activity. You may see yourself struggling, but over time getting better and better. Make your own movie; create a memory resource that will have an impact on your Basic Self and help form a new, stronger self-concept in this area.

---◆---

Positive, resourceful visualizations—creating inner experiences of strength, capacity, and success—can prepare and encourage our Basic Self to break through old barriers. But after that preparation, the best way to reeducate our Basic Self and free it from limiting beliefs is through direct experience—*doing* more than we had believed we could. Each time we do more than we thought we could, we experience a rush of joyous energy and excitement as we transcend assumed limits. Before we will allow ourselves to do this, however, we need to apply healthy skepticism and take a fresh look at our old assumptions.

Only direct experiences *over time* give us accurate feedback about our present ability in any area of life—not just one experience, but many. To base our sense of ourselves on one or two attempts is like visiting a new country and judging that country's weather by whether it happens to be raining that particular day.

Throwing Out Old Assumptions

Until we throw out *all* our old assumptions—until we freshly examine who we are, what we value, and what we can do—we remain bound by beliefs based on false data. "But I've tried to learn golf for *years*," someone might say, "and I'm still a mediocre player." That belief reflects the insidious nature of distorted self-concept. If we misunderstand our beginnings in any field of endeavor (such as golf or singing) and prematurely assume we "have little talent," we will naturally tend to tense up, try too hard, or avoid the activity altogether. We begin to focus on the problem rather than on the solution, remembering our errors rather than our successes; soon, we have a whole string of remembered mistakes or failures to reinforce our first assumption. By changing these assumptions, we open the door to a new future.

If we focus on what we can't do, we hardly notice what we *can* do. By changing the focus—looking at the solution, not the problem—we start to reach for the carrot and stop worrying about the stick. To repeat the words of the steel-worker on the 76th floor: "Don't look where you don't want to go."

Principles of Excellence

For any activity, difficulty corresponds to preparation; the stronger and more complete our preparation, the better our performance. Abe Lincoln once said, "If I had six hours to chop down a tree, I'd spend the first four hours sharpening the ax."

"Natural talent" is overrated; it can only take us so far, as Aesop's turtle reminded the hare. My first year as gymnastics coach at U.C. Berkeley, I did my best to interest a young woman named Patricia in coming to workout every day, but even though she had more talent than nearly any gymnast I had seen, she lacked the perseverance to approach her potential. Since that time, I've looked for character and work habits over flash and talent.

While some of the world's most brilliant performers in any field seem to have a rare combination of genetics, motivation, and other qualities, anyone can become *highly competent* in just about any chosen field, in one form or another, through sheer focus, intention, and work. The successful professionals I know in the fields of athletics, acting, law, medicine, and business attribute their success more to "hard work" than to "natural talent."

Eric, a past gymnastics teammate of mine, had had severe polio as a child; his legs were like sticks, and he couldn't walk without leg braces when he first came into the gymnastics room and told the coach he wanted to try the still rings. The coach welcomed him but felt dubious; we had one of the strongest teams in the nation, and it seemed unlikely that Eric could qualify. Four years later, Eric was running with the team without his leg braces, and he had performed a high, full-twisting somersault, coming down from about eight feet in the air and landing on his feet, unassisted. He became one of the top three performers in the nation, and an All-American.

Ron liked to throw frisbees; other than that, at twenty-nine years old, he really didn't know what to do for a living. His parents and friends told him, "Come on, Ron—grow up. You can't throw frisbees for a living." Ron also had a passion for world peace. One day he had an idea. He contacted a sponsor, got about five hundred frisbees that said "World Peace" in English and Russian, and went to Russia as a citizen goodwill ambassador, teaching people all over the then–Soviet Union to play frisbee (this was during the cold war). Now, Ron leads frisbee tours to Russia and to China, taking many fun-loving, kindhearted people with him—making good money doing what he loves and serving other people.

These and hundreds of other stories serve as examples of people who didn't assume limits.

Pushing Our Limits

Today we find many dramatic opportunities to test our limits. How many ancient sages could have foreseen the new rites of passage? How many shamans imagined a time when "ordinary" people would jump into space at ten thousand feet—for sport? Could the men of New Guinea, about to dive off fifty-foot towers with vines attached to their feet, have seen a vision of modern men and women, held by rubber cords, leaping out of cranes and hot-air balloons hundreds of feet high? Would the East Indian fakirs and African warriors have imagined thousands of people walking across fire during one weekend workshop and breaking boards with their bare hands the next?

These dramatic experiences are certainly not for everyone, however. The peaceful warrior's way begins where we are now and respects each person's unique needs. For some of us, expressing our deepest feelings takes far more courage than a skydiver's leap. For others, taking a five-mile walk or asking someone for a date may represent a tremendous step toward a new sense of self. We show courage, capacity, and compassion in many ways; in fact, some of those skydiving, fire-walking, and bungee-jumping daredevils may have other much more "ordinary" areas of life they haven't yet found the courage to confront—such as letting themselves cry when they feel sad, or committing to a relationship. We each have our own special challenges.

If we accept the challenge of doing something—*anything*—that breaks through our imagined limits, we are less likely to accept these limits in the future. One step up the ladder of courage tends to encourage another, so that when we run into an "I can't do that," we remember to ask, *"How do I know?"*

Experience teaches us that if we accomplish something, we *know* we can. If we *don't* accomplish it, that does *not* mean we can't; it only means that we haven't done it yet.

Staying Open to the Possibilities

I never believed I would become the trampoline champion of the world, but then again, I never believed I wouldn't. For most of us, perhaps an optimistic, open-minded "let's go for it and see what happens" works best.

When we regularly practice music, dance, sports, or anything else, we discover that *anything we do constantly, over time, tends to improve.* We can rely on this principle.

Everything and everyone evolves and changes. Today, we have almost none of the cells that made up our body seven years ago. We change and grow, and so do our abilities. What was true in the past is not necessarily true now: Ugly ducklings can become swans; the insecure recluse can, and often does, become the dynamic public speaker.

No matter what the source of our distorted self-concept, we can start now to break out of prison so that our past no longer determines our future. It isn't where we've been that matters, but where we're going.

Secrets of Capacity

We've already seen that our Basic Self is responsible for our success in the world. Our Conscious Self, however, *defines* success, and remains at the helm, ideally helping our Basic Self to understand the world. Whatever our conscious mind says or imagines about ourselves sends a message to our subconscious, which will eventually recognize these images as a reality, or pattern, and assume they are real.

If we have a habit of saying, "I'm not good at that," or "I'm such a klutz," our Basic Self will have no choice but to agree with our own negative programming and help us act like successful klutzes; soon enough, we'll have numerous glasses of spilled drinks and bumped heads to prove it. Let's pay close attention to our assumptions—to what we say about ourselves and to how we see ourselves. If we say, "I don't see myself doing that," then we probably aren't going to do it.

Knowing how the Basic Self responds to this kind of self-programming, we can turn our self-talk and imaging into a positive experience. *Affirmations, combined with clear, vivid, and positive visualizations,* create an internal experience for the Basic Self; finally, it comes to accept the positive images and begins to give us the energy that such accomplishment requires. This practice works especially well when we remember what motivates the Basic Self—survival, pleasure, and power.

If, for example, we say to ourselves, "I have an attractive presence and people like my company," and at the same time visualize people walking into the room, obviously attracted by our presence, then our Basic Self will generate the energy and subtle behaviors to attract this. In addition—since all Basic Selves are in contact—those very people we want to attract will also support our affirmation, if our Basic Selves are in rapport.

I had a friend in high school who always seemed to come up with a positive interpretation for every interaction with a woman. If a girl smiled at him, he'd say to me, "She loves me." If she put her nose in the air and ignored him, he'd say, "She's crazy about me—just playing hard to get." Whether or not Jimmy's interpretations were correct didn't matter. He felt attractive to women and he felt pleasure in their company because, after all, they all "loved" him. As I recall, Jimmy always had female company, and a big smile on his face.

◆

Expanded Possibilities: Affirmations and Imagination

1. Select an area in which you have a low self-concept – in other words, an area in which you feel you really lack talent or ability.
2. Now affirm your talent in this area. *Say this affirmation aloud.*
3. At the same time, create a vivid image, an internal experience or fantasy supporting this affirmation, drawing on the Basic Self motivators of survival (security), pleasure (fun), and power (control). The more detailed and the more enjoyable, the better.
4. Then, keeping your expectations positive, let your visualization go, and trust the process.

◆

Life has magic; the story of our lives can change with the next turn of the page. More than any other external obstacles, our limited, distorted self-concept hold our life's possibilities hostage. By breaking free of limited concepts about our capabilities, we find the power to take charge and to write our own story, turning a tragedy or drama into a joyous adventure.

Modeling Who We Want to Become

Acting may represent a divine art, a transcendental practice of stepping out of our own ego and trying on another.

Acting goes far beyond the professional or even amateur efforts on a stage or in front of a camera. We all act; it's just that most of us get locked into one character role: ourselves. We continue to pretend to be who we believe we are. Values, imposed upon us and programmed into us by well-intentioned people, continue to control us until we blow into our own sails and change course.

Acting (or role modeling) changes and expands our self-concept based on the principle "Fake it 'til you make it." Acting involves mastering the "as if" mode. Act *as if* you were beautiful, or had abundant finances, or could win the game, and soon that role becomes natural. I hope it's obvious that modeling and acting are *conscious* practices of expanding roles and repertoires, as distinguished from the largely unconscious game of "let's pretend."

Role modeling is something we've *all* done subconsciously; it's how the Basic Self learns—how, as children, we learned to walk and talk, as well as imitate mannerisms, gestures, and other behaviors. Now, we can do it consciously.

Modeling looks like imitation, but on deeper levels, it is incorporating the inner qualities, resources, and energies of another person or, as in the case of ancient warriors and shamans, taking on certain strong qualities of animals. It serves as one of our most effective means of change. We can consciously take on the positive qualities of people we have admired. Some real-life examples may help to clarify the practice and its benefits.

Several times a year, at the Peaceful Warrior Intensive Training in northern California, I teach people the core principles and movements of knife fighting (rubber knives) in order to access, at the Basic Self level, resources like courage, self-trust, commitment, acceptance, and the ability to focus attention on the present moment. A few years ago, I noticed that one of the participants, a man named Roy, seemed locked into the role of the stereotypical "nerd." He wore coke-bottle glasses; he never looked anyone in the eye; he was slight of build, soft-spoken, and very shy. And here he was, trying to move off-line and make a cut with his knife as an attacker came at him. Roy was moving with awesome ineptitude; he was a master of gawkiness.

I came over and asked, "Roy, are you having some difficulty I can help you with?"

"It's just that I'm really afraid," he confessed. "I never pictured myself a knife fighter. I still don't."

"Well, I understand why you might feel afraid; after all, this is new to you, and it can be scary if you lack confidence right now. But let me ask you this: Would Bruce Lee be afraid?"

Roy was a Bruce Lee fan: "No," he said. "This would be simple for Bruce Lee—what a fighter—fast as lightning!"

"Okay, then," I said. *"Be Bruce Lee."*

Roy had a blank, dreamy expression on his face as I walked away. A few minutes later, I looked back, and Roy was making the high-pitched noises that Bruce Lee used to make—and I swear, he did look a little like Bruce, moving like lightning.

Robin, another participant, faced the final test—which entailed staying centered, breathing calmly and, staying relaxed and in his heart, as the attacker came at him repeatedly—while the entire class watched and cheered him on. But Robin didn't hear their cheers; he was nearly numb—paralyzed with fear. Robin began to collapse before our eyes.

Just then, I remembered a film clip we had watched a few nights before, from *The Court Jester*, a classic adventure/romance. In the scene we saw, Danny Kaye in the title role dueled the dastardly villain, a master of the sword. Grizelda, the witch, had hypnotized our hero and snapped her fingers, saying, *"You're the greatest with the blade!"* When her fingers snapped, his character changed from a terrified beginner to a master of his destiny, so skilled that he merely toyed with the villain.

So I snapped my fingers and said to Robin, "You're the

greatest with the blade!" Robin remembered the film clip, and all the participants sat up straight, electrified as they saw him *instantly* snap to attention, with a devilish smile on his face, and transform himself before our amazed eyes! For the rest of that test, he *was* a master with the blade! It can happen just like that; we only need a role model—a new part to play.

The more roles we can play, the more freedom, options, and excitement we have in life. The ability to play different roles expands our self-concept and generates both freedom and balance.

Balancing Act

Some of us act out the role of a puritan who follows the rules—lean, moral, and fastidious, sometimes tense and up-tight. Others of us play the hedonist; we love to party, to follow our impulses; if it feels good, we do it. The hedonist has more fun in life—and probably more regrets, too.

But what fun to change roles: to give the puritan the day or the week or the year off—to loosen up just a bit, let our hair down, actually have a bit of cake or candy, flirt a little, and do things just for the fun of it even if they aren't constructive. And how interesting for the hedonist to go on a purifying regimen—to watch our diet, exercise more, maybe even go on a fast and clean up our act a little.

I don't suggest that we throw away deeply ingrained, cherished values if they truly work for us in a positive way. I only suggest that we have *choices*—that we can consciously *play the role* of someone with values, attitudes, and behaviors to which we might aspire, if only for a change! That way, we don't get typecast—stuck playing the same character for the rest of our lives.

When I used to coach women gymnasts on the balance beam and I noticed a gymnast tending to fall off the same side of the beam when attempting a new move, I'd ask her not to stay on the beam, but to *fall deliberately off the other side*. By working both sides, we find the middle. Balance, then, involves the ability to play both sides of any role; it means reconciling moderation with passion—playing the hedonist and celebrating life if we're at a party, and playing the puritan the next day, eating only lightly, exercising more, and cleaning out from the fun we had the night before.

Sometimes, for example, it's necessary to be rigid and tough—to be able to say no and mean it, to set limits; other times, we benefit from acting more sentimental—from getting in touch with our feelings and expressing them. Sometimes we need to play the skeptic and to discriminate between the radical and the ridiculous; other times, we need to believe in a cause, in an idea, in a friend, or in ourselves. I repeat: Play both sides to find the middle.

The balanced life, or "the middle way," can also include exploring the extremes now and then—working hard or playing hard, standing or sitting—not wobbling between the two. A hot then cold shower invigorates us more than a lukewarm one. It feels nice to be comfortable, but if we're comfortable all the time, we miss out on the chance to stretch and grow.

◆

What Roles Do You Play?

1. List all the roles you play in your daily life, both at work and at home. Ask yourself:
   • Which roles could use more practice?
   • Which roles are missing?
   • How might you expand your repertoire?

◆

A ship is safe in harbor, but that's not what ships are for. Please take a chance now and then. Go for it. Do something you fear to do. Tackle a job you might avoid because you don't think you're capable of it—because someone else didn't think you could do it. You can do, and be, more than you believe.

The Golden Eagle

A man found an eagle's egg and put it in the nest of a backyard hen. The eagle had hatched with a brood of chicks and grew up with them.

Believing himself to be a backyard chicken, he clucked and cackled. He thrashed his wings and flew a few feet into the air, just like a good chicken. He scratched the earth for worms and insects.

Years passed and the eagle grew old. One day he noticed a magnificent bird soaring in the heavens in graceful majesty. The old eagle gazed up in awe.

"Who is that?" he said to his neighbor.

"That's the eagle, the king of birds," said the neighbor.

"Wouldn't it be wonderful if we could soar like that up in the heavens?"

"Don't give it another thought," the chicken replied—"you and I are chickens."

So the eagle never gave it another thought. He lived and he died thinking he was a backyard chicken.

Anthony Demello, *The Song of the Bird*

Within each of us lives the spirit of that golden eagle; within each of us also live the hero, the magician, the adventurer, the priest/ess, and the peaceful warrior. We have all roles within us; we are made of stronger stuff than most of us yet imagine, and our bodies hold secrets yet to be revealed.

Once we realize that our self-concepts are nothing more than that—concepts—the healing begins, the fog clears, and we see a sign that says, "Path open ahead."

11

Self-Worth

If, when I come to lay down the reins of power,
I have lost every other friend on earth,
I shall at least have one friend left,
and that friend shall be down inside of me.
Abraham Lincoln

What We Deserve

In some cosmic sense, perhaps, we, as individuals and as humanity, get what we need to grow and evolve. Accepting this helps us proceed positively with our lives, even if our circumstances are difficult due to external forces such as social injustice or getting born into a materially impoverished part of the world. Many factors, both internal and external, influence the ease or difficulty we encounter in the world; perhaps part of the script is even written in the stars.

Many courageous souls have gone beyond their expected destiny, and overcome extreme hardships, to become shining examples for us all. We may not be the sole creators of our lives; we may not be entirely at the helm of fate, but we have a powerful influence on our own fortunes. To a large degree, we make or break ourselves. A major factor in what we allow ourselves to experience depends upon how deserving we feel. A sense of deservedness, or self-worth—how good we feel about ourselves as a person—may well be a key element in our life.

Les Brown grew up a black man in a poor rural area of America who was labeled "educationally retarded." He went on to excel in his education, become a popular radio talk show host, and serve in the Ohio legislature. Brown now addresses groups and corporations all over America.

In contrast, I know of some upper middle-class children, raised in expensive neighborhoods where they attended very good schools followed by college, who nearly destroyed themselves in one way or another. A key factor involved their sense of self-worth. If we have self-worth in abundance, all else follows; if we don't have it, nothing else helps.

The Master Hurdle

We may feel as handsome or beautiful as a model or movie star; we may believe we possess a great intellect; we may come from a wealthy family, or develop the skills of an athlete; but unless we overcome feelings of unworthiness, our lives cannot work well or feel satisfying—because we won't let them.

I need to make a slight distinction here between self-esteem and self-worth: We can feel considerable self-esteem about specific qualities such as our appearance, our physical skills, or our intelligence. But until we come to unconditionally *like* ourselves as people, deep down inside—until we feel like a *good* person, *deserving* and *worthy* of success, abundance, peace, happiness, love, we do one of two things:

1. We *sabotage our efforts* or otherwise avoid fulfillment. We choose or create low-paying jobs, troubled relationships, and money problems (no matter how much we make). We sabotage ourselves by taking drugs, by getting injured or sick, by running away, or by engaging in other behaviors that undermine our success or happiness.
2. We *have trouble receiving* energy, praise, or having people serve us. If we do become successful, we usually feel uncomfortable with it or unable to enjoy it; therefore, we may cycle back to sabotaging ourselves and our relationships, and our jobs seem to self-destruct before our eyes.

We don't do these things consciously. Our Conscious Self may feel excited about opportunities and desire success. However, since feelings of unworthiness date back to our childhood programming, our Basic Self feels the discomfort and creates the sabotage, leaving everyone concerned, including ourselves, wondering why we act the way we do: "I don't understand that kid; he's a great athlete, but he keeps screwing up." "Brenda is highly intelligent, Mrs. Somers—she just isn't achieving up to her abilities."

The Spectrum of Self-Worth

Of course, only a few of our lives fit any classic examples. Most of us consciously try to make all areas of our lives work better. But to the degree we lack self-worth, we limit, avoid, or subtly sabotage our own success—or find ourselves unable to fully enjoy it if we do achieve it.

If I asked, "Do you feel worthy of a life of abundance and peace?," you might answer, "Sure!" But if I asked your Basic Self, it might have a very different answer. Our Conscious Self—the tip of the iceberg—cannot know or tell the whole truth, because it remains unaware of the deeper motives that lie below the waterline. We set our own limits of self-worth; if life gets too good, we may start feeling unworthy: I've never felt I deserved my partner; he/she is just too good for me.

Marilyn Monroe couldn't tolerate the adulation and success that came to her, and tragically cut her life short. Some child actors and actresses with low self-worth face the serious jeopardy of sabotaging themselves because of the discomfort and dissonance set up by sudden wealth and adulation. Most lottery winners go through considerable stress when they win large sums of money ("But we didn't do anything for this," their Basic Selves say), and many lose it all a short time later.

The Only Way to Know

Suppose, as an exercise, we quantify how deserving we feel of all the best that life has to offer—and rate that on a scale of one to one hundred. If we're totally honest with ourselves and tune into our deepest feelings, and give ourselves less than one hundred, we have work to do on our sense of self-worth. Even if our Conscious Self responds, "One hundred, of course," the real measure of our self-worth lies with our Basic Self. Perhaps the only way to know how worthy we feel would be to *examine what our life looks like now, for it serves as a mirror of how much we feel we deserve*—a more honest indicator than what we *think* we deserve.

◆

Key Questions of Worthiness

1. Ask yourself the following questions:
   - Do you feel you have to do more, give more, or work harder to deserve or justify your existence?
   - Do you have an easier time giving than receiving?
   - Does getting presents or attention or appreciation or applause make you feel awkward?
   - When something good happens, do you say, "This can't last" and wait for the other shoe to fall?
   - Do you get sick or injured relatively often, or otherwise sabotage your efforts? (Not every illness or injury is self-sabotage!)
   - When you have money, does it "burn a hole in your pocket"? Does money seem hard to acquire?
   - Do you make "bad" choices and do things the "hard way"?
2. If your response to any or all of these questions is affirmative, then the hurdle of low self-worth remains in your path.

◆

The Irony of Worthiness

Those of us who carry the most light—those with the *highest* ideals, the highest vision, the highest standards—often have the *lowest* sense of self-worth, because we measure ourselves against our high standards and find our behavior and our performance lacking. As the sunlight of heightened awareness passes directly over the dark well of our psyches, we see our negativity and fear. On the other hand, people with low standards, who lack this level of vision or sensitivity, don't have so much to measure up to, and they seem to manifest more self-esteem than those of us who are more awake and aware!

The irony, here, is that those of us actually traveling the warrior's path—those of us who are opening our eyes to see our foibles and shortcomings—sometimes have the hardest time recognizing ourselves as peaceful warriors.

In recent years, I've worked consciously with my own self-worth issues. Among other things, I've placed an index card where I can see it every day. On that card, I've written a message that greets me every morning: *"How good can I stand it today?"* However good we "can stand it" is how good we'll get it.

Origins of Self-Worth

Our sense of self-worth begins to develop almost as soon as our sense of self. Later on, in childhood, as we become socialized, the scales of our internal sense of justice form, and start tilting one way or the other.

As young children, we learn to treat ourselves as others treat us. If our parents show us love, especially in the earliest stages of infancy—touching us, cooing at us, holding us, and *paying attention to us*—we feel good about ourselves and our bodies; we feel intrinsically valuable and worthy of attention and loving touch.

Later, as we become more verbal, if our parents praise us, forgive us, and let us know we are "good" children, we come to feel good about ourselves *not because of how we act or what we do, but because of who we are.* This is probably the greatest gift my parents ever gave me.

When we feel good about ourselves, we naturally feel open to the opportunities life presents—optimistic, ready, and willing to get what we want in life; in fact, it would never occur to us to do anything less.

The Inner Judge

Something happens, however, usually between four and ten years of age, that interferes with this pattern. As we get older, the unconditional cuddling gives way to our social training. Our parents and others in our environment begin to *reward* us for "good" behavior and *punish* us for "bad" behavior. Primary rewards can include attention, approval, affection, and praise; secondary gains include special privileges and material gifts. Primary punishments include the withdrawal of rewards (the carrot) and even physical pain (the stick).

Through these subtle or gross rewards and punishments, and accompanying verbal cues ("You are a good boy/girl." "That was wrong!"), we develop a fundamental *moral code* that may differ from culture to culture but almost always exists in one form or another.

In fact, we learn two deeply embedded rules:

1. It's better to be good than bad.
2. Good boys/girls (behaviors) get rewards; bad boys/girls (behaviors) get punished.

From these two rules, we begin to form a sense of ourselves as (relatively) good or bad, based on our own internalized standards and how we measure up.

We have all acted badly—made mistakes or misbehaved— at times in our lives. Even when our behaviors have met with approval, we know we have had thousands of "bad" thoughts— mean, petty, antisocial, or even cruel fantasies. Only some of these misbehaviors or "bad" thoughts were discovered and punished. However, none of these "transgressions" escaped the notice of our own inner judge.

When our parents or teachers don't punish us for all our "bad" thoughts and actions, we tend to spend the rest of our lives punishing ourselves out of guilt. Compounding the problem, many of us never learned to separate our mistakes or behaviors from ourselves, so instead of the sense, "I've behaved badly," we came to believe subconsciously, "I'm a bad *person* and deserve not rewards but punishments."

When our Basic Self is troubled by a deep sense of guilt and unworthiness, it punishes us through illness, accidents, failures (big dramatic ones, or strings of little ones), or other forms of self-sabotage (such as selecting a business partner who robs us, choosing an incompatible marriage partner, and so on). We make these "choices" at the subconscious level.

Those of us who have many accidents or chronic failures, then, are probably trying to balance out our self-perceived scorecard, acting out of low self-worth. "Surely we must know better than to repeat all that pain," we say. But we don't know better; that's just it. In a few cases, after serious injuries or illnesses, some of us even appear to manifest a kind of serenity in spite of our maladies; we feel we have finally been "sufficiently punished" for the "sins" in our own minds.

Healing the Past

By working with our Basic Self to regain or uplift our sense of self-worth, and by coming to love and accept ourselves at the subconscious level, we see our life improve and grow easier; we get "luckier," and new opportunities suddenly appear.

The path of the peaceful warrior may sometimes embrace work with a professional therapist, who, over time, can help us search back through the pages of childhood, understand the seeds of our present level of self-worth, and make skillful interventions to heal the wounds from our past.

Visualizations to generate self-compassion can help us begin the healing process and reprogram our subconscious as we offer our inner child—a powerful image of our Basic Self— the love and forgiveness we all deserve.

Healing the Past

1. Using all of your senses, imagine yourself as a young child.
2. As you do so, feel love, empathy, and compassion for your young self, who faces childhood confusion and fears.
3. Remember a time when you felt guilty for misbehaving, whether or not you were punished.
4. Allow this incident to play out in the theater of your mind, from a place of deep understanding and compassion.
5. Visualize your adult self with your child self, comforting your child self and explaining that he or she made a mistake, but that he/she is *good* deep down inside. Forgive your child self.
6. Now *replay* that same incident, but this time, allow your young self to *change* the perceived mistake or misbehavior – to make good in some way – returning what was taken, telling the truth, confessing and being forgiven. See the other people in the scene also forgiving your child self. *Feel* the love, and the relief.
7. Say good-bye to your child of the past with a hug that says, You have value and goodness, and you deserve to be happy.

Forgiving Our Shadows

The worst prison for our psyches, a dank hole of misery, is a feeling of unworthiness, of self-anger or self-hatred. "Bad" people don't go to hell; they are already *in* hell; that's why they act so badly. I deeply believe that people can't cause more suffering than they, themselves, already feel inside. Only disturbed people end up disturbing others.

The criminals in our society tend to reflect in exaggerated form our own shadow sides. As morally and emotionally satisfying as it may feel to shake our heads and condemn those who commit particularly violent or cruel crimes, we need to remind ourselves that it was a lack of love and self-worth that helped create that criminal in the first place. Who needs love more?

Love doesn't mean allowing criminals to continue acts that hurt others and increase their own benumbed suffering. We absolutely must stop them from further offenses, but at the same time, no matter how awful or unrepentant their personalities, we need to love the souls beneath. Once we forgive the shadows in others and in ourselves, we can truly be of service, out of a deep sense of self-worth.

The Method of Service

We know that service—helping others, doing volunteer work, or just showing a caring heart—represents goodness, morality, and kindness. Service can also change our lives.

Serving others offers one of the best ways to allow our Basic Self to balance out the scorecard of past transgressions and guilt. Because self and world mirror one another, by showing love for others, we cannot help but love ourselves more. Service presents the royal path to self-worth; through self-worth, we open a way to inner peace, happiness, and a feeling of Spirit.

A woman who called herself Peace Pilgrim walked across every state and province in the United States and Canada seven times. She carried no money, and ate only food that was offered. She didn't ask for shelter unless that, too, was offered. She walked prayerfully, speaking of world peace and inner peace:

> *Out of a very deep seeking for a meaningful way of life, after having walked all one night through the woods . . . , I felt a complete willingness, without any reservations, to . . . dedicate my life to service. I tell you, it's a point of no return.*
>
> *And so, I went into the second phase of my life: I began to give what I could, instead of to get what I*

could, and I entered a new and wonderful world. My
life began to become meaningful. I attained the great
blessing of good health; I haven't had a cold or head-
ache since. From then on, I have known that my life-
work would be work for peace . . . peace among na-
tions, peace among groups, peace among individuals,
and the very, very important inner peace.

For the Love of a Pet

In several prisons, psychologists have studied records of
the most violent, incorrigible prisoners—repeat offenders—
and found that not a single one had ever been allowed, as
a child, to have a pet, and the responsibility of taking care
of a living being.

Insightful wardens allowed an experiment in which these
same inmates were allowed to adopt a pet rabbit, bird, rat,
hamster, cat, or small dog. The results were positive, even
dramatic: Previously violent inmates grew calmer and stopped
creating as much trouble for themselves or others. Perhaps,
the study concluded, being able to show concern and caring,
to have a *service* relationship with a small creature, made a
real difference. Taking care of a pet helped these inmates feel
better about themselves, and therefore broke the cycle of violence and frustration.

Opportunities for Service

True service isn't an act, but an attitude. We can do
things for other people with all kinds of self-serving motives.
True service, however, stems from a feeling of humility, gratitude, and the essential recognition that we are in this together.
Love entails looking beneath the personality and realizing that
we are all, as Plato said, "fighting a hard battle." Service is love
in action—as simple as a friendly smile or nod to a stranger—or
as all-embracing as the life of Peace Pilgrim or Mother Teresa.

Service can take many forms, including

- helping out in hospitals;
- visiting homes for the elderly;
- working with youth;
- participating in Big Brothers/Sisters;
- staffing a suicide prevention hotline;
- staffing a teen runaway hotline;
- decorating a homeless shelter;
- teaching children something you're good at;
- working with an organization to help protect the environment.

Anytime we go out of our way to do something for someone else (as long as we feel good about doing it), we also do something for ourselves.

Taking Charge of Our Life

If we don't feel worthy of success, love, or abundance, no matter what opportunities appear we can't let ourselves have these blessings or enjoy them; our Basic Self finds ways to keep life difficult. But since this process takes place subconsciously, we don't realize we are working hard at it; instead, we feel frustrated and wonder why these "bad" things "happen to us."

No matter what methods we've put into practice from this book, no matter what principles we understand, we need to elevate our sense of self-worth if we want our life to improve. Armed with the identity of the master culprit, we can take the steps to eliminate self-destructive patterns and the false guilts that generate them.

The feeling of unworthiness, along with fear, self-doubt, and insecurity, arises from the dark force inside us with which every peaceful warrior must do battle; it remains one of our most deceptive adversaries because it wears the cloak of a judge.

The universal misunderstanding of "goodness" and "badness," and of "moral rules," "crime and punishment," and imagined "sins," has put dark clouds over our lives. Now, with the power of understanding, we have an opportunity to undermine this false belief system. At the very least, we can begin to realize that maybe we are far more deserving than we thought, and maybe we can blow those dark clouds right out of the sky.

Compassion

Most of us can understand that our parents did their best in raising us. Whether they were kind or cruel, enlightened or ignorant—and even if they made a lot of mistakes—they still did the very best they could *within the limits of their own blind spots, fears, and models of reality.*

Similarly, *we, too, have always done our best.* Knowing this, we can more easily find the ability to forgive ourselves for our imperfections. Not all of us, however, accept that we've done our best when we see our mistakes so clearly.

> *I'm not okay; you're not okay;*
> *and that's okay.*
> Virginia Satir

Perhaps in some absolute sense, we "could have done better," but with that thought we pave the road to misery. If we wake up one day with a throbbing headache, we may not do as well as the day before when we felt wonderful. *But both days we do the best we can with what we have to work with.* As we clear and balance our body, mind, and emotions, our "best" gets better all the time.

Self and World

We've all heard that it's good to love (or treat) our neighbor as we would love (treat) ourselves. Yet how can we follow the Golden Rule and love others unless we learn to love ourselves?

The better we feel about ourselves, the better we feel about the people around us. We want to live a healthier and longer life. We enjoy our own company and don't need constant distractions. Our thoughts and dreams run to more pleasant reveries instead of dark clouds.

As the feeling of unworthiness gives way to self-compassion, we can finally make use of books and trainings and experiences. Perhaps we can look back and see how many of us have made our life more difficult than it needed to be. But the past is gone; we can learn from it. The future awaits us; we can enjoy it.

Forgiveness

Those of us who believe that guilt keeps us on the "straight and narrow path" (defined by someone else's standards) might want to take another look: Modern psychology has amply demonstrated the pitfalls of guilt. Before we can forgive others, we need to forgive ourselves. Self-forgiveness helps break the old patterns and open the way for change.

I had the opportunity to meet with Gary, an old schoolmate who had sunk to the depths of self-hatred after beating his wife and battering his children. We began to talk about the vicious cycle of repeated offenses; Gary's guilt and self-loathing grew, along with his frustration, which started the cycle all over again. I referred Gary to a good psychotherapist, who helped him understand how he had developed this pattern in childhood in the context of a father who had abused both him and his mother. By opening the space for him to forgive himself, the therapist guided Gary in reclaiming the self-worth and self-respect that allowed him to clear the frustrations that had driven him to violence. (Our Basic Self learns to behave as our parents did, not as they said.)

Judgments we place on ourselves only hold negative patterns in place. The following exercise provides a simple, straightforward psychophysical means to release our self-judgments, offering profound healing to our Basic Self.

◆

Releasing Self-Judgments

1. Close your eyes for a few moments and breathe slowly into your belly.
2. Let your awareness drift to any past action or inaction you regret.
3. Say aloud or silently, "I release all judgments I've placed on myself for [whatever you wish to forgive]."
4. As you do this, inhale deeply; then, as you exhale, imagine that you are breathing out the judgments. Don't focus on the specific judgments; just *feel* yourself releasing them to Spirit.

◆

Along with practicing self-forgiveness, we can extend our circle of healing by developing the humility to ask forgiveness of others. When I've gotten so involved with my work that I act angry if one of my daughters interrupts me, I later apologize and ask her if she will forgive me. In most cases I feel an immediate warm glow envelop us both as she smiles and says yes. Simple acts of humility can help us to forgive others and ourselves.

Because the people close to us sometimes mirror our own unrecognized patterns, the actions that bother us the most in others may point to similar but unrecognized behaviors in ourselves. Forgiving others also helps us forgive ourselves of our own hidden self-judgments.

We Deserve Life

Again, *the only way to really know how deserving we actually feel is by looking at how our life is going right now.* The goodness we have allowed into our life directly reflects our level of self-worth. The more deserving we feel, the more blessings come our way, because our Basic Self, feeling good about itself, tends to put us in the right place at the right time.

How much needless suffering do we have to go through before the scoreboard is even? How many real or imagined "sins" do we have to punish ourselves for before we'll let ourselves enjoy life's riches—a happy home life, financial security, health, a meaningful life? What will we choose? What will we settle for? How *good* can we stand it?

Only when the power of unconditional self-worth reaches our Basic Self and we can say from those depths, "*I deserve better!*," do we get better—whether in our relationships, work, or finances. Self-worth cuts through any obstacle like a warrior's sword, clearing the way for a new life.

12

Good Excuses

*The great dividing line
between success and failure
can be expressed in five words:
I did not have time.*
Anonymous

The Limits of Reason

Our Conscious Self serves us with its ability to form logical premises and to apply rational thought, good judgment, and sound sense—with its ability to *reason*. Like anything else, however, logic and reason present both benefits and liabilities. When reason urges us to hold in our feelings, go with the odds, avoid all risks, and stay with the familiar, it's time to take another look. Reason has survival value, but when overused at the expense of our intuition, feeling, and spirit, reason cuts us off from discovering our full potential. Based on the reason and logic of their times, here's what some of the experts said:

Who the hell wants to hear actors talk?
Harry Warner, Warner Bros., 1927

*What use could the company make
of an electrical toy?*
Western Union, on rejecting the rights to the telephone, 1878

*Everything that can be invented
has already been invented.*
Charles Duell, Director, U.S. Patent Office, 1899

238

Heavier-than-air flying machines are impossible.
Lord Kelvin, President, Royal Society, 1895

There is not the slightest indication
that we will ever obtain nuclear energy;
the atom would have to be shattered at will.
Albert Einstein, 1932

I propose to undermine reason, or at least to take it off its pedestal. As we explore the limits of reason and the liabilities of logic, we can take a fresh look at the reasonable excuses we offer for not creating the best possible lives for ourselves. Life gives us plenty of "good" reasons for not getting what we want. Most people accept these excuses because they sound so *reasonable.*

"Good" reasons and "sound" excuses bring paralyzing inertia to our every impulse to go beyond ourselves. Reason would have told Christopher Columbus to stay home by a comfortable fire instead of risking his crews, his ships, and his life seeking land on the other side of the sea. Before the American Civil War, if Harriet Tubman had listened to reason after she escaped to the North, she would not have risked her life going back to the South again and again to help free others.

Every time we decide not to try, not to achieve, not to better ourselves, we have "good" reasons: "I don't even have a high school diploma; how can I even dream of having my own company someday?" "I want to teach martial arts, but I'm not well known enough; you have to be a champion to make a success of it." "I'd like to do healing work, but I see so many people doing bodywork and healing; I'd never be able to attract enough people to make a living at it." "I don't have enough money." "I'm not good-looking enough . . . tall enough . . . smart enough." "I lack experience." "There's too much competition." "You have to know somebody." "The odds of success are one in a million."

I don't want to know the odds!

Han Solo (to R2D2), in *Star Wars*

Twenty-one major corporations rejected Chester Carlson's vision of a device he called a Xerox machine. Twenty-eight publishers rejected Theodor Geisel's first children's book; he's also known as Dr. Seuss. Irving Stone's first historical novel was rejected seventeen times before he found a new editor.

These people didn't give up. They knew that *nothing is less important in life than the score at halftime.* They knew that we never really fail; we just quit trying.

The person with a new idea is a crank
until the idea succeeds.

Mark Twain

Playing Roles in the Theater of Life

Most of us move along, day to day, putting one foot in front of the other, doing what is expected of us—all the while never realizing that we are crossing a great stage, making entrances and exits, playing roles in the theater of life. When this realization dawns bright enough, we also realize that we can *change* roles, that we can play any role we like. Can you imagine being in a theater production and having to play the same role *your entire life?* We've forgotten the great reminder:

All the world's a stage,
And all the men and women merely players:
They have their exits and their entrances;
And one man in his time plays many parts . . .

William Shakespeare

Many of us have accepted the role and status of a bit player in our life; our spouse, our boss, our children, or our friends play producer and director. This makes no sense, because *it's our own play.* Each of us has controlling interest in our own theater production; each of us is entitled to a starring role. We never have to be bit players or victims again.

---◆---

Giving Yourself a Promotion

1. Consider the possibility that your life is a kind of stage production and that you can play a variety of roles at will, take your own authority, and manage the production.
2. If you don't like the script or story you're in, become the playwright and write a new script.
3. If the present cast of characters doesn't work for you, then take the job of casting director and hire a new cast.
4. You can be manager, producer, star, writer, and director of the play of your life. Who is better suited? You never have to take a bit part again.

---◆---

I once expressed the above ideas to a group at one of my seminars. People nodded and seemed to feel it made sense. I could tell that it had only sunk in deeply for a few people, but I had planted some seeds that would sprout later.

Sure enough, about six weeks later, a woman called me and said, "Dan, this is Mary Ann—I was in your training—and I just got it!"

"Got what?" I asked, curious.

"Remember that talk you gave—about life being our own stage production and how we could be the playwright and the director and—"

"Oh, that talk. Yes, I remember."

Sounding elated, she told me, "My husband came home last evening after work and reminded me that we were supposed to go to his boss's house for dinner. He asked me why I wasn't dressed to go out. 'I'd rather stay home,' I told him. 'I don't really enjoy visiting with your boss. You have a good time, honey; I'll just stay home and read this evening.'"

"Come *on*, Mary Ann," he told her. "This is the *boss* we're talking about, and he wants both of us there. Now come on, get dressed; we're late! We've got to go."

"No, we don't," she said. "I just rewrote the script; you're the one who's late, darling."

Mary Ann realized that it really was her production after all. She wasn't buying into anyone else's ideas about what she "had" to do. She took control of the theater of her own life. And if we don't take control of our own life, someone else will.

Getting What We Want

Living in physical bodies, we humans operate within the bounds of natural laws; yet, our destiny seems tied to expanding our limits. Human history reveals a string of "impossible" achievements, from the flight at Kittyhawk to Roger Bannister's four-minute mile. That we developed from single-celled organisms swimming in a primeval sea seems impossible to start with! This world abounds with miracles; if we can't find one when we need it, we can create one.

We cannot fly like birds, so we invented flying machines; we cannot swim like fish, but with submarines we can dive deeper and swim faster and farther than almost any fish in the ocean. As a species, we do what we can dream; this is equally true of the individual. We have more ability to shape our life and our reality than we imagine.

Imagination, the bridge to clairvoyant sight, opens the realms of exploration described by mystics and shamans. Every positive thought is a prayer, and every prayer is answered. By focusing on what we want, and by sowing the seeds in our imagination, we reap the harvest, both material and spiritual.

When We Wish Upon a Star

We always get what we want at the deepest levels, but not necessarily what the Conscious Self asks for. If we get a sprained ankle or the flu, we may think, I didn't want this. But since the Basic Self predominates in determining what people, circumstances, and situations enter our personal sphere, the only sure means of knowing what we have wanted lies in seeing what we have.

We have the option of working with our Basic Self through visualizations, prayer, clear intention, and *action* to change what we want at the deepest levels of our being.

Sometimes, when we wish or pray for something and it doesn't happen, we may believe that God didn't answer our prayers. But God always answers our prayers; it's just that sometimes the answer is no. Perhaps what we were asking for came from the Conscious Self's fear-based desires and attachments rather than from a commitment to growth and learning, which often entails letting go. True prayer is done with faith, without attachment to outcomes, with the sense, "Thy will be done."

The Conscious Self sometimes asks for things without considering whether they serve our highest good. Some years ago, I met Arthur, who used to be a professional taxi driver. In his younger years driving a cab, he didn't have much money and dreamed of having a million dollars. He prayed for it and thought about it constantly. That million in cold cash seemed like his ticket to happiness. He felt that if he focused on it long enough and hard enough, he would get it and all his dreams would come true. Such focus is a powerful thing; the universe responds to strong intention, and Arthur finally did get his million: A truck collided with his taxi, and he won a 1.6 million–dollar settlement in compensation for permanently losing the use of his arms and legs. *When we ask for something, we do well to add, "If it serves my highest good and learning."*

Do We Really Want
What We Think We Want?

The first step in getting what we want involves deciding whether we *really* want it. As Socrates told me, "Everyone wants things, but do you want it enough to do what's necessary to get it? Everything costs—time, energy, money, life— you can get it if you're willing to pay for it. Wisdom doesn't come cheaply; strength must be earned; even inner peace has a price."

Wanting to be good, to "do right," to please others, to gain approval and affection, we have been trained in the school of denial, taught to suppress what we really want to do, and to see the logic and reason in doing what others want us to do.

Thus, most of us suffer a near universal malaise; we have difficulty figuring out the difference between what we *really* want to do, and what we *think* we should want, or should do.

For example, Alan told me that more than anything he wanted a life partner. I asked how much time had passed since he'd had a long-term relationship. "About five years," he replied.

"So you feel kind of lonely?" I asked.

"Yes."

I then pointed out that, in spite of his feeling of loneliness, he, a handsome athlete, had managed to stay out of a relationship for five years—with his qualities, that must have taken some doing!—and I suggested that perhaps at a deeper (Basic Self) level, he valued his independence more than a relationship.

He said he'd think about it. He called me a few months later and said he had realized some things about his independent nature and worked out a compromise: He would find a partner who also felt a strong need for independence. Alan is now happily, and independently, married.

As in Alan's case, our lives improve when we contact our heart's desire—when we allow ourselves to dream and to remember what makes us feel excited. That's a sign from our Basic Self that we've struck gold. If we remain out of touch with our innermost desires, we have trouble deciding which direction to go, and every fork in the path up the mountain presents a crisis of decision-making agony.

If we *really* want something, we will do whatever we need to do in order to get it. By definition, if we don't do the necessary work, then we don't *really* want it enough to do what is necessary to achieve it; we only *think* we want it. Because we don't really want it, then not getting it poses no real problem, even though this may leave our Conscious Self feeling unsatisfied.

◆

Finding Your Heart's Desire

1. First, *What do you most want, right now, in your life?*
2. Ask not only your Conscious Self (which tells you what you "should" want); also ask your Basic Self. To do this, visualize what you want and see how your body feels. Ask yourself the following questions:
   * Any mixed feelings?
   * Does it truly excite you?
   * Do you feel *fully* deserving of having it?
   * How do you know you don't already have it?
   * How will you know when you have it?
   * What will happen when you have it? How will you feel?
   * What stops you from having it?

◆

Joy of the Quest

If happiness depended upon getting what we want, we'd only be happy a relatively brief time; we spend most of our time on the quest and only a small amount of time achieving our goals (before we pick more).

Like the golfer who enjoyed hitting the ball but grumbled all through the walk, many of us have never learned to enjoy the in-between. Until we stop treating our moments as ordinary, most of life lies in the realm of in-between. Our journey can be as happy and fulfilling as our arrival. Many passengers on the Orient Express didn't really need to go to Istanbul; they were just along for the elegant ride.

Getting there may be *more* than half the fun. I recall an old Chinese curse: "May you reach your goals." Then there's the Western saying: "Be careful about what you want; you might get it." Many astronauts faced bouts of depression when they returned to Earth. What they had worked so long and hard for finally came. "How do we top that one?" they asked.

Other times, when a dream becomes reality, the reality doesn't always match the dreams. Every cloud has a silver lining, but the opposite also holds true. From what I've read, quiz show winners and those who get big lottery jackpots often end up with a whole new set of problems and stresses; their newfound fortunes don't make them as happy as they had imagined.

The personal joy I've found in striving for goals came from the intensity of the quest. Without goals, we never make the journey; we just wander aimlessly. If we don't know where we're headed, it's hard to get anywhere. On the other hand, if we don't care where we are, we're never lost. In recent years, I've let go of attachment to outcomes. I just do my best, sow seeds, and see what happens, trusting whatever happens as a perfect part of my process. I've achieved most of my goals, but I've generally found more pleasure in the journey than in the arrival.

No Matter What Excuses, The Consequences Remain

Socrates once told me, "It's better to do what you need to do than not to do it and have a good reason for not doing it." When I finally figured out what he'd said—he refused to repeat himself—I realized he was right. We can always come up with a good excuse for not doing something. *But when the smoke clears and the task remains undone, what good are our excuses?*

Once, just before final exams, I didn't show up to gymnastics practice for two weeks. When I finally came into the gym, I started to tell the coach all the good reasons I had to miss practice, but he interrupted me and said, "Any excuse is good enough for me, Dan. What excuse is good enough for you?"

As it turned out, I did okay on the exams but lost the top spot on the team to my teammate Sid, who had showed up and trained a little every day. So even though I had a good *excuse* for missing practice, I missed the training time and reaped the consequences.

Most people don't get what they want because of good excuses. Through our actions, we can choose to be one of the many, or one of the few.

Excuses Large and Small

Once, while watching a gymnastics meet on television with Jon, a heavy-set friend, I heard him say to himself, "I'd give anything to be able to do a somersault."

"You could learn," I told him.

He thought I was joking. "You know I'm too heavy."

"You could lose the weight."

"Maybe, but I'm also stiff and out of shape."

"You could stretch, and get in shape."

"But I'm not strong enough."

"Ever heard of weights?"

He had no excuses left. I convinced him that he could achieve his wishes, even though the road to his goal might be longer than for someone already in good physical shape. It took Jon a year and a half, and in the process of his challenging journey, he found himself transformed—all for the love of a somersault.

Being a creative species, we humans come up with excellent excuses not to eat well, not to exercise, and so on. Fred says he would exercise "if only I had the time." Ed tells me, "if only exercise weren't so boring." Bert sighs, "if only I were more motivated," while Lucille laments, "if only I had someone to exercise with." Terry mourns, "if only I had more money to join a club or get some exercise machines." Patricia sighs, "if only I had more energy," while Mike complains, "if only exercise weren't so inconvenient."

Some of us wander up the path, winding and wavering, not getting very far because of a psychological defense strategy based on fear of failure that says, "If I don't really try, I can't really fail." True enough, but we can never fully succeed, either. Beware of the danger of relying on the fallback belief "I could have done it if I had *really* tried."

With very little effort, we can all find excuses and reasons to give up, but what would happen if we threw all the excuses away and leaped over that final hurdle?

A peaceful warrior's approach to daily life requires a willingness to put ourselves on the line, to stand by our choices for better or worse, to believe in ourselves when no one else will, and to accept the consequences of success or failure knowing we have followed through and done our best.

> *The credit belongs to the one*
> *who strives valiantly;*
> *who comes up short again and again;*
> *who knows great enthusiasm and great devotion;*
> *who spends himself in a worthy cause;*
> *and who, at the best, knows in the end*
> *the triumph of high achievement;*
> *and who, at worst, if he fails,*
> *at least fails while daring greatly,*
> *so that his place shall never be*
> *with those timid souls*
> *who know neither victory nor defeat.*
> Theodore Roosevelt

No Excuses Accepted Here

I'd like to tell you about a group of young people in the Washington, D.C., area who had many reasons they couldn't get what they wanted. They no longer had hopes or dreams. They no longer knew what they wanted—why want something you don't ever believe you can get?—they only knew what they *didn't* want. They didn't want "the Man" bothering them; they didn't want the pain they felt, or the frustration, or the low-life inferiority that had been dumped on them by what they perceived to be a hostile, uncaring world.

Most of these young people were black, along with a few Hispanics and a scattering of white kids who didn't have to deal as much with racial prejudice but who had a lot of other issues. Most of these teenagers were barely literate; most came from broken homes; some had been kicked out of school; a few of the young men and women were getting into crime— theft, vandalism, and, for the girls, prostitution. Many also took drugs.

Police and local government officials knew that these teenagers were "at risk"; balancing on the razor's edge, they could go either way. Enough funding was available to hire some social workers, a psychologist, and a coach. A sports program was started. It helped some, but the social workers had trouble achieving any kind of rapport. The teens demanded, "What do you know about *my* problems?"

Almost none of the youth could get a job, so they hung out on the streets; their lives looked pretty dim. Sometimes the social workers would say to one of these young guys, "Listen. You can make something of yourself! You've got your whole life ahead of you; you're strong, you're young—you could have a bright future." The youth would look at the social workers like they were crazy, and pull out all his excuses, which certainly sounded very convincing: "Oh, I have a bright future, huh? I'm black in a racist society, I can't read or write, and I've been kicked out of five schools."

The social workers would try to come back with something positive: "Yes, but—well, you can do it anyway . . . " This well-intentioned but empty encouragement fell on deaf ears. The words had no impact, because these kids had such *good excuses* for why they could never get what they wanted.

The local government contacted some associates of mine, who went in to work with these kids. We reached out to them in ways no one had before—offering an unusual kind of martial arts training to strengthen their Basic Selves, because as much bravado and bluff as they had on the outside, each of them had a frightened Basic Self, programmed for pain and self-loathing. The training provided a means to cultivate in them a deeper sense of self-trust, self-respect, confidence, and courage—seeding lessons about life in a way that felt practical and appealing to them.

We also went in with open hearts and bombarded these kids with love; we let them see the love we had for them, for their souls, even though some of their personalities weren't so hot. We helped them to see themselves in a new light and made sure they felt our caring, so they could begin to care a little for themselves.

We weren't reasonable; we didn't buy into all their "good" excuses; we didn't assume for a moment that they were "poor problem kids" or limited in any way. We told them we didn't care where they had been; we cared where they were going. And we started to see some changes stirring where no one had gotten through before.

Still, they held tightly to their excuses as most of us do—like shields. It wasn't going to do any good just to tell them their lives weren't written yet; all their negative beliefs and excuses and reasons were stuck too strongly for that. We had to give them some perspective.

So we told them a story about a young black girl from a very poor family in the rural South. Her father wasn't there; her mother had something like twelve children to take care of. This little girl had had a bad case of polio; her brothers and sisters had to wheel her around in a wheelbarrow or carry her. She wanted to walk more than anything in the world, and to run and play with them. But she couldn't even stand.

One day, her mother heard about a free medical clinic in the city and took her daughter there by wagon—a three-day trip on a rough and dusty road. The mother asked the physician, "Can you help my daughter?" He checked her over and said, "I think we can do something." So they cleaned her up and fit her for some leg braces and crutches.

When the mother saw her, she said, "Thank you, sir. But she doesn't want the braces; can you help her walk by herself? She wants to so badly."

The doctor said, "I'm afraid not, ma'am. She's had a bad case of polio and doesn't have enough muscle tissue left. She's not *ever* going to walk again by herself. This is the best we can do." These were powerful statements, coming from this doctor in his white coat. I'm sure he felt he had done his best; he just wanted to be realistic.

But the little girl's mother would not accept this, and neither could the little girl. They went back home, disappointed but determined; after all, the doctors could be wrong. Her mother started to massage the little girl's legs and pray over her, and give her some herbal soaks suggested by a neighbor; it was all she could do.

About six months later, the little girl's mother thought she saw some improvement, and she took her daughter all the way back to the clinic. "She seems stronger," the mother told the doctor.

A little irritated but sympathetic, the doctor checked her quickly and said, "No, ma'am—I told you—she's *not going to get better*. It's really best if you don't hold on to false hopes."

This almost crushed the little girl, and her mother, too. But still, they couldn't give up. They were completely *unreasonable*. They continued the massage and the prayer.

At the end of the story, we asked these teenagers from Washington, D.C., "Do you know why we tell you this story?

Because that little girl *did* learn to walk alone; in fact, she learned to run. She ran and she ran, until she could outrun *all* of her sisters and her brothers. In fact, that little girl learned to run faster than any woman on the planet; she won four gold medals at the 1960 Olympic Games. Her name is Wilma Rudolph."

We were met with silence. The youths just sat there, for a few moments, with nothing to say. After that true story, these ghetto kids just stared. Suddenly, their excuses—their reasons for not getting what they wanted—just didn't have the same impact: "I'm black; I've been in trouble with the law; I can't read or write." We talked; they repeated their excuses and their "Yeah, buts." We told them we were hard of hearing and deaf to excuses. We told them we didn't believe they couldn't read; we didn't believe they were lazy or dumb or any of the things others had told them.

Finally, these youngsters in Washington, D.C., didn't have any excuses left—not for us, not for themselves. Some started work-study programs; others got a Big Brother or Sister, or reconciled with family. We lost touch with some. Even those who stayed on the streets and slid downhill knew they were making a choice.

Maybe we ought to ask ourselves something: *If these teenagers, trying to climb out of very tough circumstances, didn't have any good excuses—what excuses do we have?*

Part V
The Expanded Life

Introduction

We've traversed some rocky terrain together in this book: In Part I, we laid foundations; in Part II, we faced the compulsions generated by our internal obstructions; in Part III, we covered specific practices to clear these obstructions in body, mind, and emotions; and in Part IV, we dealt with the major hurdles – our inner adversaries.

Those of us who have made it this far, through the difficult insights of earlier sections, can now enjoy the fruits of our labor as we climb farther and higher, reaching up into the domain of the Higher Self, exploring a peaceful warrior's vision of a more expanded, more loving, and happier approach to daily life.

13

Opening the Heart

Love is friendship that has caught fire.
It appears as quiet understanding,
trust, sharing, and forgiving.
Love remains loyal through good and bad.
It settles for less than perfection
and makes allowances for human weakness.
Love feels content with the present;
it hopes for the future;
it doesn't brood over the past.
Love includes the day in, day out, chronicle
of irritations, problems, and compromises;
the small disappointments, big victories,
and common goals.
If you have love in your life,
it can make up for a great many things you lack.
If you don't have it,
no matter what else you have,
it never feels enough.
Anonymous

Love, Language, and the Lies We Tell Ourselves

The word *love* may be the most battered, abused, and misused word in the English language. We have little trouble saying it, but more difficulty doing it, because so few of us *truly feel* it.

Most of the time, when we speak of love, we lie—even to ourselves. Only when our awareness resides *in the heart—*

above fear, sorrow, and anger—can we really feel or demonstrate the piercing, compassionate, open-hearted, energy of love. I mean this literally, not just poetically or metaphorically.

In learning to open our heart, we have to contend with our Conscious Self—separate and alone, a whirring computer that isn't, by nature, particularly loving. Our Basic Self knows love as physical contact—touch, cuddling, *making* love; it doesn't think or philosophize about love. Most of us, because of the obstructions we've explored, don't yet feel the love and energy of the Higher Self. But once we "see with the eyes of the heart," we can love others, and we can even love ourselves.

Until then, however, when we say, "I love you," we may mean "I feel a mixture of sexual attraction and admiration and awe," or "I feel great affection and sentiment," or "I feel I need you, and you make me feel more complete."

We feel one kind of love for our mates, another for our children, and yet another for our parents; all of these differ in kind or degree from the love we feel for our sisters, brothers, cousins, grandchildren, more distant relatives, friends, colleagues, and humanity at large.

The feelings we identify as "love" can change over time with regard to the same person. How many beautiful marriage ceremonies and declarations of eternal love end in feelings of resentment, anger, sorrow, or even fear? Where did the love go?

Love may have appeared for a brief time; we may have found a person whose total profile—appearance, personality, qualities—somehow lifted us for a time into the heart—until the obstructions below the heart pulled us back down. Falling out of love may have less to do with the other person and more to do with ourselves—with our own issues. We often look for someone else to pull us back up into the exalted space, only to find the pattern of withdrawal and self-protection repeating itself again and again.

We hear a lot of talk about love: "Love your neighbor

as you would yourself." "Love, and do what you will." "Love is the law." "Love is the Way." These are high and lofty ideals to strive for, but how do we translate such ideals into the everyday course of events? How do we show love in ways we can demonstrate easily, gracefully, and naturally, in the midst of daily life?

Little Things

Some things appear very big in the eyes of the world (owning our own home, two cars in the garage, money in the bank) and very small in the eyes of Spirit—not because there's anything wrong with them, but because they are things of the world that turn to ashes and to dust.

> *What you do may not seem important*
> *but it is very important that you do it.*
> Mahatma Gandhi

We can also do little things that appear very big in the eyes of Spirit—simple acts of altruism, of consideration, and of loving-kindness that might slip by unnoticed in the eyes of the world but that will shine like beacons when we someday look back and review our life. I can best describe these little things with some examples.

A Caring Note

Some years ago, my family and I ate at a local restaurant we'd been to many times before. On this particular evening, a new waitress was really scrambling; we found out that it was her second day, and one of the cooks had called in sick. The place was full, and she was on the verge of losing her composure. We ordered; she did okay with the order but made one mistake; she apologized, wiped her hair from her forehead, and ran the item back to the kitchen. I wouldn't call her charming that night, but she was hanging on.

When we finished eating, I left her a very big tip; I did this just to get her attention for the note—I like to put my money where my mouth is. On the note I wrote, "You were clearly having a tough time, tonight, but we could tell you were going all out—really doing your best—and we want you to know that we appreciated it." Those readers who have ever served as waiters or waitresses know what a note like that could mean on a tough night. Nowadays, I often leave notes of appreciation when my family and I eat out; I've also found that little notes can help uplift the spirits of postal workers or other people who often go unappreciated.

I don't wait around to see the person get the note, but a few times, when paying the check, a waiter or waitress has come up to me at the register. One waitress told me she had been feeling very discouraged and ready to quit; she had tears in her eyes and was obviously very moved, because of a simple note—a little thing.

It's Only Money

When I drive over the Golden Gate Bridge or other toll bridges in the area, I make it a habit to pay the toll for the car that pulls in behind me; I ask the toll booth attendant to wish that person a good day, and I wish the attendant a good day, too.

To me, strangers are friends I haven't met yet. When the people whose toll I paid reach the toll booth and learn that some *stranger* paid their toll, maybe the next time they look at a stranger, they might be more likely to give a friendly nod or strike up a conversation. Who knows, they may get such a kick out of the whole thing that they pay someone else's toll next time, *just because it feels good.*

If we happen to be on a tight budget or live in an area without toll bridges, we can have lots of fun putting money in people's expired parking meters—maybe helping them have a more pleasant day than if they found a ticket on their car window. Such an act says, "Hey, we're in this together; maybe you'll feed my meter next time" (but without expecting them to).

Anonymous Donations

Money itself is only a medium of exchange—pieces of printed paper and engraved metal. But when we give money away *anonymously*—with no strings attached, expecting no recognition—in sharing it selflessly with others, we give of our energy, our time, our labor, our love, and our life. The amount doesn't really matter; our Higher Selves and Basic Selves don't count the amount; they only note our loving sacrifice.

Making donations to people or organizations we feel good about, or sending a few dollars to someone we appreciate, celebrates our sense of abundance; it also makes a stronger impression on someone else's Basic Self because we are giving a tangible symbol of our caring and our love rather than just mouthing the words; in other words, we are putting our money where our heart is.

A Moment of Our Time

Many of us feel very busy, with no time to "waste" (read: no time to spend on something other than what we consider important). I've caught myself on numerous occasions telling my daughters that I didn't have time to play with them for a few minutes, and then accepting a call from a friend and talking for fifteen minutes about something *I* thought was important.

Giving our time and attention entails giving ourselves; it's a way of saying, "You, and your needs, are important to me." More recently, I've come to see that my children do understand when I feel busy; all they want might be one or two minutes of my time to tell me something or just to be with me. Rather than regret the past times I've refused, I turn these regrets into a resolve to set my priorities straight. Whenever people close to me want a little of my time, they get it.

These little things are among the most important spiritual work I do. They become part of my warrior's practice in the arena of daily life; they have taught me that every moment is an opportunity to create something positive.

Opening the Heart: Transcending Emotional Contraction

Love, like happiness, is a moment-to-moment state. Trying to remain loving or happy all the time is like trying to eat once and for all. From one moment to the next, our awareness either emanates from the heart or remains trapped in issues of subliminal fear, sorrow, and anger. Trusting that awareness heals, we can clear these obstructions moment to moment—recognizing and accepting them as part of our process, and then moving beyond them by applying one or more of the methods outlined here.

Opening the heart generates a deep and profound emotional healing of the entire psyche. As our awareness resides there, we feel a quality of happiness that transcends worry, fear, sorrow, anger, regret, or any of the parade of concerns that have preoccupied us. Even if our external lives don't change at all, our internal lives change instantly.

Opening our heart allows us to attain the highest levels of emotional health. In this loving state, we no longer help other people out of duty; we feel absolute joy in service; we love without caring whether we are loved in return. The practices I offer here are easy to integrate into daily life. They only require an act of conscious attention and intention; we have to *want* to love before we can practice love. Yet love is always within our immediate reach—as close to us as our own heart.

Ways to Open the Heart

The physical heart is our strongest muscle; it also functions as the core of our feeling dimension. Like any muscle, the heart grows stronger with use. *By creating a feeling connection between our heart and our voice, thought, touch, sight, and hearing, we instantly access the safest, most accessible method for opening our heart.* We create this feeling connection by allowing awareness to penetrate the heart. The moment this connection occurs, we contact the love of our Higher Self; we transcend fear, sorrow, and anger; and we heal ourselves and others.

The beauty of this process lies in its simplicity. We can practice the following five ways to open the heart anytime, anywhere, without other people even knowing we're doing it; yet they will *feel* it. In this practice, we don't merely put our mental attention *on* the heart; rather, we see and touch other people and the world *from* the heart.

◆

Feeling the Heart

1. Direct your attention to your nose or ears or feet or hands. To help you focus, you can move that part of your body and touch it; then stop moving it, remove your touch, and keep your attention there until you become more aware of that part of the body than any other.

2. Now, direct your attention to your heart by placing your right hand over it. You may notice a quality of attention you hadn't noticed with the other body part you touched – a quality of *feeling.*

3. Now, remove your hand and *just feel your heart.* Breathe, relax, and notice any emotions that come up. This act of feeling your heart is one of the deepest, most profound, and yet simplest spiritual practices of love.

◆

Having experienced feeling the heart, we can now practice the first means of opening the heart in the midst of daily
life.

The Resonant Heart

If we place two guitars next to each other and pluck the
"E" string of one guitar, the "E" string of the other guitar will
begin to vibrate as well. This principle is called sympathetic,
or harmonic, resonance. This phenomenon of acoustics also
works with the human voice: *If we speak from our mind, the
mind of the other person resonates; if we speak from our heart,
that person's heart resonates.*

Sometimes, we may choose to speak from the mind — to
explain a math problem, for example. To clarify the difference between the two ways of speaking, I'll describe an incident I experienced: Some years ago, before retiring for the
night, I checked on my little daughter. As I tucked her covers
in, I gazed down at her, and felt how much I loved her. I
wanted to tell her, but I didn't want to wake her, so I reminded
myself to tell her in the morning.

The next day I remembered my intention and told my
daughter I loved her. She heard me, but she didn't feel the
love — because in that moment, my awareness wasn't in my
heart as it had been the night before; my attention was in
my head as I *remembered* to tell her.

Nowadays, I don't even have to say the words "I love you,"
though I still do; I can just say, "How was school today?" or
"I like that outfit," but I speak from my heart, and so they
feel the love. Even the simplest words spoken from the heart
carry farther and deeper than the most eloquent poetry spoken
from the mind.

Speaking from our heart, we can even say, "I am in pain,"
or "I'd like you to do something different from what you are
doing," and our feeling expression will help to get our point
across without animosity.

♦

Speaking From the Heart

Practice speaking from your heart – to a friend or an adversary, to someone nearby or at a distance. Whether or not the person is present, the steps remain the same:

1. Feel your heart and allow yourself to feel the love there.
2. While *maintaining* that heart awareness and feeling, say, in a normal tone of voice, whatever words seem appropriate. The feeling matters more than the words.

♦

We can apply this simple practice whenever we'd like to uplift someone's spirit. Let's say we get to the bank just before closing time, and we have a lengthy transaction to make. The teller, seeming frazzled or weary, looks at us, then glances at the clock and sighs. Instead of getting defensive, suppose we notice that the teller has a nice-looking scarf or tie and we feel our heart and say, "You know, that scarf (tie) really looks good on you."

This compliment may seem a kind or thoughtful gesture, but we make such gestures all the time for a variety of motives. But it's our own openhearted feeling that provides the key to opening the heart of the teller or anyone else. This gesture of human kindness makes a subtle but important difference for others as we touch their lives. Again, the key to the process lies not just in opening our mouths, but in opening our hearts.

Such a simple act—such a little thing—also makes a difference for us, because the moment we speak from our heart we will almost certainly notice that we have transcended whatever fear, sorrow, or anger had been troubling us.

A Kind and Loving Thought

When we can't conveniently say something out loud— for example, when the recipient is absent, or ill, or in a coma, or busy, or angry with us and anything we say will only inflame the situation, we can practice *inner blessings*.

Offering an inner blessing is a simple process: We get in touch with our heart, and say *internally* (not aloud), "*I wish you well,*" or words to that effect. Inner speech helps heal those who feel upset, and it also serves to lift the spirits of those around us—perhaps a bus driver, or a clerk across the counter—without our saying something out loud that might sound odd from a stranger.

I had just begun practicing inner speech when an incident I already described occurred—the time Joy felt angry with me for getting home late with the car and I had only fueled the fire by suggesting she "watch her breathing." As Joy continued expressing herself, I remembered to feel my heart. Internally, I said, "I wish you well, I love you, God bless you." To my surprise and delight, Joy stopped speaking for a moment, then smiled, and said, "What are you doing?" Her anger and my fear vanished. Though the outcomes of inner speech are not always so dramatic, healing always takes place.

I enjoy inner speech because it's like an underground spiritual movement; we can go around placing blessings on people—planting seeds of love in people's energy fields, leaving them happier for having been in our presence. I hope this book will plant the seeds so that many of us can become "secret spiritual healers." Little things can make a big difference.

We can use inner speech with someone across the room or across the world. We can use it with friends or adversaries. It can be *especially* powerful with adversaries or those who annoy us. We don't have to be feeling profound love for the person we "bless." For example, as I drove up a freeway on-ramp, a man in a souped-up car sped by me; apparently thinking I was driving too slowly, he made an "obscene" gesture as he passed. The lanes converged, so he almost cut me off and I had to swerve.

My first impulse was anger—a natural reaction—but I remembered my practice and felt my heart. The moment I did so, I realized: "There goes a human being, like me. There goes someone who is suffering as I've suffered; someone who, like me, will lose loved ones someday. There goes a schoolmate on planet Earth who is having a bad day."

This all happened in an instant; then I could honestly get in touch with my heart and say, "I wish you well; God bless you." I didn't have to repress or deny my initial anger; I transcended it, for in feeling the heart we rise above emotional contractions.

Take an opportunity to practice this very simple exercise in opening the heart. Select as many people as you wish, one at a time—a friend, an intimate, a parent, a stranger, an adversary (an ex-spouse will do very well).

---◆---

An Inner Blessing

1. Picture the person you want to bless (if not physically present).
2. Remember the line "There goes a human being like me . . . " and feel your heart.
3. Coming from the heart, say internally, while looking at (or visualizing) the person, "I wish you well."
4. Feel whatever comes up.

---◆---

Enjoy the surprise if the people you contact in this way telephone you soon after "out of the blue," say they were thinking about you, or show some other sign of contact or reconciliation. Even if nothing obvious happens, know that you have practiced a very real act of loving-kindness. Inner speech can also enhance the spirit and effectiveness of any volunteer or service work we may offer.

Speaking from the heart and inner speech are always available to us; we can practice them any time—at work or at home. We could all use loving-kindness, and we can all give it.

Spiritual Senses

When we connect the three primary senses of sight, touch, and hearing to our heart, subtle but magical things happen, all of which open heart channels to our Higher Self.

Spiritual Touch

Touch is the first and most primal of all senses because it provides contact. Young animals who receive no touch often grow depressed, stop eating, and die. The same thing can happen with humans (Basic Selves, like children, have many qualities in common with animals).

Shaking hands or other socially acceptable forms of skin-to-skin contact stem from this universal need, and open our Basic Selves to one another in ways that words cannot touch. While we all need and deserve privacy and a sense of space, we also can "get through" to others more powerfully if we make a physical connection. Using touch in addition to speaking from our heart can double the impact.

Clearly, touch is more appropriate at some times and places than at others. (Refrain from practicing spiritual touch with a stranger on an empty subway train!) When it feels right, however, even a slight touch on the arm, connected with heart feeling, reminds our Basic Self that love and safety and caring exist in the world.

Touching the Heart

1. Simply feel your heart.
2. Touch another person in an appropriate way, such as a gentle pat on the back or a light touch on the arm.
3. Combining spiritual touch with inner speech or speaking from the heart enhances the effect of both.

Opening the Windows of the Soul

We all appreciate the sense of sight. But we may forget that while we seem to look out through our eyes, they are also receptive. We don't just see out; others see in, if we let them. The eyes have rightly been called the "windows of the soul." Most of us, however, don't really open our eyes; in fact, we have signs of strain and tension around them.

Spiritual sight, in practice, entails feeling our hearts and *letting other people "see" our hearts through our eyes.* In other words, by keeping our eyes open, relaxed, and receptive, we let others see the love we feel for them as human beings.

In this practice, we don't project anything out of our eyes; we simply let others look *inside* as we stay aware of our heart. Even if our eye contact lasts no more than a split second, the heart message is there. And the moment we let others see our hearts through our eyes, the healing happens.

———————————◆———————————

Spiritual Sight

1. At your next opportunity, make eye contact with someone nearby. You've probably done this many times before even though many of us have issues about eye contact.
2. Feel your heart and remain aware of it while your eyes make contact with that person's eyes.
3. As the person glances or looks into your eyes, feel as if your eyes are receptive as you continue to feel your heart.

———————————◆———————————

Spiritual Hearing

Epictetus, a Greek sage, reminded us, "Nature has given to us one tongue, but two ears, that we may hear from others twice as much as we speak." Often, when we listen to someone, even if we are a good listener, we spend part of the time thinking about something else, or about something we can tell them that may be helpful.

Using spiritual hearing, instead of focusing on our mind, or thinking of what we're going to say next, we place our awareness in our heart and connect that heart feeling to our ears. Like the heart, the ears are receptive, and miracles can happen when we *just listen.*

Because Basic Selves are in contact, and because our Higher Self communicates to us *through* our Basic Self— through our feelings and intuitions—if we listen with our heart as a friend describes a problem, even if we say nothing our friend will often come up with the same "answer" we might have suggested.

◆

Listening From the Heart

1. The next time someone talks with you, especially your children or someone else close to you, notice if you tend to space out or go on automatic pilot and anticipate what you think that person wants to say – and start formulating an answer.
2. *Stop thinking.*
3. Remain aware of your ears, and listen from your heart.
4. Just listen, *feel,* and give that person your full attention, as if you had all the time in the world. Treat what that person says as vitally important.

◆

Just by listening deeply
we alleviate pain and suffering.
Buddhist saying

Uses and Misuses

These conscious acts of kindness—these deceptively simple means to open the heart, heal the emotions, and connect with our Higher Self—send out ripples of caring that continue to grow as they expand into the world of human relations. Like any tool or method, however, they can be misused. The Conscious Self tends to take in whatever information it learns, compartmentalize it, and apply it as a mental technique to get results. Like the rest of humankind, those of us practicing the peaceful warrior's way need to subordinate our minds to our hearts if we are to evolve into our full potential.

Salespeople who temporarily forget their sense of ethics—who may not have their clients' best interest in mind but simply want to make a commission—sometimes use the techniques of touching their clients, listening intently, or making good eye contact. If these salespeople are dealing with security or "survival" issues and trying to use these tools to manipulate us for their own ends, our Basic Self will know it very quickly; we will sense the absence of the heart.

On the other hand, one of the most spiritual people I know works as an insurance salesman, financial planner, and stockbroker. Lew uses all of the spiritual senses with every client—because he loves to lift people's spirits, and it makes him feel better about his work. Lew just uses his job as an excuse to get in the door. When he leaves his clients, they feel better than when he arrived, whether or not they do business. I see Lew as a spiritual healer disguised as an insurance salesman.

Physicians, attorneys, bakers, secretaries—people from all walks of life—can explore new dimensions and possibilities by opening their hearts, and the hearts of others, in the midst of daily life. And, like Lew, they won't have to search for more "meaning" in their work.

Emotional Needs:
A Message From the Universe

Every one of us shares the same fundamental emotional need to feel loved, understood, and appreciated. The way we dress, the way we speak, and the exercise we pursue (or want to pursue), our occupation, the money we make, the car we own, where we live, and many other choices we've made and achievements we've worked for are *all* related to our need to feel loved, understood, and appreciated.

And yet, despite all our efforts, our needs for love, understanding, and appreciation rarely feel satisfied. This stems from a deeply rooted misunderstanding between our Higher Self, Basic Self, and Conscious Self—a misunderstanding so common it is almost universal: We have formed a dependence on the world outside us to fulfill our internal needs. Ultimately, however, external sources cannot satisfy inner needs.

The Need-to-Give Principle helps clear up this internal confusion by stating:

> *If we want carrots, we need to plant carrots;*
> *If we want radishes, we need to plant radishes;*
> *If we want love, we need to plant love;*
> *If we want understanding, we need to become understanding;*
> *If we want to feel appreciated, we need to appreciate others.*
> *If we want to feel loved, we need to give love.*

This principle may sound familiar to most of us. If we take an honest look, however, we can observe that most of us give in order to get something back: We act loving so that people will love us back; we listen with understanding so that others will listen back; we appreciate and compliment others so they will return the favor—all acts driven by need. These manipulations don't work; they have too many strings attached.

The Need-to-Give Principle involves a deeper level of understanding, and a universal principle: *Whatever we feel we most need is our Higher Self's way of telling us what we most need to give.*

In other words, the message from our Higher Self creates a feeling in the Basic Self that our Conscious Self interprets as a feeling of lack: "I need to feel loved (or understood or appreciated)." The feeling we interpret as "I need to feel understood" is our Higher Self's way of letting us know through the Basic Self that we need to become more understanding of others.

Once we understand and align ourselves with this principle, our emotional disposition changes from neediness to expansiveness, from an energy vacuum to an energy radiator, from a source of sorrow to a beacon of joy.

14

The Power of Happiness

Who is the happy Warrior?
Who is he
That every man in arms would wish to be?
William Wordsworth

The Capacity for Happiness

Happiness, like *love*, has many different levels and meanings. Eating when we're hungry; looking forward to rest, recreation, or entertainment; or, for some of us, just stopping the pain with the next fix or drink or sexual encounter can make us feel happy.

This chapter is not about trying to be happy all the time; it's about being happy at *will*, being peaceful at *will*, being loving at *will*, through *an act of attention*.

The ability to do this takes practice, like anything else. Through biofeedback and conscious direction of the Basic Self, some people have learned to control certain physiological functions such as body temperature and heartbeat that were formerly believed to be involuntary. Many of us have assumed that deep feelings of happiness, love, and peace are also "involuntary," dependent on random external circumstances.

Rather than leaving body, mind, and emotions at the mercy or whim of circumstance, peaceful warriors bring a balance of spontaneity, vulnerability, and self-control into daily life.

Happiness Defined

We know *about* that all-too-fleeting feeling of love, satisfaction, perfection, and peace we call happiness, but how

272

many of us *live* it? In our younger years, as we model our society's culture of emotional denial, we are taught how to *look* happy, to smile and "put on a happy face"; but no one taught us how to *feel* happy.

In contrast to the cultural messages about looking happy and "smiling for the camera," *true happiness is the ability, developed over time and with practice, to radiate positive energy* regardless of external *or* internal circumstances. In other words, this ability to radiate happiness is independent both of how our life happens to be going *and* of whatever emotional state we're experiencing. With this understanding, we can express fear, sorrow, or anger, and still remain aware of an *underlying* happiness.

To retain this underlying happiness even in the midst of external and internal difficulties, we need to have developed the ability to clear emotional and mental contractions. Once we've developed the practice of clearing these contractions, we can experience emotions without getting caught up in them. If Joy and I have an argument and raise our voices, I may experience anger or sadness. Over time, I've found that beneath these emotions I still feel an undercurrent of happiness that cannot be diminished by whatever drama I'm going through at the personality level.

Shadows of Guilt and the Power of Radiance

Many of us have come to accept the guilt-based belief structure that says, in effect, "Happiness is a callous middle-class pursuit for those who have free time on their hands. How can I be concerned about my own happiness when so many people are suffering in the world? The rain forests are in peril, millions are starving and homeless, and here I am, seeking fulfillment. I ought to be ashamed!" Beliefs like this are enough to push anyone's guilt button.

Those of us who find happiness offensive don't end up finding much of it at all. Postponing happiness until everyone else in the world feels good seems more masochistic than altruistic—like not eating until everyone in the world has been fed.

> *I'm not for voluntary poverty;*
> *I'm against involuntary poverty.*
> Joan Baez

Let me state strongly that we all need to recognize, confront, and redress the pain, suffering, and social ills yet to be resolved in our world. Along with the beauty, pleasure, and blessings of this world, suffering exists; people are starving, physically and emotionally; children are abused; millions of us have lost sight of the meaning in our work and in our lives. This world leaves much room for improvement, much that needs to be done on internal, individual, family, national, and global levels.

The simple fact remains, however, that the stronger and more radiant we are, the more we can serve as a positive influence in the world. *The more happiness we bring into the world, the better it is for everyone.* Happiness (or love) serves as a master key to open every doorway to social progress. Happy people create happiness; it's the most contagious energy on Earth. Fearful, sad, angry, or miserable people only tend to spread these same qualities, even if working in the name of "social conscience." Do we imagine that Mother Teresa got up every morning and said, "Oh, damn, I've got to go work with those lepers again"? Of course not! She said she saw Jesus in the eyes of each person she served; she found an essence to love and care for. Mother Teresa's healing power stems in large part from her ability to radiate happiness.

> *We're here to learn to go with joy*
> *among the sorrows of the world.*
> Joseph Campbell

The Elusive Quest

No matter what we want in life—a partner, more money, good health, a fulfilling career, or enlightenment—it all comes down to the same thing: Behind all the wishes, behind the desires, beyond every symbol, we *want to feel happy*. After all, if we feel completely happy, what more do we need? And if we don't feel happy, no relationship or career or success can satisfy us.

If we look closely at our lives, most of us don't feel terribly happy very much of the time because we focus our attention on what *doesn't* make us feel good. We find the quarry of happiness so elusive because we aren't sure what it looks like—happiness appears to each of us in different forms and seems to depend on what we feel we want right now.

◆

Whatever Makes You Happy

1. Imagine that you find an old bottle on the beach, you open the cap, and a genie appears. If the genie gave you *one* wish for yourself – for *anything* at all (except for more wishes) – what would you choose? Name your ultimate desire.
2. Assume that the wish comes true, and then the genie comes back. "Now that you have your ultimate desire, do you still want anything else? Name it!" What else would you wish for?
3. You get that wish, too; then the next. Think about this a bit further; consider it deeply and continue to come up with wishes/wants until you can't think of anything else you could want.

◆

Seeking

Working toward material success, expanded awareness, and love helps make life exciting and meaningful. The urge to find happiness motivates humanity. Despite our achievements or material success, the sense of longing, or "something missing," spurs us up the mountain path to find the state we call happiness.

In both the worldly and spiritual traditions, *seekers* have been lauded and idolized. Yet we base our seeking upon a subtle rejection of life right now, of happiness right now. *Seekers suffer under the delusion that when they grasp the object they desire, it will finally make them happy.* Happiness may be the most universal "addiction" of all, because so many things make us feel happy for a little while, but all tend to be temporary. We build up a tolerance, and spend most of our days—and time and money—seeking ways to find it. In the end, however, seeking only reinforces the sense of dissatisfaction that sends us seeking in the first place. Seeking stems from resisting life as it is right now; yet only now exists— so we can only feel happy now, or never.

Where Happiness Isn't

The best thing about going to college is that we learn it doesn't make us happy. Those of us who never went to college may harbor a belief for years that if we'd only gone to college our life would be happier. But those of us who have graduated know that happiness doesn't come with the diploma.

The same applies to making a lot of money. In a survey done several years ago, interviewers asked hundreds of people at random whether they believed they would be happier if they had a million dollars. Not surprisingly, 76 percent said, "Yes, absolutely." The interviewers also spoke with ten millionaires and asked if having a million dollars made them happier people. All ten millionaires agreed on the answer: "No."

Well, then, what about finding a partner who fits our ideal of friend, companion, and lover? Surely *that* would do the trick! Those of us who do have such a person in our lives know about the challenges of relationship; we know that even the best marriage doesn't bring happiness; neither does having children.

Maybe the answer lies in meaningful work; that must be it—a form of service that makes us excited about getting up every morning. Well, while meaningful work certainly seems preferable to work we dislike, those of us who have meaningful work we enjoy know that it doesn't guarantee stable happiness.

Then it's got to be good health, we tell ourselves. After all, if we don't have our health, what have we got? At least, that's what my grandfather said. But I know some superbly healthy specimens—right now, I'm one of them—and by itself, health doesn't bring happiness either; it only brings less distraction, less pain, and more energy. We could go on and on with this, because the list is as long as our lives, as long as our hopes and our dreams.

Of course, there's nothing wrong with going to college or with getting married, having children, making money, finding a good career, or staying healthy—all of these things are natural and useful parts of life. They all have the power to make us *conditionally* happy for a little while; almost *anything* we desire and then obtain can make us feel pretty good for a few minutes or hours or days or even weeks. Nothing in the world can offer permanent happiness, however, because the nature of life is change.

A Moment-to-Moment Practice

Happiness is a moment-to-moment practice, accessible at any time we choose. If we can't find it here and now—no matter what our circumstances—then we are not going to find it elsewhere. Though we can certainly always improve our situation, if life meets our basic needs for clothing, food, and shelter, then any suffering we feel comes from our mind's resistance. If we take this same mind with us into the future, the suffering remains, no matter what our external circumstances.

Only when we can love hell
will we find heaven.
Anonymous

The Ultimate Discipline

Before I closely examined my own beliefs, I had identified "happiness" as a personal, private, gleeful feeling inside — a feeling that came and went at random. When I didn't feel it, I sought it, usually through the easiest, quickest means: a "kiss" or a "candy bar." I've learned to see happiness not as something that happens to me, but as something I *do*; not as something I get out of life, but as something I bring to life. Radiating positive energy is not the goal of the peaceful warrior's way; it's the internal attitude we maintain as we journey; it's the warrior's ultimate discipline.

In order to enjoy an underlying state of happiness despite the vagaries and difficulties of daily life, we need the courage and the willingness to radiate positive energy not only in the face of external difficulties but *in spite of what's going on inside.*

I practice happiness as a warrior's discipline when I'm working on a writing deadline and I've worked for six hours writing material that isn't fit to feed the dog, or when I've written two hours' worth of inspired material and the fuse blows and I forgot to save it and I lose it all — and then my little daughter knocks on my office door and says, "Daddy, will you play with me?"

That's the moment of truth — will I practice happiness, or not? I don't always do this perfectly or even very well; when I do practice, I can open the door to my office feeling frustrated and depressed inside, and say, "Hi, honey!" I can give my daughter a hug and a smile, and ask about her day at school. I can give her a few minutes of my time even though thoughts like, "Damn! If only I had remembered to save the material . . . " and "Why did that fuse have to blow?" pass through my mind. I observe the thoughts, acknowledge them for an instant, and then go play with my daughter, giving her positive energy and attention. Just because I'm having my own private little crisis doesn't mean the whole world has to suffer with me. In fact, *I* don't have to suffer, either!

I don't mean to imply that this is easy; any process of learning involves mistakes at first, "blowing it," feeling overwhelmed by the upset, observing ourselves without judgment, and, over time, opening up little by little until we feel a new capacity to be happy.

The discipline of radiating positive energy doesn't mean playing "let's pretend," which involves fooling ourselves. When we practice happiness, we fully acknowledge what we feel; we remain aware of what's going on inside and outside. We just don't dramatize it. Thus, *being* unconditionally happy differs from just *saying* we're happy, or bravely *pretending* to be happy. The discipline of radiating happiness also differs from the passive state of feeling good. It's the only happiness I know of that is not dependent on outside circumstances.

Such happiness, like a surging river, flows beneath and rises above all circumstances, all situations, and even our own obstructions. We all have the inherent capacity to radiate positive energy at any time. However, the worse we feel or the more difficult our circumstances, the more challenging this discipline becomes. Therefore, the more obstructions we've cleared in our body, mind, and emotions, the easier the practice becomes (never easy—just easier).

Like any other consistent practice, radiating positive energy despite our inner and outer circumstances improves over time, especially as we learn not to take our mind so seriously. We need patience while the ability to radiate happiness matures. We crawl before we walk; we walk before we run. We start from where we are now, and continue up the path.

The Conscious Self Will Never Be Happy

People ask me many questions, but they all boil down to the same theme: What about *my* relationship? *My* direction in life? *My* job? *My* family? *My* education? *My* dilemma! I feel hurt, angry, afraid.

Why aren't you happy?
It's because ninety-nine percent
of everything you do, and think, and say,
is for yourself —
and there isn't one.

Wu Wei Wu

When I was three years old I had an experience that serves as a parable of the search for happiness through self-satisfaction. My first visit to the circus felt disorienting and awe inspiring; there were so many things I'd never seen before. One of these new things was a paper cone with a bunch of pink fluffy stuff sticking out of it. As my sister handed it to me, she said, "Here's some cotton candy." I quickly threw the pink stuff on the ground and looked inside the cone for the candy. As I stared into the empty cone, my sister informed me, "You just threw away the candy, Dumbo."

Our Conscious Self tends to throw away the candy, then looks inside the hollow cone of experience for happiness.

In Any Moment

Beth and Jerry are engaged in the middle of a tense, hurtful, and painful argument when they hear the doorbell ring. Jerry, still feeling bitter and upset, opens the door and sees Michael J. Anthony from the old television series "The Millionaire" standing there wearing his pressed tuxedo and his pleasant smile as he announces he has been authorized to give them a cashier's check for one million dollars on which the taxes have already been paid.

At first, Beth and Jerry don't believe him — surely this is some kind of prank or sales pitch — then, finally, they realize he's genuine. "Wow!" they respond. Suddenly, everything has changed — a million dollars! They can pay off the car, buy another house, invest, go on vacation, start new careers, give money to charities.

In the meantime, Jerry and Beth have forgotten their silly little argument. They feel expansive, happy, radiant! And *they could have felt just as happy the moment before they heard the doorbell ring.* The check only gave them a *reason* to be happy — until the next reason to be unhappy comes along.

Once we *fully* realize that radiating happiness is an internal state, we can take responsibility for our own internal states and begin to practice. Those of us who choose the peaceful warrior's way take responsibility for our happiness or unhappiness, and for the beliefs behind these states.

Expansion-Contraction: Unreasonable Happiness

Fundamentally, no matter who we are or what we look like, no matter where we live or what our life circumstances, we always have the power of one choice: *We can expand, or we can contract.* We can expand and radiate positive energy, or we can contract and collapse on ourselves — whether we call that contraction fear, sorrow, or anger.

I make no judgments here; I propose no shoulds or oughts. We have the right and the power to choose what we will.

Anyone can be happy when life is going well. It takes a warrior to be happy when life is hard. We can always find good reasons to be unhappy. We have a harder time finding the reasons to be happy. So we can choose to be *reasonably unhappy* or *unreasonably happy.*

Some of us may argue that there are times our unhappiness feels fully appropriate and justified. Suppose we just had a terrible argument with a loved one, or a friend just died, or we broke our leg or lost our job — are we supposed to feel *happy?*

Certainly, putting a happy face on any of these situations seems inappropriate. But if we remember that peaceful warriors view happiness not as an outward pose or self-deception but a conscious *choice* about how we will act—to radiate or not—we can choose to radiate in spite of our situation.

A Fundamental Lesson of Life

Once, several years ago, while teaching a workshop in the midst of a winter storm in Columbia, Maryland, I heard a knock on the door. Someone informed us that a very large tree had just blown over, fallen, and crushed four cars in the parking lot. We took a break and everyone rushed outside in the roaring wind to see whose cars had been destroyed.

Life alternates between convenience and inconvenience; four people had just experienced the latter. That's all this turned out to be; no one had been injured, and they all had insurance. They would have to call a tow truck, contact their insurance agent, get estimates, find a body shop, get a rental car, and wait for a settlement.

Each person who owned one of the flattened cars had a different response. I want to relate two of the more interesting ones: One man I'll call Jack was sitting slumped over, mourning his new Porsche. Though I felt compassion for Jack's attachment to his new car, I found Jane's reponse even more enlightening: Trying her best to respond constructively to her flattened Fiat, Jane started pacing back and forth and asking herself, "What's the *lesson* in this? What's the *lesson* in this?" Then I saw her glance out the window just as a large raven flew past. She interpreted this as a bad omen—she may have been reading too many Carlos Castaneda books—and said, "I knew it! That's the lesson; I shouldn't have come today. I should have known!"

Jane's reaction indicated more about her state of mind than about the lessons of a flattened car or a raven in flight. Since we don't know what anything really *is*, and since nothing ultimately *means* anything, we see that we make up our own meanings, interpretations, and lessons. Those of us who feel balanced and healthy make up positive, constructive meanings and lessons; others of us make up negative meanings.

It seems to me that all incidents we tend to resist teach the same lesson, embodied by the question "Can I be happy anyway?"

For some incidents, like a flat tire, we may be able to stay expanded with only a little effort and a little perspective ("In a hundred years, who's going to care?"). For other, more traumatic incidents, however, such as the sudden death of a loved one, radiating positive energy even as we mourn may seem almost impossible. Nevertheless, the challenge remains: "Can I be happy anyway?" Each time we transcend a particular incident — each time we practice expanding and radiating in a difficult circumstance—we further develop our capacity to practice unconditional happiness, which is the *same* as unconditional love.

Of course, in any circumstance, we can accept, recognize, and fully experience the waves of emotion—the obstructions and contractions that arise and pass. We can feel whatever it is we're feeling. We can cry, shout with passionate anger, or express fear, and yet remain expanded beneath it all, serving as support for others even while we deal with our own inner pain rather than collapsing and becoming an energy drain. We are not responsible for what comes to us, only for what we hold on to.

Happiness is love, and while love can be smothered, it can't be stopped; therefore, happiness, like love, is the greatest power in the Universe. But like any power, it must be earned. And so, the question remains: *How can we stay happy as we face everyday problems?* When we run into difficulties at work or home, how do we manage to expand and radiate—how do we go with joy among the sorrows of the world and the difficulties of daily life?

How to Be Happy

We can become happier by learning how to direct our attention. This practice stems from the old principle of the glass of water. We interpret the glass as half empty or half full, depending upon our attitude and perception, depending upon how we *choose* to look at it. Since nearly everything has both positive and negative aspects, and both are "true"—the glass truly *is* half empty or half full—we can choose whether to place our attention more on the positive or on the negative.

Some of us have developed a habit of looking at the negative because we believe this is prudent, necessary, and realistic. Others of us have formed the habit of looking at the positive, because we have found life feels better that way.

◆

The Direction of Happiness

1. The next time any emotionally charged incident occurs, *stop* for a moment before reacting in your habitual way.
2. *Remember* the bigger picture; think of something more important in your life that makes you feel good. It could be
   * something you feel grateful for;
   * something that generates wonder, awe, or appreciation;
   * something you're looking forward to;
   * something that helps put this incident in perspective.
3. Hold your focus there, feel good, and realize that what you feel depends upon the direction of your attention.

◆

No matter what incidents or issues we confront—even if someone *did* say or do something terribly unkind or unfair—we can still develop and apply the ability to direct our attention elsewhere, to remember the bigger picture, so that the momentary impact of a slight or offense takes on far less force.

The great secret always remains the same; we have the power to shift our attention from petty details, problems, and self-concern to the larger universe, filled with awe-inspiring beauty and wonder.

Remember the Movie

When small children watch a movie on television, or at the theater, they *believe* it. If the film is funny, the children laugh; if it is happy, they smile; if the film is sad, some of them may cry. In that moment, *the movie becomes their reality*. If the film becomes frightening, we adults can remember that it's only a movie. Though the experience may feel real, and powerful—even traumatic—we can step back from it and remember that "it's only a movie."

Young children (or Basic Selves), however, do not yet have this perspective. It is for us parents (or Conscious Selves) to teach them, as they become ready. We need to remember our inherent but latent ability to see our own lives as "only a movie." We can play it as if it's real, but we can also maintain the ability to step back.

As peaceful warriors, we can develop the ability to engage life—to be in the picture and connect fully—or to disengage, step back, and see it all from a distance. If we *habitually* remain detached from life, creating a wall or buffer between us in our experience, we end up wondering why daily life has lost its attraction, excitement, and passion. On the other hand, if we lose our perspective and get too attached, too wrapped up in the drama as reality, we experience more than enough excitement and passion, but also a surplus of stress and suffering. As in all things, we are wise to seek both flexibility and balance.

Over the years, through the practice of radiating happiness, I've developed the ability to see my own drama and the dramas of those around me with compassion and understanding, yet remain free of attachment. And from that vantage point, I've found a measure of peace and happiness in spite of what arises in the arena of daily life. I just handle what's in front of me, grateful for the intensity and the chance to lift some "spiritual weights," to learn something more, and to take another step up the mountain path.

A Shift of Perspective

Another tool in the peaceful warrior's inventory is the ability to shift our perspective. Socrates once graphically demonstrated this shift to me while we were walking in the wooded hills above Berkeley, I asked him a question about "the meaning of happiness." He took one look at me, then suddenly grabbed my backpack and ran off with it. If you've read *Way of the Peaceful Warrior*, you know that Socrates was a very fast runner. He was so unpredictable, I knew he might do anything with that pack, including throw it away, just to make some point.

I ran after him, panting. "Damn it, Socrates!" I yelled. "I have a term paper in that pack; I worked for weeks on it, and I want it back!" A few moments later, behind some foliage, I saw papers flying in every direction. He was apparently littering the Berkeley hills with my term paper!

In a panic, I ran into the bush and found Socrates, picking up some blank pages and grinning from ear to ear. He handed me my backpack. Everything was in order, including the term paper.

Very much relieved and happy to have the pack back, I asked, "What was that all about?"

"I take your pack and you get upset; I return it, and you're happy. Now you know about conditional happiness," he replied.

Stable happiness doesn't come from getting everything we want, because we never will; true happiness comes from wanting whatever we get.

I sometimes have a chance to apply "wanting what I get" at restaurants: If I order carrot juice and the waitress tells me, "I'm sorry, we're out of carrot juice," I generally respond, "Wonderful! Because I *really* want orange juice, instead." Even a moment's resistance—"I really wanted carrot juice and you should have it; it says so right here on the menu!"—creates stress. It's not worth it.

At first, practicing "wanting what we get" may feel as if we're playing "let's pretend," but later this practice becomes a natural way to develop mental flexibility.

Once we develop the ability to want (accept and enjoy) whatever we have, then *everything* can make us happy. Wanting everything we get is easier said than done, however. Following this principle requires a huge leap of understanding — beyond attachment, beyond the Conscious Self's habitual ways of thinking and the Basic Self's habitual ways of reacting. We can make the leap anytime; it only takes a shift of perspective. It's as simple as remembering two rules:

1. Don't sweat the small stuff.
2. It's all small stuff.

Shifting our perspective so that we appreciate and value whatever happens takes practice. Our biggest challenges involve personal loss: separations, deaths, accidents, or the varieties of illness or pain. How could we possibly *want* those things? Here I use *want* not in the sense of "desire," but as an active acceptance of whatever happens as a part of our process of growth and learning.

We don't desire difficulties or pain, but if and when we experience them, we can do our best to remember that our Conscious Self will never know what serves our highest good, or the good of the whole. We can come to trust in what life offers with faith in the inherent wisdom, meaning, and perfection of all that occurs. This perspective may not turn our pain to delight, but it does bring us more serenity, and at times even gratitude.

In the conditional world, happiness remains a challenge. We will continue to face gain and loss, ups and downs. Sometimes it seems that all we can count on are paradox, humor, and change. As we increase our capacity to face the world squarely, we can share the sentiments of the pianist Arthur

Rubinstein, who once said, "Even when I'm sick and depressed, I love life."

The Big Picture

Life seems very serious when we only see it through our own two eyes. To those of us locked into the sense of separate self, disconnected from the larger picture, others' gains seem to be our losses. How do we expand our perspectives beyond this limited view, in order to embrace all of life?

---◆---

Expanding Beyond Yourself

1. Take a few slow, deep breaths down into your belly; relax your body and make sure it feels comfortable.
2. Imagine your awareness floating up and out of your body. See yourself from above, then imagine yourself a hundred feet in the air, no longer attached to your individual concerns or desires.
3. Rising much faster, see yourself above your entire city, then state, then country, until you can see the curve of the earth, this blue-green ball, receding in the vastness of space.
4. Experience our solar system receding in the distance as you expand farther out into space, beyond the billions of stars in the Milky Way, then farther, until all the galaxies, all the star systems, merge into a point of light and you see it all from the very edge of creation.
5. Feel the balance, the mystery, the vastness. From your vantage point, let your mind pierce the void, with its floating specks of matter, and find a small star system called the Milky Way. Then find the tiny star that is our sun, surrounded by a few whirling bits of matter, the planets. And somewhere, on one of those specks of matter, on a planet called Earth, see yourself, thinking, Oh, my, what am I going to do about my relationships, my job, my hairdo, my money?

6. Allow yourself to feel the humor that comes from seeing the larger view, then come back into your body. Retain the memory of the bigger picture, and know that in any moment you have the ability to leap beyond yourself and see life in perspective.

Looking at ourselves from a distance helps restore our humor. Even when I'm concerned about something in my life—my writing, for example—a larger part of me is out there, in the vastness of space, watching it all, reminding the little me that "life, death—all of it—is small potatoes" from that distance. This ability to shift from the Conscious Self to the bigger picture helps more than anything else to keep life from getting too serious.

Humor and Transcendence

Many of us foster the secret hope that one day we will experience a sudden and dramatic transformation. Life, however, rarely seems to work that way; years of work and discipline may bring only modest change: We extend our useful life span, but we still wear out and die. We improve our health, but we still get ill on occasion. Our responses to difficulties change, but we continue to face new challenges.

And yet, even though the challenges of our lives remain, the work of personal evolution brings one quality common to all forms of genuine transformation: *We don't take ourselves so seriously anymore.* When I find myself beginning to take myself too seriously, I remember Sam. I met Sam during an intensive training in which we both participated, and I soon noticed that Sam stuttered badly; when we talked, I had to wait patiently for him to complete every sentence.

I ran into Sam a few years later, at a reunion. I learned that he, like me, had pursued more advanced work in balancing his body, mind, and emotions since our last meeting. As he explained all the work he'd done on himself, I noticed that he still stuttered. Curious, I commented, "Sam, after all the spiritual work you've done on yourself, you still stutter."

"Y-y-yes," he said. "But, n-n-now I d-d-don't *give* a damn!"

Maybe that's what life is all about—not self-improvement, but self-transcendence. Maybe we've already transcended everything but haven't yet realized it. Maybe all we have to do is open our eyes.

This moment is the moment of reality, of union, of truth.
Nothing needs to be done to it or to you for this to be so.
Nothing needs to be avoided, transcended, or found
for it to be so.
Da Avabhasa (also known as Da Free John)

Perhaps we come to this planet for one great purpose: to develop a *terrific* sense of humor. Maybe laughter provides the key that finally unlocks the door to happiness.

15

The Time Is Now

If I am not for myself,
Who will be for me?
And if I am only for myself,
What am I?
And if not now, when?
Hillel

One night, Socrates did two uncharacteristic things: First, he handed me a pen and some paper and told me to take notes; second, without further explanation, he spoke for as long as I'd ever heard him speak at one time.

"You find yourself here, in the midst of an experiment in human evolution," he began. "What you set in motion now, in your personal life, as a part of the body of humanity, will have farther-reaching consequences than you can possibly imagine. We humans are still children, playing with forces larger than ourselves. But we are growing up fast.

"The challenge and the opportunity of this moment in history is only beginning to dawn on us. We are just waking up.

"You will be tempted again and again to fall back to sleep, to fall back into your personal dilemmas, and in that tunnel vision, to lose sight of the bigger picture. You will find yourself treading water in a sea of concerns, with only moments of peace and flashes of happiness to interrupt the parade of problems.

"But is that what life is about? Are we merely here to spend our lives treading water? Or is there something else?

"In order to find the answer, you need to take a realistic

and compassionate look at yourself and your situation. See your own part in it, your responsibility, and your power of choice within the larger context.

"We all know that life has ups and downs; you've experienced both. And though you can't always control what happens outside you, you can choose how you will *respond*. You can treat life as a dance rather than a wrestling match. You can become an active participant rather than a victim of circumstance.

"There are times to let things happen, and times to make things happen. Now is that time. You will either make things happen, watch what happens, or wonder what happened.

"Do you want to live as a peaceful warrior, or a soap opera star? Choose now what you will do and who you will be. The choices you make today sow the seeds for the future.

"Do you have the courage for it? Do you have the love? If you have enough of one, you will develop the other.

"But if you fall asleep, you miss the show! If you lose sight of the bigger picture, you may also lose your sense of humor and become fearful or frustrated.

"If you choose the warrior's way, the challenges of life remain; they may even intensify. And, yet, everything changes: You begin to recognize this world as a training ground, a school for souls. We are all humans in training.

"Whatever life hands you, tackle it. Handle what is in front of you. Do whatever you have to *in spite of* fear or insecurity or doubt. Don't wait to feel motivated! Life rarely lays out a red carpet between you and your goals; more often, it's a swamp. But remember that your stumbling blocks can become stepping-stones.

"Someday, at the moment of death, your whole life will pass before you. In a few fractions of a second — because time no longer applies — you will see many incidents from your life in order to learn. You will review your life with two questions in your consciousness: Could I have shown a little more courage in these moments? Could I have shown a little more love?

You will see whether you let fear stop you from expressing who you are, how you feel, or what you need. You will see whether you were able to expand into these moments, just a little, and show love, or whether you contracted.

"Don't wait until you die to learn the warrior's way. Do it now, each night, just before you drift off to sleep. As you review your day, consider these two questions of courage and love. Learn from each day, so that each day you can show a little more courage and a little more love. Then, as incidents occur, you may rise to the occasion and look back at the end of your life and feel good about the way you have lived.

"You are not only here to grow up and go to school and work and make money and marry and raise children and retire. These occupations only form the backdrop in the Theater of Life. They provide the wrapping, but they are not the gift—only the means of your education—important aspects of life, but not the purpose of it, not the whole of it.

"Life develops what it demands. The issues you face are the spiritual weights you lift to strengthen yourself. Your task is to shine *through* the petty details of your life, not to get preoccupied with them. And when life puts hurdles in your path, my friend, you had better become a hurdler.

"There may come a day when you begin to see beneath the surface of life, and read the meaning between the lines. There may come a day when you *welcome* the hurdles and obstacles of daily life as the means of your training. Then you will thank Spirit for *everything* that is given, whether you call it good or bad, easy or difficult. Your preferences will begin to drop away, and you will embrace what *is*.

"Your path will lead you over some lofty peaks and down into some dark forests. From each peak, you'll see the bigger picture and feel on top of the world and closer to God. Down in the shadows of the forest—your own shadows—you'll confront necessary challenges and discover the strength within you. So both the highs and lows are useful in their own ways.

"When you reach a peak, take advantage of that opportunity to see the higher nature of the world. Do not take it for granted or assume you'll be there forever, because if you fail to take advantage of the peak times, a doorway of opportunity closes; you'll have to wait until the next peak to see what you can see.

"Don't wait until next time. *This* lifetime, this moment, is an astonishing time in the history of the planet, an incredible time, still beyond your comprehension. Now is the time to prepare yourself — a time for courage and commitment.

"If you coast because it's comfortable and things are going well, you may one day look back and realize what you missed. At the end of your life, you will see the opportunities you had to stretch toward your potential but that you let go because things were easy and you could always do it later. Do it *now* — while you have the time for it, while you have the energy for it, while you are alive.

"Maybe you think you're too busy to grow into your higher self; maybe you're too busy just staying afloat. It's easy to let physical problems, relationships, money, and work monopolize your attention. You may think that you've got no time for happiness — that you have too many things to do — so the war rages on, and inner peace gets buried at the bottom of the "in box." But with a simple shift of attention, you could enjoy it all now. So I ask you: What do you want to look back on?

"Right now, whether or not you are aware of it, a great battle is waging inside you. Fears and concerns distract you; doubt and insecurity urge you to sit this one out, to go back to sleep. They lull you with comfort and convenience; they weave false hopes and fairy tales. You will, at times, feel a strong temptation to crawl into a cocoon or put your head in the sand where it's quiet.

"Why do I tell you this? Because you are still caught between waking and sleeping. *Now* is the time to wake up fully. This is the great time, the great battle. Don't be caught unaware. Now is the time of the greatest work, the greatest challenge, and the greatest growth. The doorway has opened. Step through! Now, in this lifetime. Now is the time. *Now.*

"Where is your commitment? What do you want to look back on? Do you have the courage to explore who you are beyond your limiting beliefs? Are you willing to take responsibility for your habits and your fears, then slash through them?

"You can change your life with a simple shift of attention. But to make that simple shift, you have to find your heart. It's the only way. Accept yourself, then transcend yourself. Make this great work the center of your life.

"Daily life is more than it seems. Use it! Find the courage and love to adapt to and live a happy life of loving-kindness — not because it will "get you somewhere," but because you understand the way of the peaceful warrior.

"I, and others like me, only serve as a bridge between you and the heart of the universe until the time comes when you no longer need any bridges — when you realize that you *are* the universe, you are the heart."

Socrates stopped as abruptly as he had begun. A light rain started pattering on the office window as I shook out my hand from taking rapid notes and gathered the papers. I knew he had told me something important, but I didn't realize how I would share it, until now.

On my own adventures, I've found more to the world than meets the casual eye. I've come to appreciate the mystery and paradox — the humor and change. In closing, I offer you the same reminders I give to myself: Be gentle with yourself. Think less and feel more. Be as happy as you can. You only have this moment.

Appendix

Getting Started

The Universe is my way.
Love is my law.
Peace is my shelter.
Experience is my school.
Obstacle is my lesson.
Difficulty is my stimulant.
Pain is my warning.
Work is my blessing.
Balance is my attitude.
Perfection is my destiny.
Guillermo Toloentino

Soon after I first met Socrates, I walked into the station one night and found him pumping gas. He nodded to me, tossed me a squeegee, and pointed to the windshield. But I was more interested in asking questions than in washing windows. He had said something to me the previous night about how I had a lot of knowledge but little wisdom. Still put off by his comment, flipping the squeegee in the air and catching it again, I asked, "So what's the difference between knowledge and wisdom?"

He paused, then spoke slowly, as if talking to someone for whom English was a second language. "You *know* how to clean a windshield."

"So?" I said, again tossing the squeegee.

"Wisdom is *doing* it."

The Peaceful Warrior Week
for Body, Mind, and Spirit

This one-week program embodies a peaceful warrior's approach to daily life—a way to translate what you've learned into something you can *do*. I believe you will find it simple, practical, and uplifting. It will help you to

- balance the body, lighten the mind, and open the heart;
- develop a stronger connection between your Conscious Self and your Basic and Higher Selves;
- detoxify and purify the body;
- experience greater energy and awareness; and
- feel better than you have in a while, on many levels.

The program works best if you do each practice listed below once each day for the next seven days. Few of us will do this "perfectly." Keep in mind that you get *out* what you put *in*, but be easy with yourself—a little of something is better than a lot of nothing. This is not an assignment, but an opportunity to feel pleasure in a way you may not have experienced before.

Twenty Minutes of Physical Exercise

Practice any continuous, balanced form of exercise such as the Peaceful Warrior Series (ordering information at back of book), walking and breathing deeply, or moving to music—whatever works for you.

Twenty Minutes of Spiritual Exercise

This can be meditation, contemplation, visualization, or communion—remembering and breathing Spirit—or any other form of inner work you find uplifting, such as walking in nature, listening to inspiring music, or reading a book that connects you to the feeling of Spirit.

A Purifying One-Week Diet

Incorporate the following principles into your daily diet as much as possible:

- Eat less (or no) meat, fish, and poultry.
- Eat less (or no) milk, cheese, and eggs.
- Eat less (or no) refined sugar (read labels).
- Use less (or no) alcohol, tobacco, and other nonprescription drugs. If you smoke, quit as soon as you can, but not this week, or withdrawal symptoms may interfere with your enjoyment of the program; the same applies to caffeine.
- Enjoy fresh salads, steamed vegetables, pastas, fresh fruit, yams, potatoes, and rice and other cooked grains.

Please note:

1. This diet is intended as a gentle, enjoyable discipline, not a spartan routine. Do not deprive yourself. Don't go hungry. Eat what you wish of the healthful foods listed above; just don't overeat.
2. Avoid "all-or-nothing" thinking. Do your best within your present limits, and remember that a little of something is far better than a lot of nothing.
3. Specialists in human nutrition now recognize this kind of diet as optimal for health, vitality, freedom from most food allergies, a feeling of lightness and well-being, and a longer life. Not everyone thrives on exactly the same diet, however; it took me some years to adopt to this program as a lifestyle. Go with your instincts. Be gentle with yourself, eat consciously, and enjoy the blessings of good food.

Here and Now

At least once each day, when you notice your mind wandering or you feel rushed or anxious, pay attention to what is happening right now, in the moment. Are you relaxed? Are you breathing easily? Are you moving with attention and grace?

Expansion-Contraction

When you might reasonably feel upset, remember to feel unreasonably happy instead—just for the fun of it. Expand instead of contracting.

Opening the Heart

Practice each of the spiritual senses each day: speaking from the heart; offering an inner blessing; and touching, seeing, and hearing from the heart.

Need-to-Give Principle

Once each day, when you feel a need for appreciation, understanding, courtesy, respect, love, or attention, give it to someone else, without attachment to outcomes.

Little Things

Do a "small thing" for at least one person each day—whether for a friend, an adversary, or a stranger. Help uplift that person's spirits.

Prayer or Positive Wishes

Twice daily—the first thing on arising and just before going to sleep—say a short prayer or positive wish, from the heart. This can be as simple as, "Spirit, if you're listening, I pray for my sisters and brothers in Africa (or India, or anywhere else)."

Summary:
The Week in Review

At least once each day, practice the following:

1. Physical exercise: Move, breathe, and stretch for twenty minutes.
2. Spiritual exercise: Remember Spirit for twenty minutes.
3. Improved diet: Feel the power of healthful eating.
4. Here and now: Take one moment to breathe, relax, and move with grace.
5. Expansion-contraction: Be unreasonably happy.
6. Opening the heart: Connect your heart to voice, thought, touch, sight, and hearing.
7. Need-to-Give Principle: Give what you most feel you need.
8. Little things: Do a small thing to uplift someone.
9. Prayer or positive wishes: First thing in the morning and the last thing in the evening, pray from the heart.

A Final Word

Every moment of every day, even as we do apparently ordinary things, we are at the same time climbing the mountain path—traveling the way of the peaceful warrior. We cannot lose our way, even though it seems like it at times. On our journey together, as we stumble and soar toward the Light, bless us all.

An introduction to
Dan Millman's best-selling
The Life You Were Born to Live

If you've found enjoyment and value in *No Ordinary Moments* and want to take another step on the peaceful warrior's path, we invite you to open the covers of *The Life You Were Born to Live: A Guide to Finding Your Life Purpose.*

This international best-seller has been praised by many, including Deepak Chopra, M.D., who commented, "The Life-Purpose System as expressed in Dan Millman's new book is *absolutely amazing* in its predictive value. It will help you sort out the conflicts in your life and guide you on the path of fulfillment."

Of all the systems Dan has studied over the last three decades, he considers this the clearest and most powerful bridge to self-knowledge and compassionate understanding he's ever found.

The Life You Were Born to Live describes the thirty-seven paths of life; a precise method to determine your own life path and the life paths of others; the core issues, innate talents, and special needs related to your path, including areas of health, money, and sexuality; guidelines for finding and enjoying a livelihood consistent with your own drives and abilities; and finally, the hidden purpose of your relationships.

Whether you believe such a book could truly help clarify your life purpose, even if you don't usually read "this kind of book," we think you will be amazed when you go to a bookstore, open page four of *The Life You Were Born to Live*, learn the simple method to determine your life path, and then read the six or seven summary pages about your life path (or the life path of a loved one).

The Life You Were Born to Live also features key laws specific to your life path to help you fulfill your personal destiny. This modern method based on ancient wisdom has helped thousands to find new meaning, purpose, and direction. It may change the course of your life.

Books by Dan Millman

Available at your local bookstore or by calling
1–800–833–9327

The Peaceful Warrior Series
Way of the Peaceful Warrior
The story that has touched a million lives.

Sacred Journey of the Peaceful Warrior
The adventure continues as Dan meets a woman shaman
in a Hawaiian rain forest.

Guidebooks
No Ordinary Moments
A peaceful warrior's principles and practices for living.

The Life You Were Born to Live
A guide to finding your life purpose.

The Laws of Spirit
A book of timeless wisdom, containing twelve universal
principles.

The Inner Athlete
A guide to developing talent for sport and life.

For Children
Beautifully illustrated, award-winning stories of wisdom,
magic, and mystery for children four to ten years of age.

Secret of the Peaceful Warrior
Aided by a girl named Joy and an old man named
Socrates, young Danny overcomes his fears by applying a
wonderful secret.

Quest for the Crystal Castle
Danny's journey through a magical forest reveals the
power of kindness and each child's ability to overcome
life's obstacles.

For information about
Dan Millman's tapes and trainings:

Box 6148, San Rafael, CA 94903

Phone: (415) 491-0301

Fax: (415) 491-0856

e-mail: wpwdan@aol.com

Internet website: http://www.danmillman.com

ALSO FROM H J KRAMER

CREATING MIRACLES:
Understanding the Experience of Divine Intervention
by Carolyn Miller, Ph.D.
The first scientific look at creating miracles in your
life. These simple practices and true stories offer new
wisdom for accessing the miraculous in daily life.

SON-RISE:
The Miracle Continues
by Barry Neil Kaufman
The astonishing real-life account of an autistic
boy's journey from silence to health through the
extraordinary love and commitment of his parents.

JOURNEY INTO ONENESS:
A Spiritual Odyssey
by Michael J. Roads
A compelling adventure beyond all known reality—
a superbly crafted metaphysical work.

THE BLUE DOLPHIN
A parable by Robert Barnes
An inspiring and moving story of dolphin life, which
serves as a powerful metaphor for human existence.

FULL ESTEEM AHEAD:
100 Ways to Build Self-Esteem in Children and Adults
by Diane Loomans with Julia Loomans
"*Full Esteem Ahead* is the best book on
parenting and self-esteem that I know."
—Jack Canfield, author of *Chicken Soup for the Soul*

TO ORDER BOOKS, PLEASE CALL (800) 833-9327